ANTI-VEILING CAMPAIGNS IN TURKEY

ANTI-VEILING CAMPAIGNS IN TURKEY

State, Society and Gender in the Early Republic

SEVGİ ADAK

I.B. TAURIS

LONDON • NEW YORK • OXFORD • NEW DELHI • SYDNEY

I.B. TAURIS
Bloomsbury Publishing Plc
50 Bedford Square, London, WC1B 3DP, UK
1385 Broadway, New York, NY 10018, USA
29 Earlsfort Terrace, Dublin 2, Ireland

BLOOMSBURY, I.B. TAURIS and the I.B. Tauris logo are
trademarks of Bloomsbury Publishing Plc

First published in Great Britain 2022
This paperback edition published 2023

A catalogue record for this book is available from the British Library.

A catalog record for this book is available from the Library of Congress.

ISBN: HB: 978-1-7845-3792-0
         PB: 978-0-7556-3506-1
      ePDF: 978-0-7556-3503-0
     eBook: 978-0-7556-3504-7

Typeset by Integra Software Services Pvt. Ltd.

To find out more about our authors and books visit www.bloomsbury.com
and sign up for our newsletters.

In loving memory of my grandmother, Fatma Gazalcı.

CONTENTS

ACKNOWLEDGEMENTS

This book grew out of my PhD dissertation, which I defended at the Leiden University, the Netherlands. Since beginning the research some twelve years ago, numerous institutions, colleagues and friends have crossed its path and contributed to its development in various ways.

First of all, I am immensely indebted to my PhD supervisors, Erik Jan Zürcher and Touraj Atabaki for their unfailing support and encouragement. It is mainly on account of their guidance that I was able to muster up the courage to dive into the social history of the early Turkish republic, still a largely unknown sea at the time, which proved to be an extremely rewarding endeavour, intellectually, academically and personally. Erik also extended his support in the later stages, when I was working on the final version of the book manuscript, for which I would especially like to thank him. I have been fortunate to have Deniz Kandiyoti as my mentor since the completion of my doctoral studies. She has not only influenced my work enormously through her scholarship, intellectual rigor and wisdom, but has also always been there whenever I needed advice. I will always remain in her debt. I would like to thank Berteke Waaldijk and Nicole A.N.M. van Os for their comments on the dissertation, which helped me improve the text while turning it into book. I also would like to thank my colleagues and especially the dean, Leif Stenberg, at the Aga Khan University, Institute for the Study of Muslim Civilisations, where I have been a faculty member for the last six years, for their support. Special gratitude goes to Gianluca Parolin for our many walks together at the Regent's Park, Sanaa Alimia for the encouragement and Farouk Topan for his insight and humour.

The research for this book took place in archives and libraries in four different countries. I would like to thank the staff of the Presidency of State Archives of the Republic of Turkey in Ankara, the National Archives of the United Kingdom Foreign Office Records, the United States National Archives and Records Administration, Leiden University Library, the library of the International Institute of Social History in Amsterdam, Beyazıt Library in Istanbul, Kent Kitaplığı in Izmir, the Municipal Library and Kent Kitaplığı in Bursa, the ISAM library in Istanbul and the British Library in London for their assistance. I had the opportunity to discuss different parts of my research for this book with many scholars at conferences, workshops and invited lectures in the last decade. Although it is impossible to list all of them here, I want to mention in particular the conference on the anti-veiling campaigns in the Muslim world held at the St Anthony's College, University of Oxford, where I presented an earlier version of Chapter 3. I would like to thank the organizer, Stephanie Cronin, for involving me, and the other contributors of the edited volume that came out of that conference, as their work has been critical in the shaping of my comparative reflections on the Turkish case.

My special thanks go to Sylvia Zeybekoğlu and Mark David Wyers for meticulously editing the manuscript. I would like to thank Rory Gormley and Yasmin Garcha of Bloomsbury Publishing for their help and patience, and Vishnu Muruganandham for copyediting. I am also grateful to the anonymous reviewers of the manuscript for their comments and suggestions, which helped me refine some of my analyses.

Many thanks are in order for my wonderful friends who over the years not only supported me but helped me to stay on track with my work. Eva Forrai accommodated me during my initial research at the National Archives in Kew. Aysel Yıldız helped me with some of the archival documents. Umut Azak, Alexandros Lamprou, Gülhan Balsoy and Şebnem Oğuz engaged with various parts of my research over the years and contributed to my thinking on the early republican history, feminist historiography, social and political theory and Turkish politics. I am grateful to all of them. I am indebted to my London friends, particularly Selin Kesebir, Berfin Emre and Ece Kocabıçak, and to my feminist bunch in Istanbul, especially Selin Dağıstanlı and Banu Paker, for helping me through the most difficult times and after. I owe special thanks to Ece as my writing companion; I would never have been able to work as productively as I did in the last two years without her unshakable determination to make sure I was okay and on course with writing. Last but not least, I would like to thank Hande Ersoy, Ayşe Bilge Yılmaz and Şafak Pesen for simply being there for me for almost thirty years now.

I would not have been able to finish this book without the support of my family. I am grateful to my parents for enduring some very tough moments with me and for ensuring that I survived them. My sister Ezgi has always been my confidant, and my nephew, Güney, my source of joy. Ezgi also helped me with my research at the Izmir Kent Kitaplığı, for which I am especially thankful. My uncle and aunt, Mustafa and Müzeyyen, and my cousins Cemal and Can, hosted me in their homes in Ankara several times when I was working at the Turkish state archives. I thank them for their generosity. And finally, Paolo always made sure that I had enough pasta, laughter and peace of mind to be able to work. I am grateful for his serenity, kindness and love, which made London, unexpectedly, home.

INTRODUCTION

One summer day in the early 2000s in my mother's hometown of Güney, a small district in the province of Denizli in Turkey's Aegean region, I was sitting in the garden of our house listening to a conversation between my grandmother and her niece, who was only two years younger than her. My grandmother's niece was complaining about a persistent pain she had in her leg, saying that she had been suffering from it since the day she fell down while trying to escape from a gendarmerie soldier when she was a teenager. When I asked why she had to run away from the soldier, she answered that the gendarmerie had tried to stop her in the street because she was wearing the local *peştamal* veil.[1] 'The *peştamal* was banned in Güney those days,' she said, referring to the late 1930s; nevertheless, her father would not let her go out without wearing one.

The *peştamal* was an ordinary, local-style veil. I have known it as the usual outdoor veil worn by women in Güney since my childhood. In fact, it was still relatively common among older women at the time of this conversation; my grandmother, her niece and other women from their generation would wear it when they went out in the town. When they travelled to a larger urban setting, to the provincial centre, for example, they would prefer wearing an overcoat and a headscarf instead. The *peştamal*, then, survived the ban that was imposed on its use in the 1930s. But how? If the ban had been put into practice by force to the extent that the gendarmerie was employed in its implementation, how did the *peştamal* endure this intervention for decades? And why was the *peştamal* banned in the first place? How was it banned? What were the reactions to the ban? How did women experience such an intrusion into how they dressed? How did they respond when they found themselves trapped between a political authority that imposed a ban on certain veils, and their families, who insisted on their continuing to wear them, as in the case of my grandmother's niece?

The literature on early republican Turkey available at the time was not helpful in answering these questions, especially those regarding ordinary people's experiences. In fact, until quite recently, the predominant argument in the

---

1. The *peştamal* is a full body covering veil made from locally produced fabric that is used especially in rural areas. While it might be still possible to encounter women wearing *peştamal* in rural settings in contemporary Turkey, it has largely been abandoned.

literature was that although the Kemalist single-party regime (1923–45) under the Republican People's Party (*Cumhuriyet Halk Partisi*, hereafter party or RPP) had celebrated a new, 'modern' Turkish woman and thus generally 'discouraged' veiling, there was no direct state intervention in women's clothing except for the attire worn by women who were state officials. The standard comparison has been with the aggressive attitude of the regime in changing men's clothing; while there was a law banning the wearing of the fez and other traditional men's headgear, there was no law banning women's veils.

The disparity between the way the single-party regime has been dealt with in the scholarly literature and the real-life experiences of ordinary people who lived under that regime has marked the historiography of the period. This period, which constitutes the formative years of the Turkish republic, has been depicted as an era of authoritarian modernization characterized by a number of very radical reforms formulated by the ruling elite and imposed on society in a top-down manner. Usually described as 'modernization from above', the Kemalist experience has been studied through a state-centred approach that is preoccupied, essentially, with the high politics of the political elite in Ankara, the capital of the country. As a result, the historiography of early republican Turkey has largely been built upon the analysis of intellectual inspirations, ideological underpinnings and the political discourses of the regime elite, particularly placing Mustafa Kemal Atatürk and his vision, ideas and 'projects' at the centre.

This tendency to narrate a process that was dominated and shaped by Mustafa Kemal and the elites within his close political circle was not limited to those works that follow the Kemalist interpretations of the era. Studies critical of Kemalism and the single-party regime have also focused primarily on the doings of the regime as they could be followed in Ankara, and thus predominantly confined to the sphere of political history.[2] The changes in the theoretical frameworks with which the single-party era has been studied since the 1960s have made little difference in terms of shifting the focus away from the state, the elite and their ideology. In classical narratives built on the modernization theory, the state appears as an autonomous institution controlled by a modernizing elite and it is seen as the main agent of social change.[3] The scholarship that follows this theory tends to present the republican state established in 1923 as the driving force in the formation of a modern Turkish society, which is a process seen as the logical result of the modernizing efforts undertaken by the Kemalist modernizers' Ottoman antecedents.[4]

---

2. Gavin D. Brockett, 'Collective Action and the Turkish Revolution: Towards a Framework for the Social History of the Atatürk Era, 1923–38', *Middle Eastern Studies* 34, no. 4 (October 1998): 44–66.

3. Wolfgang Knöbl, 'Theories that Won't Pass Away: The Never-Ending Story of Modernization Theory', in *Handbook of Historical Sociology*, eds. Gerard Delanty and Engin F. Işın (London: Sage Publications, 2003), 96–107.

4. Bernard Lewis, *The Emergence of Modern Turkey* (Oxford: Oxford University Press, 1961); Niyazi Berkes, *The Development of Secularism in Turkey* (Montreal: McGill University Press, 1964).

Another set of works, which are framed by what came to be called 'the strong state approach', also continued, and even reinforced this central place of the state in modern Turkish history.[5] In this reading, the state tradition the republic inherited from the Ottoman Empire was 'a strong and centralized state, reasonably effective by the standards of its day, highly autonomous of societal forces, and occupying a central and highly valued place in Ottoman political culture'.[6] Within this framework, society appears to be weak and predominantly passive or unimportant compared to this vastly autonomous and powerful state. Even those approaches that were sociologically oriented and emerged as a critique of the modernization school, such as the centre–periphery analysis of Şerif Mardin, did not go beyond this dualism and actually contributed to the reproduction of the state–society dichotomy.[7] Although social actors, the periphery, were given more agency in that type of analysis, the distinction between the state and society as fixed entities positioned in opposition to each other remained intact and the Kemalist policies were largely analysed on the basis of the ideology of the elite rather than how they were implemented and the ways they were contested, consumed and negotiated by social actors in practice.[8]

This book takes its point of departure from the critique that the dominant frameworks used in studying single-party Turkey, which were briefly outlined above, fail to bring to light the complexity of the socio-historical reality on the ground. It argues that they underestimate the readiness of state actors to negotiate and compromise with the dominant practices and structures in society, and the tendency of societal actors to tackle reform processes in various and quite creative ways. In the literature, the roles of non-state elite actors, such as religious leaders or local notables, are either largely neglected or incorporated into the analysis as forces of 'traditional' opposition.[9] The Kemalist regime is thus portrayed as completely detached and alienated from the 'people' (*halk*), who are imagined to

---

5. For example, see Metin Heper, *The State Tradition in Turkey* (Beverley: Eothen Press, 1985).

6. Ergun Özbudun, 'The Continuing Ottoman Legacy and the State Tradition in the Middle East', in *Imperial Legacy: The Ottoman Imprint on the Balkans and the Middle East*, ed. L. Carl Brown (New York: Columbia University Press, 1996), 133.

7. Şerif Mardin, 'Center-Periphery Relations: A Key to Turkish Politics?', *Daedalus* 102, no. 1 (Winter 1973): 169–90.

8. For example, Mardin claimed that 'the meaning of [Kemalist] laicism as a project is best highlighted not by a description of its practice but by its relation to the primordial goals of the republican regime'. Şerif Mardin, 'Religion and Secularism in Turkey', in *Atatürk: Founder of a Modern State*, eds. Ali Kazancıgil and Ergun Özbudun (London: C. Hurst & Co., 1981), 211.

9. This is quite a prevalent assumption since the history of non-Western countries has been seen as a struggle between the forces of modernity and tradition. For a critique of this assumption, see Stephanie Cronin, 'Introduction', in *Subalterns and Social Protest: History from Below in the Middle East and North Africa*, ed. Stephanie Cronin (London: Routledge, 2008), 1–22. In the case of Turkey, exceptional in this regard are the works by İsmail Beşikçi.

consist of uneducated, quite religious and conservative masses. Within this rigid dichotomy, the regime vs. the *halk*, there is little room for acknowledging the multiplicity of actors and discourses at all levels and taking up the complexity of their interactions. The role that lower-level elites played in the way the regime functioned, for example, does not receive enough attention, and the fact that a considerable number of people were involved in Kemalist policies, supporting and shaping them in critical ways, is overlooked. The agency of non-elite groups and subordinated sectors of society is also largely ignored. This has resulted in a lopsided analysis: Much is known about the visions of the Kemalist political elite, their ideological tenets and motivations, and the main frameworks of the reforms and policies they formulated. However, far less is known about how these reforms and policies were implemented. Not much is understood about how the main political and ideological parameters drawn in Ankara travelled to the provinces and became translated into the daily mechanisms and conduct of the state, or how they actually entered the everyday life of ordinary citizens and were consumed by individuals and communities. In other words, 'the meeting ground of fact and fiction' in Kemalist modernization,[10] the encounter and interaction between the power of the modernizing state, and the limits of and myths about that power, remain largely unexamined. The aim of this book is to address this gap through a study of the regulation of women's clothing during the single-party period, namely, the anti-veiling campaigns of the 1930s.

The early Turkish republic through new theoretical lenses

Obtaining a more nuanced understanding of the social change under the Kemalist regime requires a change in our approach to the question of state–society relations. This refocusing makes it possible to draw upon a number of alternative theoretical and methodological debates. One of these entails the theoretical break put forward by the critical historiography of the 'history from below' school and subaltern studies. Both emerged as a challenge to traditional elitist perspectives, emphasizing the agency of the subaltern classes and the historical experience of the common people.[11] The rank and file of the history from below school aimed at bringing back the common people as actors in their own history.[12] Likewise, subalternist historians strove to 'rectify the elitist bias'.[13] They also challenged Eurocentrism

---

10. Joel Migdal, 'Finding the Meeting Ground of Fact and Fiction: Some Reflections on Turkish Modernization', in *Rethinking Modernity and National Identity in Turkey*, eds. Sibel Bozdoğan and Reşat Kasaba (Seattle: Washington University Press, 1997), 252–60.

11. Vinayak Chaturvedi, 'Introduction', in *Mapping Subaltern Studies and the Postcolonial*, ed. Vinayak Chaturvedi (London: Verso, 2000), vii–xix.

12. Eric Hobsbawm, *On History* (London: Weidenfeld & Nicolson, 1997), 201–27.

13. Ranajit Guha, 'Preface', in *Subaltern Studies I. Writings in South Asian History and Society*, ed. Ranajit Guha (Delhi: Oxford University Press, 1982), vii.

and suggested rewriting the history of the modernization in non-Western societies by analysing the politics and agency of societal actors.

Alternative understandings of state–society interaction have also been informed by studies that look at the questions of power and agency in a relational manner and go beyond an understanding of the state as a clearly bounded, autonomous institution that is distinct from society.[14] They try to 'conceptualize "the state" *within* (and not automatically distinct from) other institutional forms through which social relations are lived'.[15] In such an understanding, the state–society boundary is more elusive than fixed. This, however, does not mean that the distinction should be erased altogether; nor does it mean that the state has to be conceptualized as a pure social construct. Rather, it means that it is necessary to revise the dominant understanding of state–society relations in oppositional terms and as a unidirectional interaction formed and dominated by the state.

Anthropological perspectives on state–society relations have similarly demonstrated that the interaction between state officials and common people in local contexts is essential to grasping how the state operates in practice and manifests itself in everyday life. Echoing the significance of the micro in studying the macro and emphasizing the critical role of 'the micropolitics of state work', they suggest that it is this encounter with the state in the local context by which people create their own means to cope with larger political processes.[16] In appreciating the strategies of common people in tackling the state, James C. Scott, for example, points at 'everyday forms of resistance'; acts that avoid direct confrontation with the authorities in the quest for largely immediate, de facto gains.[17] Scott suggests that each form of control is likely 'to generate its own distinctive forms of quiet resistance and counter-appropriation'.[18] By the same token, different ways in which societal actors respond to control and domination bring about different state policies in response. The crucial point is that whatever the response, the reaction of the common people changes or at least narrows the policy options available to the state.[19] Therefore, it is this interplay that determines the outcomes of state–society interactions and of the processes that are shaped by this interaction.

Joel Migdal's state-in-society approach most directly deals with the question of how to understand state–society relations in a less dichotomous way. It shares the assumptions regarding the analytical separation of state and society and the

---

14. For example, see Mustafa Emirbayer, 'Manifesto for a Relational Sociology', *The American Journal of Sociology* 103, no. 2 (1997): 281–317.

15. Aradhana Sharma and Akhil Gupta, 'Introduction: Rethinking Theories of the State in an Age of Globalization', in *The Anthropology of the State: A Reader*, eds. Aradhana Sharma and Akhil Gupta (Oxford: Blackwell Publishing, 2006), 9.

16. Ibid., 17.

17. James C. Scott, *Weapons of the Weak: Everyday Forms of Resistance* (New Haven: Yale University Press, 1985), 33.

18. Ibid., 34.

19. Ibid., 36.

significance of states as agents of change.[20] However, it diverges from state-oriented approaches in seeing the state as an agent situated in a certain social setting (thus 'state-in-society') and susceptible to the influence of social forces. In other words, the state-in-society approach is a critique of the perspective that sees the state as the fulcrum of the process of domination and change, as a force capable of shaping people's lives entirely.[21] In contrast, it maintains that the state is by no means the only force that matters: 'societies affect states as much as, or possibly more than, states affect societies'.[22] In this sense, state autonomy and effectiveness are always constrained, and even in countries with authoritarian regimes, the reach of the state is more limited than it is usually assumed to be.[23]

The state-in-society approach also suggests shifting the focus from the centre of state power to the periphery, from the topmost institutions of the state to its diffuse parts. Rather than clear-cut boundaries, the state-in-society approach sees blurred and constantly changing boundaries between the state and society. It argues that it is in the study of these boundaries, these junctures of encounter, conflict, negotiation and compromise, that we can better evaluate state power and its effectiveness, as well as the power of societal dynamics and the extent of social change. By referring to Scott's analysis of the failures of state plans in *Seeing Like a State*, Migdal claims that 'state policy implementation and the outcomes in society have ended up quite different from the state's original blueprints. Even the boldest state plans, as Scott has demonstrated in his discussion of the designs of modernism, can turn into disastrous follies.'[24] This is why the state-in-society approach suggests that in order to understand the processes of domination and change, we should examine the practices of the state while also recognizing the 'image' of the state.[25]

Migdal's state-in-society approach has been particularly inspiring for scholars studying authoritarian regimes, including single-party Turkey.[26] In fact, Migdal himself commented on the Turkish experience of modernization. He asserted that if we want to understand the social transformation initiated by the Kemalist regime, one should look at the 'effects' of the modernity project, which 'can be found not in

---

20. Joel S. Migdal, Atul Kohli and Vivienne Shue, 'Introduction: Developing a State-in-Society Perspective', in *State Power and Social Forces: Domination and Transformation in the Third World*, eds. Joel S. Migdal, Atul Kohli and Vivienne Shue (Cambridge: Cambridge University Press, 1994), 1–6.

21. Joel S. Migdal, *State in Society: Studying How States and Societies Transform and Constitute One Another* (Cambridge: Cambridge University Press, 2001), 7–8.

22. Ibid., 2.

23. Migdal, Kohli and Shue, 'Introduction', 3.

24. Migdal, *State in Society*, 12. See also James C. Scott, *Seeing Like a State: How Certain Schemes to Improve the Human Condition Have Failed* (New Haven: Yale University Press, 1998); Micheal De Certeau, *The Practice of Everyday Life* (Berkeley: University of California Press, 1984).

25. Migdal, *State in Society*, 22.

26. For example, see Senem Aslan, *Nation Building in Turkey and Morocco: Governing Turkish and Berber Dissent* (Cambridge: Cambridge University Press, 2014).

an examination of elites and their institutions exclusively, nor in a focus solely on the poor or marginal groups of society, but on those physical and social spaces the two intersect'.[27] This has precisely been the aim of a new body of literature that emerged as a critique of the state and elite-centred analyses of modern Turkey. Diverse in focus, methods and sources, this recent scholarship nevertheless reflects a common perspective, concerned with examining the dynamics of state–society relations, restoring the agency of people as social actors and looking at the everyday politics of modernization as a relational process. Michael Meeker, for instance, ascertained the ways in which the Turkish state was embedded in local society and how this embeddedness remained basically intact in the transition from the Ottoman Empire to the Turkish republic.[28] Thanks also to the opening of the state archives of the early republican period, new sources were scrutinized to shed more light on the complexities and contradictions of the state policies, as well as the mechanisms through which the societal actors negotiated the 'projects' of the Kemalist elite.[29] Studies that focus on the implementation process of a particular reform have enriched our understanding of the discrepancy between the visions and plans of the Kemalist elite in introducing that reform, on the one hand, and what had actually happened in practice when the plan was confronted by the micro mechanisms of interaction and negotiation between the forces of the state and society, on the other.[30]

This book is a part of and contributes to this developing body of literature on the social history of the early Turkish republic. Drawing on the theoretical insights briefly discussed above, particularly Migdal's state-in-society approach, it aims to understand the ways in which the Kemalist policies and reforms were received, interpreted, negotiated, compromised and/or resisted by actors in the provinces. By looking at the anti-veiling campaigns as a space/field where these negotiations took place, it aims to understand how state–society interactions were drawn and redrawn during the course of these campaigns, contesting and blurring the boundaries that are imagined to clearly separate the regime and the *halk*. In addition to this intervention in the historiography on modernization and social change in

---

27. Migdal, 'Finding the Meeting', 253–4.

28. Michael Meeker, *A Nation of Empire: The Ottoman Legacy of Turkish Modernity* (Berkeley: University of California Press, 2002).

29. For example, see Yiğit Akın, 'Reconsidering State, Party and Society in Early Republican Turkey: Politics of Petitioning', *International Journal of Middle East Studies* 39 (2007): 435–57; Sevgi Adak, 'Kemalist Laikliğin Oluşum Sürecinde Ramazanlar (1923-1938)', *Tarih ve Toplum Yeni Yaklaşımlar* 11 (Fall 2010): 47–88; Murat, Metinsoy, 'Kemalizmin Taşrası: Erken Cumhuriyet Taşrasında Parti, Devlet ve Toplum', *Toplum ve Bilim* 118 (2010): 124–64; Hale Yılmaz, *Becoming Turkish: Nationalist Reforms and Cultural Negotiations in Early Republican Turkey, 1923–1945* (Syracuse: Syracuse University Press, 2013); Alexandros Lamprou, *Nation Building in Modern Turkey: The 'People's Houses', the State and the Citizen* (London: I.B. Tauris, 2015).

30. For example, see Meltem Türköz, *Naming and Nation-Building in Turkey: The 1934 Surname Law* (New York: Palgrave Macmillan, 2018); Senem Aslan, '"Citizen Speak Turkish!" A Nation in the Making', *Nationalism and Ethnic Politics* 13, no. 2 (2007): 245–72.

interwar Turkey, the book also strives to provide a more nuanced understanding of the formation of a new gender order in the early republic by looking at the complex ways in which women responded to the anti-veiling campaigns. I argue that women had as much an impact on the shaping and implementation of the Kemalist reforms like the anti-veiling campaigns as they were influenced by them and they used the opportunity spaces opened up by such policies to negotiate their social positions and roles. In the light of this argument, I suggest that the feminist historiography on the early republic should also be revisited in order to better reflect women's role in the shaping of the Kemalist experience.

Feminist historiography, the early republic and women under Kemalism

Very few bodies of scholarship have altered the way we analyse the Turkish state and its ideological underpinnings as radically as the feminist scholarship that has flourished in Turkey since the 1980s. Although the issue of gender is still sometimes treated by some as a relatively peripheral component of a more serious 'bigger picture', feminist scholars of modern Turkey have established that the political debate around gender roles and women's rights and liberties has been on the centre stage of Turkish politics since the establishment of the republic, and that the foundations of the Turkish state were shaped by a gender regime radically redefined to meet the necessities of the new nation-state.

Although a number of studies have explored the situation of women in Turkey until the late 1970s (particularly in the field of demography, women's health and sociology of the family), it has really been since the beginning of the 1980s that a feminist scholarship with an exclusive focus on women and gender has emerged. While some of the earliest examples of this scholarship maintained a 'critically Kemalist' approach,[31] the core of the feminist thinking soon came to be dominated by a radical feminist stance entirely critical of Kemalist modernization. This coincided with the advent of the second-wave feminist movement in Turkey in the 1980s. The focus of the scholarship also shifted to analysing the early republican era and problematizing the modernist-Kemalist discourse on women's emancipation.

This radical feminist scholarship still emphasized the achievements of the period, such as the adoption of a secular civil code.[32] Nonetheless, rather than following what had been the hegemonic narrative until then, that these rights were given to women by a benevolent regime, feminist historians demonstrated that these issues had long been on the agenda of the women's movement, which had flourished in the late Ottoman Empire and became institutionalized after the establishment of the new nation-state in the Turkish Women's Union (*Türk Kadınlar Birliği*) in 1924. As they unearthed the Ottoman and early republican women's activism through their

---

31. See Nermin Abadan-Unat, ed., *Women in Turkish Society* (Leiden: Brill, 1981).

32. For a critical assessment of the impacts of the Civil Code, see Ece Kocabıçak, 'What Excludes Women from Landownership in Turkey? Implications for Feminist Strategies', *Women's Studies International Forum* 69 (July–August 2018): 115–25.

pioneering research, feminist scholars successfully challenged the narrative that the Kemalist state was the sole initiator and thus ultimate guardian of women's rights in Turkey. In fact, this independent women's movement inherited from Ottoman women, characterized as first-wave feminism in the literature, was not tolerated by the Kemalist single-party state. The eventual suppression of first-wave feminism not only marked the beginning of a troublesome history in terms of the relationship between the state and women's rights activism in Turkey, but it also put the state, and particularly its ideological manifestation, Kemalism, at the centre of the feminist critique and scholarly inquiry. Consequently, the feminist criticism of Kemalist reforms and discourse (and thus, mainly the feminist scholarship on the early republican period) was central to the shaping of gender research and scholarship in Turkey. Even the analyses of some contemporary issues in the field, such as the Kurdish women's movement or new female religiosities, include an often-implicit reference to a particular feminist reading of the founding gender regime of the Turkish state and the consequences of this regime for women. One can see here the parallelism between the feminist scholarship's focus on the Kemalist discourse on women and the hegemonic approach to the single-party period and Kemalism in the literature that prioritizes the study of the policies and discourse of the central elite.

The feminist criticism of Kemalist modernization produced a very rich literature indeed. Although there are many layers to its richness, three points stand out as its key and most influential arguments. The first is the class bias of the republican reforms, which benefitted mainly urban middle-class women.[33] Accordingly, while the Kemalist regime paved the way for a very limited number of urban elite women to become professionals and equal subjects in public life, it left the lives of the majority of women largely unaffected. Even if it did manage to touch their lives, its message for these women was nevertheless very different. They would be part of the modernization of the nation by playing the role of disciplined housewives and mothers. A derivative of this class bias argument would be criticizing those elite Kemalist women for embracing and internalizing the Kemalist emancipation narrative, becoming its forerunners and doing their share in modernizing 'other' women.[34]

The second point emphasized by the feminist scholarship is that the Kemalist project of women's emancipation was inherently patriarchal and particularly keen

---

33. Deniz Kandiyoti, 'Emancipated but Unliberated? Reflections on the Turkish Case', *Feminist Studies* 13, no 2 (1987): 317–39; Yeşim Arat, 'The Project of Modernity and Women in Turkey', *Rethinking Modernity and National Identity in Turkey*, eds. Sibel Bozdoğan and Reşat Kasaba (Seattle: University of Washington Press, 1997), 95–112; Deniz Kandiyoti, 'Gendering the Modern: On Missing Dimensions in the Study of Turkish Modernity', in *Rethinking Modernity and National Identity in Turkey*, eds. Sibel Bozdoğan and Reşat Kasaba (Seattle: University of Washington Press, 1997), 113–32.

34. Arat, 'The Project', 101. See also Şirin Tekeli, '1980'ler Türkiyesi'nde Kadınlar', in *1980'ler Türkiyesi'nde Kadın Bakışaçısından Kadınlar* içinde, ed. Şirin Tekeli (Istanbul: İletişim, 1990), 15–49; Serpil Sancar, *Türk Modernleşmesinin Cinsiyeti: Erkekler Devlet Kadınlar Aile Kurar* (İstanbul: İletişim, 2012).

on controlling women's bodies and female sexuality.[35] This has been, I would argue, the most significant, paradigm-shifting contribution of the feminist scholarship, the implications of which have not yet been fully explored. The third argument has to do with the characterization of the Kemalist approach to women's rights as 'state feminism', as formulated by Şirin Tekeli.[36] According to this analysis, Kemalist modernizing reforms that aimed at achieving women's rights were instrumental in nature. The Kemalist elite had used these reforms to underline the modern and democratic aspirations of the new state and it was through these reforms that the Kemalist state could position itself as the guardian of gender equality. This argument complemented the previous two in calling attention to the problematic aspects of the Kemalist discourse of women's emancipation and highlighted how it had the effect of impeding the development of a feminist agenda of women's liberation. This finds its most salient and famous formulation in Deniz Kandiyoti's much-cited article depicting women as 'emancipated but unliberated' citizens of the new republic.[37]

As apparent from this very brief overview, the primary focus of the feminist scholarship in Turkey has been the state, and more specifically, the discursive and ideological manifestations of the Kemalist women's emancipation project. I argue that as innovative and transformative as it has been in its critique of both the Kemalist and revisionist (but equally blind when it comes to gender) narratives of the single-party period, the feminist scholarship too has been shaped by an approach that sees the state and society in dichotomous terms, overestimates the role of ideology and elite discourses, and underestimates the capacity of women of all strata to negotiate with elite discourse and imaginations on the ground. Because the state and its ideological manifestations were at the centre of the critique and scholarly inquiry and because decoding their patriarchal nature and restoring women's roles in the nation-state formation were urgent tasks, feminist scholarship has also focused, almost exclusively, on women's movements and organized political activism. As a result, again, we know a great deal about the 'ideal Turkish woman' celebrated by the Kemalist regime, the male elite discourses around new gender identities promoted by the nationalist-modernist ideology and various manifestations of these visions and discourses in state policies, in legislation, in public debate in newspapers, in major elements of the visual culture and in women's journals. We also have now detailed studies of women's organizations and activism in the first three decades of the twentieth century and the various ways in which this women's movement tried to negotiate state policies regarding women. However, our knowledge is much more limited when it comes to ordinary women,

---

35. Kandiyoti, 'Emancipated'; Arat, 'The Project'; Fatmagül Berktay, 'Cumhuriyet'in 75 Yıllık Serüvenine Kadınlar Açısından Bakmak', in *75 Yılda Kadınlar ve Erkekler*, ed. Ayşe Berktay Hacımirzaoğlu (Istanbul: Tarih Vakfı Yayınları, 1998), 1–11; Ayşe Saktanber, 'Kemalist Kadın Hakları Söylemi', in *Modern Türkiye'de Siyasî Düşünce*, Cilt 2, *Kemalizm*, ed. Ahmet İnsel (Istanbul: İletişim, 2001), 323–33.

36. Tekeli, '1980'ler Türkiyesi'nde'.

37. Kandiyoti, 'Emancipated'.

women living in the provinces, women who did not openly engage in political activism, and their experiences of the so-called Kemalist reforms.

Understanding women's experiences of modernizing reforms and their reactions to or involvements with them requires a more nuanced appraisal of the Kemalist experience than one finds in the existing feminist literature. This refined understanding needs to reflect the complexities of the transformation of everyday lives of ordinary women and their 'ordinary' agencies. Such an approach entails rethinking the class-bias argument of the feminist scholarship and challenging the idea that apart from a group of urban middle-class women, women's lives were largely unaffected. The assumption that those women who 'complied' with the Kemalist policies were passive carriers of their message needs also to be revisited. These imperatives involve 'going local' and focusing on the provinces. They require linking the micro and the macro, the lives of ordinary women in a certain locality to larger processes of the transformation of the gender order. If we turn our attention from the discourse and reforms of the Kemalist elite in Ankara and look more at the ways in which state policies were implemented and negotiated at the local level, we can see that women were able to influence these policies in many different ways. The case of the anti-veiling campaigns of the 1930s is one rich terrain that can be used to trace such influences of women on the modernization process.

Anti-veiling campaigns in interwar Turkey

In her article on unveiling in early twentieth-century Egypt, Beth Baron indicates that the veil has been 'the quintessential metaphor for Middle Eastern women'.[38] Indeed, this has been the case for Muslim women in general.[39] Although its history did not begin with Islam and it has been a complex and changing issue with multiple aspects that cannot be reduced to religious questions, the practice of veiling and the wider system of gender segregation have been overwhelmingly associated with Muslim societies, marking their 'difference' from their 'Western' counterparts.[40] When modernization and 'catching up with the West' became the primary agenda of the modernist political elites and nationalist intellectuals of the Muslim-majority societies, the so-called 'woman question' was soon the main issue; everywhere, women were 'localized as a sphere of backwardness and defined as individuals who were to be uplifted' for the good of the nation.[41] The

---

38. Beth Baron, 'Unveiling in Early Twentieth Century Egypt: Practical and Symbolic Considerations', *Middle Eastern Studies* 25, no. 3 (July 1989): 370.

39. For a detailed discussion, see Meyda Yeğenoğlu, *Colonial Fantasies: Towards a Feminist Reading of Orientalism* (Cambridge: Cambridge University Press, 1998).

40. For a detailed analysis, see Leila Ahmed, *Women and Gender in Islam: Historical Roots of a Modern Debate* (New Haven: Yale University Press, 1992).

41. Omnia Shakry, 'Schooled Mothers and Structured Play: Child Rearing in Turn-of-the-Century Egypt', in *Remaking Women: Feminism and Modernity in the Middle East*, ed. Lila Abu-Lughod (Princeton: Princeton University Press, 1998), 143.

veil, in particular, was of central concern in this uplifting; its removal would be the most visible symbol of the social change the modernist Muslim elites envisaged. Unveiling thus became an agenda item for the modernization discourses across the wider global Muslim context from the late nineteenth century onwards, paving the way in a number of countries to more systematic attempts to do away with veiling practices during the interwar period.

The anti-veiling campaigns in 1930s Turkey were part of both this wider picture, the surge of 'reforming' the veil in Muslim countries and the Kemalist reforms that were concerned with clothing in general. The importance of clothing for the Kemalist regime stemmed primarily from the power it had to shape identities in the public sphere. As Alev Çınar argues, clothing can be considered as 'one of the most powerful tools for the display of identities due to its temporally and spatially proliferative quality',[42] and this quality was what concerned the Kemalist regime the most, in terms of both controlling and regulating society and transforming it into a modern, civilized nation. The Hat Law in 1925 was the most apparent and earliest manifestation of this Kemalist concern. Only regulating men's clothing, the law nevertheless made it explicit that one fundamental aspect of the Kemalist project of building a secular nation state was to create new, 'modern' subjects who would transform the public sphere into a modern domain through their very existence. In contrast to its determination to directly intervene in men's headgear, the Kemalist regime was more reluctant to apply the same approach to women's veiling and clothing.

The main strategy Ankara followed regarding the issue of unveiling was to transfer the matter to the local level and encourage the local administrative bodies and their actors to deal with it. In other words, despite the fact that there was no law or decree banning women's veiling country-wide, there were anti-veiling campaigns organized at the local level that were clearly encouraged by Ankara, albeit in some cases, they could also stem from the local elite's own initiatives. Thus, there was state intervention in women's clothing during the early republic, but it was local in character, shaped and implemented mainly by actors on the ground. Given the complicated involvement of Ankara in the process and its reluctant attitude, which swayed between promoting local efforts and limiting them, combined with the diversity of the attitudes and reactions of the local elite, women and other societal actors, the process at the local level was in fact quite complex. The local character of anti-veiling campaigns and the lack of solid and consistent policy guidelines

---

42. Alev Çınar, *Modernity, Islam, and Secularism in Turkey: Bodies, Places and Time* (Minneapolis: University of Minnesota Press, 2005), 57. For a discussion on the role the anti-veiling campaigns played in reorganizing the public sphere, see Sevgi Adak, 'Women in the Post-Ottoman Public Sphere: Anti-Veiling Campaigns and the Reshaping of the Urban Space in Early Republican Turkey', in *Women and the City, Women in the City: A Gendered Perspective on Ottoman Urban History*, ed. Nazan Maksudyan (New York: Berghahn, 2014), 36–67.

led to space for discussions, negotiations and local variations, which, in the end, resulted in a more multidimensional and less radical transformation of women's clothing and gender norms in the provinces. Moreover, although Europeanization of women's dress was the ideal, the anti-veiling campaigns mainly aimed at the removal of the *peçe* (face veil) and the *çarşaf*,[43] and certain local equivalents of the *çarşaf*, such as the *peştamal*. The covering of the hair was never openly targeted. This limited scope of the campaigns provided certain room for women's selective adaptation, and created possibilities of maintaining the existing dress norms, except for the use of the *peçe*, *çarşaf* and *peştamal*.

Since veiling encompassed the whole system of the seclusion of women,[44] unveiling entailed a direct intervention in deeply rooted gender codes. As such, the example of anti-veiling campaigns offers a very rich milieu ideal for exploring the attitudes, strategies and actions of the central state actors, local elites and women, and the ways in which they interacted and negotiated. As profoundly gendered processes, these interactions and negotiations played a significant role in the transformation of the dominant gender regime, and thus the transformation of state–society relations. In other words, anti-veiling campaigns cannot be understood within the framework of clothing change only. Nor can they be compartmentalized as a sub-field, yet another Kemalist reform, as the gender aspect is often seen in relation to 'more important' processes of social change. As Kandiyoti has emphasized, politics of gender is '*intrinsic* rather than *incidental*' to understanding the ideology and character of a political regime.[45] Consequently, the anti-veiling campaigns constitute a terrain upon which it is possible to explore not just the transformation of the gender regime in the early republic, but the dynamics of how the state worked as well as interacted with various segments of the society, shaping the contours of the social change under Kemalism.

Despite their significance, however, the number of studies on the anti-veiling campaigns in early republican Turkey is very limited. The Turkish case received significantly less attention compared to some other Muslim contexts where similar attempts were made almost synchronously, such as Iran and Uzbekistan. The first scholarly work that mentioned local bans on the *peçe* and the *çarşaf* that were put into place by a number of local administrations was Bernard Caporal's doctoral dissertation entitled 'La Femme turque à travers le kémalisme et le postkémalisme (1919–1970)', which was published in Turkish in 1982.[46] Caporal, however, did not

---

43. The *çarşaf* is a long, full-body cover that also envelops the head. It is usually black. Although it can be used together with the *peçe*, the *peçe* is not a standard part of it.

44. Baron, 'Unveiling', 370.

45. Deniz Kandiyoti, 'Locating the Politics of Gender: Patriarchy, Neoliberal Governance and Violence in Turkey', *Research and Policy on Turkey* 1, no 2 (2016): 103.

46. Bernard Caporal, *Kemalizmde ve Kemalizm Sonrasında Türk Kadını (1919–1970)* (Ankara: Türkiye İş Bankası Kültür Yayınları, 1982).

discuss these bans in any detail and only mentioned the few bans he could locate. This short note by Caporal remained largely unnoticed until women's headscarves became an issue at Turkish universities and were transformed into a matter of political controversy in the public debates from the late 1980s onwards. Those women who faced the headscarf ban at universities became increasingly politicized. Devout women intellectuals in particular began to search for the historical grounds on which women's veiling came to be linked to political debates on modernity, secularism and the public sphere in Turkey. One of those women, Cihan Aktaş, published a detailed account of the history of state intervention in the way people dressed in the Ottoman/Turkish context based on secondary sources, in which she also used a few oral historical accounts on the *peçe* and the *çarşaf*.[47] In the first major scholarly works that were published on the headscarf debate and Islamic women's identity in the early 1990s, a discussion on the question of state intervention in women's veiling in the early republic was still missing, apart from the emphasis on the Kemalist project of creating a modern and national Turkish womanhood.[48]

A short article by Metin Çapa provided the first account of the banning of the *peçe* in one province, Trabzon, in 1926.[49] Another article, by Hakkı Uyar, enlarged Çapa's analysis of this early banning of the *peçe* in Trabzon by bringing in the coverage in local newspapers and established that the *peçe* and the *çarşaf* had in fact became an issue in Turkey in the mid-1930s.[50] Kemal Yakut's article was the first to use a few documents from the archive of the RPP on the anti-veiling campaigns after the opening of the state archives.[51] These three short but important articles published in Turkish did not receive the attention they deserved in subsequent scholarly works. Although they had been able to unearth only a few examples of anti-veiling campaigns, they provided some significant insights as to how research on the anti-veiling campaigns could be expanded. Following these insights, Hale Yılmaz devoted a chapter in her book on the regulation of women's clothing in the early republic.[52] Yılmaz's work brought the anti-veiling campaigns into the English-language literature on the early Turkish republic and expanded the discussion on them based on new documents from police archives and oral historical accounts. Her own interview with a woman from an educated middle-class family in Trabzon, combined with previously published oral historical

---

47. Cihan Aktaş, *Tanzimat'tan 12 Mart'a Kılık-Kıyafet ve İktidar*, 2nd ed. (Istanbul: Kapı, 2006).

48. See Aynur İlyasoğlu, *Örtülü Kimlik* (Istanbul: Metis, 1994); Nilüfer Göle, *Forbidden Modern: Civilization and Veiling* (Ann Arbor: University of Michigan Press, 1996).

49. Mesut Çapa, 'Giyim Kuşamda Medeni Kıyafetlerin Benimsenmesi ve Trabzon Örneği', *Toplumsal Tarih* 30 (June 1996): 22–8.

50. Hakkı Uyar, 'Çarşaf, Peçe ve Kafes Üzerine Bazı Notlar', *Toplumsal Tarih* 33 (September 1996): 6–11.

51. Kemal Yakut, 'Tek Parti Döneminde Peçe ve Çarşaf', *Tarih ve Toplum* 220 (April 2002): 23–32.

52. Yılmaz, *Becoming Turkish*, 78–138.

accounts from other provinces,[53] allowed us to hear the voices of women who had lived through the anti-veiling campaigns. More recently, an edited volume by Stephanie Cronin brought together examples of fresh research on the anti-veiling campaigns in Muslim contexts, with three chapters on the Turkish case.[54]

This book is the first monograph on the anti-veiling campaigns in the early Turkish republic. It is an endeavour to go beyond an analysis of these campaigns that is rooted in the discourse and strategies of the high-level state actors. It is novel in that it attempts to avoid employing the kind of elite-centred analysis that has in fact shaped much of the literature on clothing change in the Middle East. As Tapper and Ingham have noted, studies on dress and clothing changes in the region have exclusively focused on the role of political or religious authorities.[55] According to this approach, the impetus for change in the way people dress comes only from above and inevitably and automatically changes social and cultural identities in the way the imposer of the change/reform imagined. In contrast, this book examines the anti-veiling campaigns of the 1930s as they were implemented through concrete strategies and actions at the local level and shaped through the interaction of various actors. Its contribution to the existing literature on the anti-veiling campaigns in Turkey specifically is twofold. First, it presents a detailed trajectory of the debates on and attempts at women's unveiling in Turkey starting from the late Ottoman Empire onwards. It discusses the anti-veiling campaigns of the 1920s separately as weak but significant attempts that created certain patterns for later campaigns and focuses on what I call the main wave of anti-veiling campaigns in the mid-1930s. Thus, this book gives the most comprehensive account of the anti-veiling campaigns in the early Turkish republic, scrutinizing the general political discourses behind

---

53. Sevil Atauz, 'Cumhuriyet'in İlk Yıllarında Gaziantep'te Gündelik Yaşamın Dönüşümü: Bir Sözlü Tarih Çalışması', in *Bilanço 1923–1998, Türkiye Cumhuriyeti'nin 75 Yılına Toplu Bakış Uluslararası Kongresi Cilt 1: Siyaset, Kültür, Uluslararası İlişkiler*, ed. Zeynep Rona (Istanbul: Tarih Vakfı Yurt Yayınları, 1999), 217–29; Arzu Öztürkmen, 'Remembering through Material Culture: Local Knowledge of Past Communities in a Turkish Black Sea Town', *Middle Eastern Studies* 39, no. 2 (April 2003): 179–193; Arzu Öztürkmen, 'Rethinking Regionalism: Memory of Change in a Turkish Black Sea Town', *East European Quarterly* 39, no. 1 (March 2005): 47–62.

54. Kathryn Libal, 'From Face Veil to Cloche Hat: The Backward Ottoman versus New Turkish Woman in Urban Public Discourse', in *Anti-Veiling Campaigns in the Muslim World: Gender, Modernism and the Politics of Dress*, ed. Stephanie Cronin (London: Routledge, 2014), 39–58; Sevgi Adak, 'Anti-Veiling Campaigns and the Local Elites in Turkey of the 1930s: A View from the Periphery', in *Anti-Veiling Campaigns*, 59–85; and Murat Metinsoy, 'Everyday Resistance to Unveiling and Flexible Secularism in Early Republican Turkey', in *Anti-Veiling Campaigns*, 86–117.

55. Nancy Lindisfarne-Tapper and Bruce Ingham, 'Approaches to the Study of Dress in the Middle East', in *Languages of Dress in the Middle East*, eds. Nancy Lindisfarne-Tapper and Bruce Ingham (London: Curzon Press, 1997), 14–15.

them and dissecting the legal and institutional mechanisms through which they were formulated and implemented. It provides a snapshot of the campaigns in all aspects and as a general reform experience. By drawing upon a large survey of provinces, this study clearly demonstrates that the anti-veiling campaigns were not limited to a few provinces or confined to specific regions but a countrywide phenomenon.[56]

Second, while looking at the main characteristics of the anti-veiling campaigns across the provinces and analysing them as a widespread reform process, this study also probes deeper into the local context. With a strong emphasis on the significance of studying the local, it analyses the campaigns within the complexities of their local settings and politics. However, digging into the local context does not mean that the book focuses on a small number of cases. It does not discuss a particular anti-veiling campaign in a specific locality in its full detail, for example. Nor does it aim at such an exhaustive analysis. In other words, this is not a study of the local as micro history. Rather, the book delves into the local to see the micro dynamics of the campaigns across various cases.

This twofold focus of the study, the general discursive, legal and institutional framework within which the anti-veiling campaigns were shaped and implemented country-wide, on the one hand, and the micro dynamics of this process at the local level, on the other, was made possible thanks to a selection of diverse sources. First, this book makes extensive use of local newspapers. Twelve local newspapers from eight provinces (Adana, Antalya, Bursa, Izmir, İçel, Kars, Konya and Trabzon) were examined. This not only provided a very rich and new body of information with which to see the details of the situation at the local level, but also made it possible to draw the most comprehensive map of the anti-veiling campaigns in the 1930s existing in the literature so far.[57] Second, documents from the Turkish state and the police archives, as well as the American and British consular reports were used. The British consular reports, in particular, were extremely helpful as a way to enrich the analysis of the local context, since they provided very rare observations of the situation at the local level, which could be compared and contrasted with the reports from Turkish state sources in the provinces. In fact, it is the combination of these three different sources of information – the local newspapers, the Turkish state and police documents, and the consular reports – that provided a very broad lens through which a general picture of the patterns of interaction between the actors at various levels could be gotten, while at the same time making it possible to dig into the local to see the complexity and diversity in the periphery of the country.

---

56. In other words, the campaigns were not concentrated in any particular region. Yılmaz, on the other hand, thinks that the bans on the *peçe* and the *çarşaf* appear to be more common in the Western provinces and in the coastal and border towns. Yılmaz, *Becoming Turkish*, 102.

57. The list of the local bans that I could locate is provided in the Appendix.

Organization of the book

The book is composed of five chapters. Chapter 1 focuses on the debates on women's un/veiling and attempts that were made to launch anti-veiling campaigns before the 1930s. It begins with a discussion of the Ottoman legacy, demonstrating that the debate on the *peçe* and the *çarşaf* originates from questions of modernization, progress and women's roles in the context of a rapidly changing Ottoman society in the nineteenth century. The chapter then looks at the nascent Turkish republic, early Kemalist visions of women's clothing, the Hat Law of 1925 and the question of how the regime's intervention in male clothing was linked to the question of women's veiling. A number of anti-veiling campaigns that were initiated at the local level in the second half of the 1920s are discussed within the context of a general campaign on the modernization of dress that the Hat Law of 1925 sparked. The chapter concludes by discussing the patterns and mechanisms these early attempts set for the following anti-veiling campaigns in the 1930s.

Chapter 2 discusses the anti-veiling campaigns in the 1930s as the main wave of women's unveiling and situates them within the broader context of 1930s Turkey. Following a discussion of the 1930s as a turn to a more authoritarian regime, the chapter analyses the increasing stigmatization of the *peçe* and the *çarşaf* as 'uncivilized' clothing in the 1930s and the regime's greater emphasis on women's emancipation. Following sections tackle three main questions: Why did the main wave of the anti-veiling campaigns begin in the mid-1930s, and more specifically, in 1934? What were their scope and content, and through which discourses were they legitimized? Upon what legal bases were they organized and implemented? The last section of the chapter outlines the position of Ankara on the anti-veiling campaigns and traces the gradual increase in Ankara's tendency to intervene in the local context and control the situation in the provinces while at the same time remaining hesitant to intervene in people's lives 'too much' in terms of un/veiling. This somewhat ambivalent position of Ankara, it is argued, widened the space of action for local elites.

Chapter 3 turns the focus to the local. It first discusses the place of the local in the literature on the single-party era in Turkey. It provides a working definition of the concept of local elite and examines how this concept can be used to see the diversity of actors at the local level. The second section looks at the various ways local elites influenced the shaping and the implementation of the anti-veiling campaigns. It shows that as a composite group, the attitudes of the local elites were diverse and their tackling of the question of women's unveiling ranged from 'being more royalist than the king' to openly resisting it. The last section discusses attitudes and reactions of the ordinary people with the contention that the importance of the local cannot be fully highlighted by looking at how the local elites negotiated Kemalism only. It looks at the reactions of non-elite actors, defined as popular resistance, and the extent to which this resistance could influence the shaping of the anti-veiling campaigns.

Chapter 4 focuses on reactions of women as the primary target of the campaigns. It situates women as 'visible' actors of the campaigns whose agency could not be reduced to the dichotomy of passive compliance and open resistance. Through a detailed analysis of the quite diverse and innovative ways women dealt with the campaigns, the chapter argues that the campaigns opened an 'opportunity space' for women to negotiate their position in the society and the prevalent gender norms shaping their lives. The emphasis, therefore, is on women's roles as subjects of Kemalist modernization in the provinces, rather than its objects, and on their capacity to manipulate, adapt, modify and domesticate the new dress codes in complex ways. As such, the chapter also engages in a critical dialogue with the feminist literature on the Kemalist regime.

The last chapter situates the anti-veiling campaigns in 1930s Turkey within the wider context of predominantly Muslim societies during the interwar period. It discusses the Turkish case together with other experiences of state or elite-initiated campaigns for women's unveiling and deals with the question of how these experiences informed each other. Following a brief, general discussion on common trends and discourses, as well as variations, the chapter focuses on three cases, Turkey, Iran and Albania, as closest comparable experiences. It provides a comparative discussion with the aim of understanding the Turkish case more vividly by sharpening the analysis of its distinguishing features outlined in the previous chapters. The chapter shows how the relative diversity of local actors and institutions in the Turkish case, as well as the relatively larger capacity of the Turkish state to accommodate them, can be factors making the anti-veiling campaigns in 1930s Turkey relatively more effective and less conflictual when seen within the wider Muslim context.

Chapter 1

THE UN/VEILING ISSUE: FROM THE LATE OTTOMAN EMPIRE TO THE REPUBLIC

Women's clothing has been a matter of intense debate in Turkey since Ottoman times. The Ottoman state issued various directives and regulations seeking to control women's dress, specifically to monitor Muslim women's adherence to Islamic dress codes by intervening in the length of veils or the thickness of the fabric used for them. The colour, size and form of women's dress were all subject to state regulation. As Quataert emphasizes, these regulations were part of a long tradition of Ottoman clothing laws that aimed at extending state control over society and disciplining the behaviour of its subjects.[1] In the eighteenth century, for example, when upper-class Ottoman women began to wear fancy *feraces*,[2] the Ottoman state felt a need to impose restrictions on *ferace* styles, especially by banning tight models and thin fabrics as a result of pressure from the ulema.[3] Regulations demanding modesty in women's clothes, and, above all, admonishing Muslim women against imitating Christian women or European styles, were on the rise with the increasing influence of the West in the nineteenth century. Although the extent of this influence was uneven in different provinces of the empire, it was clearly visible in major urban centres like Istanbul, which seem to be where the clothing regulations regarding women's dress were directed.[4]

---

1. Donald Quataert, 'Clothing Laws, State, and Society in the Ottoman Empire, 1720–1829', *International Journal of Middle East Studies* 29, no. 3 (1997): 403–25.

2. The *ferace* is a long mantle, a full coat with wide arms, body and skirt that reaches the floor. The *ferace* changed significantly over time, especially in the nineteenth century. Its form and colour diversified and it was transformed into a long overcoat-like outfit by the end of the empire. Reşat Ekrem Koçu, *Türk Giyim Kuşam ve Süslenme Sözlüğü* (Istanbul: Sümerbank Kültür Yayınları, 1969), 108–11.

3. Aktaş, *Tanzimat'tan*, 54; Serpil Çakır, *Osmanlı Kadın Hareketi*, 2nd ed. (Istanbul: Metis, 2011), 247.

4. Most of the time, the sources are not clear about the targeted geography of the Ottoman clothing regulations regarding women's dress. Koçu indicates that the first regulation that prohibited Ottoman women from dressing inappropriately (meaning, not properly covered) was issued in the eighteenth century during the reign of Sultan Ahmet III. This regulation was concerned only with the clothing of the women in Istanbul, for example. Likewise, the regulations in the Hamidian era seem also to be limited to Istanbul. Koçu, *Türk Giyim*, 8–9.

Western influence could be seen in the ongoing changes in women's social roles and dress that had begun in the Tanzimat era, particularly as regards the tendency of upper-class Ottoman women in urban areas to follow and adopt European fashions following the Crimean War.[5] Şeni indicates that in its transformed form, elite Ottoman women's outdoor clothing was in fact very similar to that worn by European women in the late nineteenth century, something that was criticized in the Ottoman satire of the time.[6]

Women's attire had become a central issue and a locus of struggle for the supporters of various political positions towards the late nineteenth century. In the 1870s, a set of regulations concerning women's dress prohibiting the use of transparent face veils and light-coloured *feraces* were issued.[7] This was also a period when the *çarşaf* increasingly replaced the *ferace* as Ottoman women's outdoor attire.[8] However, in 1881, Sultan Abdülhamid II issued a regulation based on the advice of the *Şeyhülislam*, the highest religious officer of the Ottoman state, which banned the use of the *çarşaf* in public and crowded places, limited its use to side streets, and urged the police to report women wearing thin face veils and gathering in groups in public places.[9] Regulations on women's clothing continued throughout the reign of Abdülhamid II, but the restrictions had little effect and various kinds of women's outdoor dress continued to co-exist in public spaces. In 1889, the use of the *ferace* was restricted and only women residing in the palace were allowed to wear it.[10] This resulted in an increase in the use of the *çarşaf* especially by urban women. Nevertheless, due to the security concerns of the sultan, who was worried that the *çarşaf* would be used to hide the wearer's identity,

---

5. Yakut, 'Tek Parti'; Sarah Graham-Brown, *Images of Women, The Portrayal of Women in Photography of the Middle East, 1860–1950* (New York: Columbia University Press, 1988); Fanny Davis, *The Ottoman Lady: A Social History from 1718 to 1918* (New York: Greenwood Press, 1986).

6. Nora Şeni, 'Fashion and Women's Clothing in the Satirical Press of Istanbul at the End of the 19th Century', in *Women in Modern Turkish Society*, ed. Şirin Tekeli (London: Zed Books, 1995), 30.

7. Meral Akkent and Gaby Frager, *Başörtü* (Frankfurt: Dağyeli, 1987), 106.

8. According to some scholars, the *çarşaf* originated in the Arab provinces and the first woman that appeared in Istanbul in the *çarşaf* was the wife of the Syrian governor Suphi Pasha in the mid-nineteenth century. Akkent and Frager, *Başörtü*, 105; Melek Sevüktekin Apak, Filiz Onat Gündüz and Fatma Öztürk Eray, *Osmanlı Dönemi Kadın Giyimleri* (Ankara: Türkiye İş Bankası Kültür Yayınları, 1997), 103; Aktaş, *Tanzimat'tan*, 68–70. It is argued that it was adopted as a reaction to the cultural Westernization of nineteenth-century Ottoman society since the *çarşaf* was supposed to offer better veiling compared to the *ferace*. Muhaddere Taşçıoğlu, *Türk Osmanlı Cemiyetinde Kadının Sosyal Durumu ve Kadın Kıyafetleri* (Ankara: Akın Matbaası, 1958), 23.

9. Akkent and Frager, *Başörtü*, 106.

10. Servet Muhtar Alus, 'II. Abdülhamid Devrinde Kadın Kıyafetleri', *Resimli Tarih Mecmuası* 2, no. 13 (January 1951): 544–7. Koçu argues that this decision proved to have little effect. Koçu, *Türk Giyim*, 9.

it was banned in 1892.[11] This ban also proved ineffective and women continued to use the *çarşaf* as a common veil.

Public debates over the *peçe* and the *çarşaf* intensified in the aftermath of the 1908 Constitutional Revolution. In fact, according to foreign observers, one of the immediate changes the 1908 revolution ushered in was a decrease in the number of women wearing the *peçe* and the *çarşaf* in Istanbul.[12] The latest trends in European fashion, which came to be associated with progress, were often adopted by elite women.[13] *Çarşaf* models became shorter and more diversified, and began to resemble cloaks.[14] Continuous warfare in the 1910s also had dramatic effects on the lives and public presence of Ottoman women. Many women began to work in governmental offices, workshops and trades, thereby significantly increasing women's participation in public life.[15] This created more room for women's freedom and eased the pressure of seclusion. Further relaxation of women's veiling in urban centres was criticized by conservatives on the grounds of women's dignity and the duty of the Ottoman state to abide by Islamic regulations. The idea of making the *çarşaf* compulsory for women by law was proposed by some in journals like *Sırat-ı Müstakim*.[16] In 1912, Şeyhülislam Abdurrahman Nesib Efendi issued a statement declaring that changes in the styles of women's *çarşaf*s would not be tolerated and women should abide by the Sharia norms regarding clothing. Yakut indicates that while the statement had little effect, similar measures were attempted by other conservative state officials in following years and the question of controlling women's veiling continued to be a concern.[17] Women who adopted more modernized versions of the *peçe* and the *çarşaf* were severely criticized. There were even attacks on women in the streets of Istanbul.[18] To counter

---

11. Akkent and Frager mention that the sultan had prohibited the use of the *çarşaf* in 1883 as well. Akkent and Frager, *Başörtü*, 106–9.

12. Caporal, *Kemalizmde*, 146. Some women were attacked in Istanbul for not abiding by religious norms. Yakut, 'Tek Parti', 23–4.

13. Brummet indicates that in the satirical press of the era, Ottoman women's attraction to *allafranca* lifestyle was severely criticized. Palmira Brummet, *Image and Imperialism in the Ottoman Revolutionary Press, 1908–1911* (Albany: State University of New York Press, 2000), 226–30.

14. There were different *çarşaf* styles in use, such as baggy *çarşaf* (*torba çarşaf*) and cloak *çarşaf* (*pelerinli çarşaf*). Apak et al., *Osmanlı Dönemi*, 104. There was also a type called tango *çarşaf*, which was a name used for the Europeanized *çarşaf* models with shorter skirts and cloaks. Taşçıoğlu, *Türk Osmanlı*, 53.

15. Yavuz Selim Karakışla, *Women, War and Work in the Ottoman Empire: Society for the Employment of Ottoman Muslim Women (1916-1923)* (Istanbul: Ottoman Bank Archives and Research Centre, 2005).

16. Caporal, *Kemalizmde*, 81.

17. Yakut, 'Tek Parti', 24.

18. Yaprak Zihnioğlu, *Kadınsız İnkılap: Nezihe Muhittin, Kadınlar Halk Fırkası, Kadın Birliği* (Istanbul: Metis, 2003), 109–10; Nicole A.V.M. van Os, 'Feminism, Philanthropy and Patriotism: Female Associational Life in the Ottoman Empire' (PhD diss., Leiden University, 2013), 220. In 1912, the Ministry of the Interior had issued an order that would exile foreigners who published pieces in opposition to veiling from the Ottoman Empire. Ibid., 221.

the popular propaganda that the Balkan Wars had been lost because of uncovered women, Mehmet Tahir decided to write and publish a small brochure in which he tried to convince the public that these women had made important sacrifices and aided the Ottoman army.[19]

In contrast, reformist male intellectuals emphasized the social harm that women's seclusion had inflicted on Ottoman society. They openly condemned women's veiling, especially the use of the *peçe*, maintaining that it excluded women from social life, prevented them from getting an education and therefore impeded their social development. For Abdullah Cevdet, one of the most prominent Ottoman intellectuals of the time, the *çarşaf* was one of the reasons for the degeneration in Ottoman society. He argued that veiling was not meant to segregate women from public life but protect their dignity.[20] Likewise, for another modernist author, Selahaddin Asım, Ottoman women had lost their social function and become sexual objects; as he argued, women's veiling was one of the reasons for the worsening situation in Ottoman society.[21] Kılıçzade Hakkı, another advocate of reform in women's clothing, claimed that veiling was the reason behind women's ignorance, moral decadence and the backwardness of the Ottoman state.[22] It was thus, he claimed, not reasonable to maintain such a harmful practice in the name of a religious and national tradition.[23] In his ideal Ottoman society, women would dress as they wished and nobody would interfere in their choice; in short, there would be no state regulation of women's veiling. For Ziya Gökalp, a prominent ideologue of Turkish nationalism in the late Ottoman period, continuation of such an ancient and primitive tradition like veiling was an insult to Turkish women, and he asserted that it should be abolished.[24] In the final years of the empire, the newspaper *İleri*, published by Celal Nuri and Suphi Nuri, well-known Unionists of the era, became a platform for discussions of women's problems, including the issue of reforming women's clothing.[25]

The subject of women's veiling was also a concern for the Ottoman women's movement. Although the primary points of struggle for the members of the movement were women's right to education and participation in public life, they also began to discuss the proper form of women's veiling in the public sphere and what form the 'national dress' (*millî kıyafet*) of Ottoman women should assume.[26] For many,

---

19. Mehmet Tahir, *Çarşaf Meselesi* (Istanbul: Sancakciyan Matbaası, 1915).

20. Niyazi Berkes, *Türkiye'de Çağdaşlaşma* (Ankara: Bilgi Yayınevi, 1973), 390–1; Caporal, *Kemalizmde*, 89.

21. Selahaddin Asım, *Türk Kadınlığının Tereddisi yahud Karılaşmak* (Istanbul: Resimli Kitab Matbaası, n.d.).

22. Kılıçzade Hakkı, 'Pek Uyanık Bir Uyku', *İçtihad* 55 (21 February 1328[1912]).

23. Kılıçzade Hakkı, 'Kadın ve Tesettür Meselesi', transcribed and reprinted in 'Kılıçzade Hakkı'nın Tesettüre İlan-ı Harbi', *Toplumsal Tarih* 66 (June 1999): 34–6.

24. Aktaş, *Tanzimat'tan*, 114.

25. Zihnioğlu, *Kadınsız İnkılap*, 85–8.

26. For more on the 'national dress' debate in the late Ottoman Empire, see Nicole A.N.M. van Os, 'Millî Kıyafet: Ottoman Women and the Nationality of Their Dress', in *The Turks*, vol. 4, eds. Hasan Celal Güzel, C. Cem Oğuz and Osman Karatay (Ankara: Yeni Türkiye Yayınları, 2002), 580–92.

Ottoman women's veiling was improper; it was argued to be in line with neither the Islamic veiling codes nor the necessities of public life.[27] Among women's journals, the journal *Kadınlar Dünyası* (Women's World) was particularly vocal in advocating for change in women's veiling and underlining the necessity to define the national dress of Ottoman women.[28] The journal even voiced the idea of founding an association to nationalize women's clothing.[29] This idea was not realized, however. Nevertheless, the Association for the Defence of Women's Rights (*Müdafaa-i Hukuk-u Nisvan Cemiyeti*), one of the women's organizations that flourished during the Second Constitutional Era, declared in its programme that one of its primary goals was the reform of women's clothing, increasing their participation in the workforce and eliminating traditions that had deleterious effects on Ottoman women.[30]

The main target for Ottoman supporters of women's rights was the *peçe* since there was near consensus among the reformists concerning its non-Turkish character and its negative impact on women's health and social roles; the main argument was that it impeded their participation in the workforce. Reformists criticized the inconsistency surrounding women's veiling. Women in Anatolia, in villages, did not wear the *peçe*, and there was a great deal of variation even among the districts of urban centres like Istanbul.[31] It is important to note that one of the concerns these women's journals expressed as regards suggesting reforms in women's veiling was the extent to which the reform complied with Islamic norms. The claim that the *peçe* and the *çarşaf* were not Islamic was used to support the idea that they could be eliminated.[32] However, women's rights advocates were equally cautious in their criticism of the *peçe* and the *çarşaf* as they did not want to lead the way towards excessive Westernization in women's clothing. Their campaign for a reform in women's dress was shaped within a nationalist framework, one that emphasized national economy, saving, consumption of national goods and the dangers of following Western fashion to the extreme. It was a search for the 'national dress' of Ottoman Muslim women[33] in which even the most radical

---

27. One of the women who criticized the social pressure on women regarding veiling was Emine Semiye Hanım. Zihnioğlu, *Kadınsız İnkılap*, 54. For other examples, see Çakır, *Osmanlı*. Even before this period, there were a few Ottoman women intellectuals like Fatma Aliye Hanım who openly criticized the *peçe* and the *çarşaf* and claimed that they were non-Islamic pieces of clothing adopted from foreign cultures. Ekrem Işın, 'Tanzimat, Kadın ve Gündelik Hayat', *Tarih ve Toplum* 51 (March 1988): 22–7.

28. Aynur Demirdirek, *Osmanlı Kadınlarının Hayat Hakkı Arayışının Bir Hikayesi* (Ankara: İmge, 1993), 105.

29. Çakır, *Osmanlı*, 249–50.

30. Tarık Zafer Tunaya, *Türkiye'de Siyasi Partiler I: İkinci Meşrutiyet Dönemi 1908–1918* (Istanbul: Hürriyet Vakfı Yayınları, 1984), 481–2.

31. Çakır, *Osmanlı*, 253–6.

32. On the other hand, there was no consensus on the question of veiling in general. In *Kadınlar Dünyası*, for example, there were also those who argued that women's veiling was a condition of Islam. Çakır, *Osmanlı*, 258–9.

33. For more on this point, see Çakır, *Osmanlı*; Os, 'Feminism, Philanthropy'.

members of the women's movement, like Nezihe Muhiddin, could be critical of the 'cultural degeneration' that Westernization had brought, particularly by non-Muslims.[34]

Women's dress in urban settings changed even more especially after the First World War. The use of the *peçe* decreased, and particularly in Istanbul, more women began to wear overcoats or cloaks instead of the *çarşaf* along with various models of headscarves.[35] As in previous decades, these changes went hand in hand with attempts to control women's clothing, and women's veiling continued to be a matter of concern for the state authorities as well as the subject of an intense debate with wider political implications until the end of the empire.[36] At the same time, an increasingly important component of the modernist Ottoman elite's political vision was the idea of the 'new woman', i.e., the woman who broke with old traditions, participated in public life, and worked with men to save the nation and the state. As early as 1913, in her novel *Yeni Turan* (The New Turan), Halide Edip, the most important female figure of the Turkish nationalist movement, had imagined this new Turkish woman dressed in an overcoat with her hair covered by a headscarf; in other words, she had removed her *peçe* and *çarşaf*.[37]

The question of veiling under the republic

Although there is strong continuity between the late Ottoman Empire and the Turkish republic in the emphasis on the 'new woman' and her central role in the nationalist agenda, the male elite of the republic had to face, to a much greater degree than did their Ottoman counterparts, the difficult task of reconciling the ideal 'national woman' with the ideal 'modern woman'.[38] In other words, it was difficult to bring together the image of the new Turkish woman as the embodiment of national values and identity and the new modern woman as a reflection of the

---

34. Zihnioğlu, *Kadınsız İnkılap*, 75.

35. Akkent and Frager, *Başörtü*, 186.

36. In 1915, for example, women were allowed to remove the *çarşaf* during working hours at government offices. However, the length of the skirts worn by women officials was subject to police control. Aktaş, *Tanzimat'tan*, 132. For an announcement of the Istanbul Police Department in 1917 asking women to avoid wearing shorter skirts, corsets and thin *çarşafs*, and a subsequent announcement declaring the previous order null and void, see Caporal, *Kemalizmde*, 147–8; Graham-Brown, *Images of Women*, 130. For examples of various statements issued by the office of *Şeyhülislam* between 1912 and 1919 concerning women's adherence to Islamic veiling, see Yakut, 'Tek Parti', 24–5.

37. Taşkıran describes the novel *Yeni Turan* as a reflection of the mental transformation regarding women's roles in Ottoman society. Tezer Taşkıran, *Cumhuriyetin 50. Yılında Türk Kadın Hakları* (Ankara: Başbakanlık Basımevi, 1973), 59–60.

38. Fatmagül Berktay, 'Osmanlı'dan Cumhuriyet'e Feminizm', in *Modern Türkiye'de Siyasi Düşünce I: Tanzimat ve Meşrutiyet'in Birikimi*, ed. Mehmet Ö. Alkan (Istanbul: İletişim, 2001), 348–61.

Europeanized face of the new state. Especially in the first years of the regime following the War of Independence (1919–22), the emphasis on the role of women in the war, particularly on the self-sacrifices of Anatolian women, became the image along the lines of which the new Turkish woman would be envisioned. There was a glorification of the traditional peasant woman of Anatolia as the essence of national womanhood. At the same time, however, women were called into the public sphere to take part in national development and to play a role as the symbols and carriers of modernization. The issue of women's clothing and outward appearance was perhaps the terrain where this paradox became the most crystallized.

Even in the women's movement inherited by the republic from the empire, which became institutionalized as the Turkish Women's Union, the emphasis on the 'national' was quite strong during the years of transition to the new regime. While the organization backed the republican project of modernization, its supporters carefully avoided compromising national identity and morality.[39] The *çarşaf* had acquired new meaning during the national struggle; at the very first protest organized in Istanbul in reaction to the invasion of Izmir by the Greek army in 1919, all women in attendance were wearing black *çarşaf*s, even though it had become very rare in the capital by then.[40] In 1923, when asked about her views on women's veiling, Nezihe Muhiddin, the head of the Turkish Women's Union, which was the most active and radical women's organization in the early republic, maintained that women's veils were a national form of dress and that the *çarşaf* was an obstacle neither to progress nor to women's participation in public life.[41] As Zihnioğlu suggests, Muhiddin likely adopted that attitude in order not to overshadow the primary point of the struggle carried out by the union: acquiring political rights for women. However, it reflects the atmosphere at the dawn of the republic regarding women's veiling. Although the founders of the Women's Union appeared in the press in 1923 having removed their face veils, they were all covered, many of them wearing the *çarşaf*, which was still considered to be the national dress of Turkish women. Two delegates who represented Turkey at the congress of the International Alliance of Women in Rome in 1923 also wore this 'national' dress, albeit in its quite modern form and without the *peçe*.[42]

---

39. See Zihnioğlu, *Kadınsız İnkılap*, 76–7. For similar concerns among Ottoman Armenian feminists of the time, who appreciated Muslim women's unveiling as it erased the 'difference' among the women of different religious communities in the public sphere while at the same time being equally concerned with the branding of Europeanized Armenian women as 'immoral', see Lerna Ekmekçioğlu, *Recovering Armenia: The Limits of Belonging in Post-Genocide Turkey* (Stanford: Stanford University Press, 2016), 146–50.

40. Halide Edip was one of the speakers at the demonstration and she had become a symbol of women's participation in the national struggle in her black *çarşaf*. She was not wearing the *peçe*, however.

41. Zihnioğlu, *Kadınsız İnkılap*, 113.

42. Ibid., 142.

It was, in fact, quite apparent even in the first years that the new regime favoured the modernization of women's clothing, and more particularly, the abolition of the *peçe*. Although Mustafa Kemal never directly addressed the issue of unveiling or referred to the necessity of organizing anti-veiling campaigns to change women's dress, it was obvious in a number of his speeches that he believed that the general habits of dress that were widespread among women in Turkey in the early years of the republic did not have a modern or national character.[43] In one of his speeches in Izmir in 1923, having mentioned that the most important aspect of social life that draws foreigners' attention in the cities of Turkey was women's veiling, he emphasized that women's attire should be simple and not prevent them from participating in public life. He also said that this was the kind of dress dictated by Islam.[44] During his visit to Konya in March 1923, he argued that women's education and participation in public life should be the main concerns, and that the issue of clothing was secondary. He also stated, however, that what had to be taken into consideration in the issue of veiling were both the spirit of the nation and the necessities of the times. Without mentioning the *peçe* or the *çarşaf*, he advised women to abstain from going too far in either direction: meaning, to neither veil nor unveil to excess. He also mentioned that the kind of veiling used should be simplified.[45]

It is important to note that in Mustafa Kemal's public speeches, there was no overt censure of covering women's hair. In fact, he was critical of women who tried to imitate European women and carried the change in their style to extremes, and he urged Turkish women to maintain their modesty.[46] However, his preference, reflected in the way women around him dressed and in the general discourse of the regime on women's modernization, was Turkish women's adaptation to 'civilized' norms in every field, including clothing. While the number of these norms governing women's clothing increased over the years, during the early years of the republic, women's emancipation was very much associated with women revealing their faces to the world. Grace Ellison, a British author who interviewed Mustafa Kemal right before he married Latife Hanım in 1923, quotes him as saying that women would be liberated in a year's time, meaning that they would uncover their faces and take their place in public alongside men.[47] Until their divorce in 1925, Latife Hanım always appeared in public without the *peçe* and accompanied her spouse in public, which was something extraordinary at the time and a dramatic change for many of

---

43. Price quotes him saying that in Turkish villages women live with men without segregation and that gender segregation and the *peçe* are Arab traditions. G. Ward Price, *Extra-Special Correspondent* (London: Harrap, 1957), 141.

44. *Atatürk'ün Söylev ve Demeçleri I-III* (Ankara: Atatürk Araştrma Merkezi Yayınları, 1989), 85.

45. Ibid., 91, 154.

46. Zehra Arat, 'Turkish Women and the Republican Reconstruction of Tradition', in *Reconstructing Gender in the Middle East: Tradition, Identity and Power*, eds. Fatma Müge Göçek and Shiva Balaghi (New York: Columbia University Press, 1995), 62.

47. Grace Ellison, *Ankara'da Bir İngiliz Kadın*, trans. Osman Olcay (Ankara: Bilgi Yayınevi, 1999), 211.

her contemporaries, men and women alike. Most of the news about the couple did not fail to mention that Latife Hanım did not wear the face veil though she wore the *çarşaf* occasionally and certainly used a headscarf all the time.[48] Foreign journalists and correspondents also stressed how she was different from the majority of the Turkish women by referring to her removal of the face veil.[49]

Mustafa Kemal was mainly concerned with gender segregation and women's exclusion from the public sphere, which was the general norm in most parts of the country. In 1923, during their tour in Western Anatolia, he and Latife Hanım had not met a single woman in the places they visited, and so he was relieved when they were welcomed by a group of women, including school teachers and the wives of a few professionals living in the town of Edremit, a small seaside town in the north of Izmir; they were dressed in the *çarşaf* but without the face veil. Mahu Hanım, one of those women and the owner of the house where Mustafa Kemal and Latife Hanım stayed in Edremit, recalled that Mustafa Kemal thanked her for the only civilized night they had experienced during the entire trip; it had been 'civilized' because of the participation of women.[50] In the 1920s, even Ankara, the capital of the new republic, was famous for the fact that there were very few women around. Many of the bureaucrats and parliamentarians had not brought their families to the city, and the few women who did come from Istanbul were a source of gossip when they were seen in public places in their 'Istanbul style' *çarşaf*, meaning 'modernized' type of *çarşaf* that was too loose to appropriately cover the body.[51] Even some of the leading elite of the new regime seemed to have reservations about women's public visibility and mixed-gender gatherings that were newly emerging in the capital.[52]

Women's veiling and segregation were so prevalent in the first years of the republic that Latife Hanım's abandonment of the *peçe*, her modern way of dressing, her appearance at public meetings and the fact that she accompanied her husband on visits were points of critique for the opposition; her clothing and attitude were described as being an indication of the anti-religious character of the regime that Mustafa Kemal and his followers were trying to establish. At the beginning of 1923, one of the opposition groups, the Ottoman Revolutionary Committee of Anatolia (*Anadolu Osmanlı İhtilal Komitesi*), distributed a handout calling on Muslims to resist Mustafa Kemal. On the handout, there was a picture showing Latife Hanım

---

48. On one occasion, at the funeral of Mustafa Kemal's mother in 1923, she wore a black coat and a black face veil. İpek Çalışlar, *Latife Hanım* (Istanbul: Doğan Kitap, 2007), 103.

49. See for example Issac F. Marcosson, *Turbulent Years* (New York: Dodd, Mead & Company, 1938), 170.

50. For Mahu Hanım's memoirs and Mustafa Kemal's recall of the experience, see Nazmi Kal, *Atatürk'le Yaşadıklarını Anlattılar* (Ankara: Bilgi Yayınevi, 2001).

51. Falif Rıfkı Atay, *Çankaya* (Istanbul: Bateş Atatürk Dizisi, 1998), 353, 386, 410.

52. For the observations of Geoffrey Knox, the acting British Consul in Ankara in 1927, especially about the reservations of Fevzi Pasha [Çakmak] and Abdul Halik Bey [Renda], see Despatch from Sir G. Clark to Sir Austen Chamberlain, the National Archives of the United Kingdom Foreign Office Records (hereafter FO) 371/12320, 20 June 1927.

sitting with Mustafa Kemal and a few other men at a public meeting, with her hair covered but her face uncovered.[53] She was identified as the embodiment of the new Turkish woman that Mustafa Kemal's regime aimed to create. The handout implied that Muslims had to resist Mustafa Kemal if they did not want to see their wives and daughters behaving so immorally. Even Latife Hanım's crossing of her legs while sitting was taken to be a sign of immorality. During the visit of Mustafa Kemal and Latife Hanım to Adana in March 1923, the *müftü* of Adana issued a public declaration, which was published in the newspapers of the time, assuring readers that Latife Hanım's accompanying her husband was not contrary to Islam, and that her clothing was in line with Sharia.[54] The Adana *müftü's* statement was probably seen as necessary to prevent a public reaction. In a way, it was also a declaration that the removal of the face veil was not against Islamic dress codes.

On the other hand, the modernization of women's clothing that had begun in the late Ottoman Empire was continuing, even accelerating, in the newly founded republic. *Çarşaf* styles had already been changing considerably in the larger cities; cloak-like *çarşafs* with shorter lengths were common, and more modernized forms of covering the hair had become fashionable. In major cities, more women had begun to remove their *peçe* and to replace their *çarşaf* with overcoats, and they also started covering their hair with draped turbans and black rectangular scarfs tied at the back of the neck, which was called the *sıkmabaş* style.[55] The educated and elite segments of the population were the forerunners since they had already been adopting European styles in their daily lives even before the republic came into being. The general public's perception of what Atatürk preferred with respect to women's clothing also played a role in women's adoption of modern styles. Some women removed their *peçe* and *çarşaf* and adopted an overcoat and a headscarf because they heard that Atatürk had told women to do so.[56] Female teachers were the vanguard since the dress code of state officials had been determined by a number of state regulations, one of which banned the use of the *peçe* for school teachers on 15 January 1924.[57] The existence of a considerable number of women who had already removed their *peçe* and *çarşaf* was also important for legitimizing the new forms of women's clothing as the modern and national norm and for consolidating them as symbols of these norms. The press in particular played a significant role in promoting new dress norms for men and women alike, regularly publishing the latest trends in Western fashion as a guide for readers.[58] Women's

---

53. Çalışlar, *Latife Hanım*, 179.

54. Mehmet Önder, *Atatürk'ün Yurt Gezileri* (Istanbul: İş Bankası Kültür Yayınları, 1998), 5–6.

55. Caporal, *Kemalizmde*, 646; Akkent and Franger, *Başörtü*, 186. Taşçıoğlu states that this transition continued throughout the 1920s but that the hat would spread among urban women only in the 1930s. Taşçıoğlu, *Türk Osmanlı*, 58.

56. For an example of such an account, see Akkent and Frager, *Başörtü*, 194.

57. Yakut, 'Tek Parti', 26.

58. In 1925, one could even see a picture of a woman in her bathing suit as the cover of a journal. *Resimli Ay* 7, August 1341 [1925].

journals also had a crucial impact on transforming women's dress and trying to create a national synthesis of Western styles and local traditions, the latter believed to be authentically Turkish. Mixed-gender public meetings became the norm and European-style entertainment, such as balls or tea parties, began to characterize social life in the republic, especially in big cities. These gatherings were events where unveiled women would appear confidently as new participants in public life. In this way it can be seen that there had already been a gradual change in women's dress starting in the early years of the republic. In the 1920s, a more radical change, however, would take place in men's clothing through direct state intervention.

The republic's first clothing reform: The Hat Law of 1925

In almost all major studies on early republican Turkey published both in Turkey and abroad, the introduction of the European hat as a replacement for the Ottoman fez is considered to be one of the most significant, if not the boldest, of Kemalist cultural reforms, and it has become widely known as 'the' dress reform of the new regime. The debate over the modernization of men's headgear had in fact begun earlier in the nineteenth century and intensified during the Second Constitutional Period after 1908.[59] Thus the hat was not a total novelty in the 1920s, at least not for the elite segments of the population. Some Ottoman intellectuals, for example, had proposed a clothing reform in the army and argued that all soldiers should wear the modern hat.[60] However, with the Balkan Wars and the First World War, and especially during the occupation of Istanbul and parts of Anatolia, the hat again came to be associated primarily with foreigners, occupiers and 'infidels'.[61] The fez continued to signify Muslim-Turkish identity, while the *kalpak*, a black Turkic wool cap, would become the symbol of the Turkish national struggle since it had been worn by the leaders of the resistance movement in Anatolia.[62]

The introduction of the hat as 'modern men's headgear' came about during the visit of Mustafa Kemal to Kastamonu and İnebolu in August 1925. To the surprise

---

59. The hat was criticized by some Ottoman modernists as a symbol of religious reactionism. Patricia Baker, 'The Fez in Turkey: A Symbol of Modernization?', *Costume* 20 (1986): 72–85.

60. See Kılıçzade Hakkı, 'Pek Uyanık'.

61. See Arnold J. Toynbee, *Survey of International Affairs 1925, vol. I: The Islamic World since the Peace Settlement* (London: Oxford University Press, 1927), 74, fn. 1. See also Orhan Koloğlu, *İslamda Başlık* (Ankara: Türk Tarih Kurumu Basımevi, 1978), 64–5.

62. As a Central Asian form of headdress, the *kalpak* was already a popular form of headgear among Turkish nationalists in the late Ottoman Empire. Koloğlu mentions that the first attempt in the late Ottoman Empire to change men's headgear was to replace the fez with the *kalpak* and *kabalak* (a khaki cloth cap) in the military. Koloğlu, *İslamda*, 62–3. The idea of introducing the *kalpak* as national headgear was proposed to the first parliament established by the nationalist movement in Ankara in 1920, but at that time no action was taken. Mahmut Goloğlu, *Üçüncü Meşrutiyet 1920* (Ankara: Başnur Matbaası, 1970), 176–7.

of many, he first arrived in the city of Kastamonu bareheaded holding a Panama hat and he emphasized the importance of modern clothing during his meetings with different segments of the population.[63] Two days later, in his speech in İnebolu, having characterized contemporary Turkish forms of dress as neither national nor international, he introduced the hat as 'civilized headgear' and proclaimed it to be a necessity of modern life.[64] On his return to Ankara on 1 September 1925, the people who came to welcome Mustafa Kemal were all wearing a hat. The next day, a governmental decree made it compulsory for state officials to wear hats.[65] On 16 October 1925, a group of deputies introduced a bill to parliament proposing that the hat should be compulsory for state officials, and that all men's headgear other than the hat, including, of course, the traditional Ottoman fez, should be banned.

The reasoning behind the bill was that the issue of headgear, though in fact an insignificant matter in itself, had special importance for the Turkish nation, whose aim was to join the family of contemporary civilized nations.[66] It was argued that the fez had become a symbol which set the Turkish nation apart from civilized nations and that it was necessary to eradicate this identification and replace it with the common headgear of all modern nations: the modern hat. Nurettin Pasha, a deputy of Bursa, argued that the law's aim of limiting people's choice of headgear was a violation of the constitution.[67] His proposal was harshly critiqued in parliament.[68] The main argument of the supporters of the bill was that the hat had already been adopted by many in society. In the end, the law required that all state officials and members of the parliament wear hats, stated that the hat was the headgear of the Turkish nation, and banned the 'continuation of any habit that was incompatible with this'. In this way, wearing traditional or local headgear such as the fez was prohibited. Article 3 of the law stated that parliament and the council of ministers were responsible for monitoring the implementation of the law.

---

63. Mahmut Goloğlu, *Türkiye Cumhuriyeti Tarihi I: Devrimler ve Tepkileri (1924–1930)* (Istanbul: Türkiye İş Bankası Kültür Yayınları, 2007), 154–5.

64. Houcheng Chehabi, 'Dress Codes for Men in Turkey and Iran', in *Men of Order: Authoritarian Modernization under Atatürk and Reza Shah*, eds. Touraj Atabaki and Erik J. Zürcher (London: I.B. Tauris, 2004), 214.

65. For the text of the decree, see Baker, 'The Fez'.

66. *T.B.M.M. Zabıt Ceridesi* [Turkish Grand National Assembly Minutes], vol. 19, Meeting 14 (25 November 1925), 221.

67. Nurettin Pasha, known as Sakallı Nurettin Pasha, was one of the army commanders during the Turkish War of Independence. He is known particularly for his responsibility in the brutal repression of the Kurdish uprising in 1921 (the Koçgiri Rebellion in Dersim), and atrocities against the Greeks in Western Anatolia. Mete Tunçay, *T.C.'nde Tek-Parti Yönetimi'nin Kurulması (1923–1931)*, 2nd ed. (Istanbul: Cem Yayınevi, 1992), 117–20.

68. Nurettin Pasha was even declared to be a reactionary in the press. Later, Independence Tribunals informed the government that Nurettin Pasha's speeches against the Hat Law in parliament partly caused the mass protests against the hat reform. Ergün Aybars, *İstiklal Mahkemeleri I-II (1920–1927)* (İzmir: Dokuz Eylül Üniversitesi Yayınları, 1988), 412.

The hat reform stirred up numerous reactions in society. According to Halide Edip, among all of the Kemalist reforms that had been implemented until that time, it was subject to the most opposition.[69] A number of protests occurred in provinces such as Sivas, Malatya, Erzurum, Kayseri, Rize, Giresun and Maraş.[70] The protests were harshly put down, the people involved were deemed to be reactionaries and counter-revolutionaries by official discourse and in the press, and many protesters were tried by the Independence Tribunals, which had been established and granted enormous powers after the Sheikh Said Rebellion, a Kurdish-Islamic uprising that had quickly spread in the south eastern provinces of Turkey at the beginning of the same year. The trials resulted in the persecution of some people and the arrests of many more.[71]

The economic aspect of the reform also created social discontent since hats were scarce in the country, and when available, they were very expensive. This was particularly difficult for the poor masses. Because going out bareheaded was considered inappropriate, there were individual instances of non-observance of the law.[72] In fact, although the law stated that headgear other than the modern hat was banned, punishment remained unclear, as the criminal law had yet to be amended. That did not occur until 1939, when the wearing of headgear other than the hat became punishable by up to three months imprisonment.[73] Yet, many people faced police action for continuing to wear the turban, fez or other local headgear, not only right after the enactment of the law but continuously (though irregularly) throughout the single-party era and even later.[74]

The Hat Law and un/veiling: Formation of a national campaign for modern dress

There were two aspects of the hat reform that were particularly relevant to the issue of women's un/veiling. On the one hand, the Hat Law marked a turning point in public debates on modern and national clothing. The law itself and the

---

69. Halide Edip, *Turkey Faces West: A Turkish View of Recent Changes and Their Origin* (New Haven: Yale University Press, 1930), 224.

70. For a more detailed discussion, see Brockett, 'Collective Action'; Goloğlu, *Türkiye Cumhuriyeti*; Koloğlu, *İslamda*; Aybars, *İstiklal Mahkemeleri*; Baker, 'The Fez'.

71. For more, see Aybars, *İstiklal Mahkemeleri*.

72. For example, there were people who did not go outside to avoid being seen bareheaded. Koloğlu, *İslamda*, 95; Aktaş, *Tanzimat'tan*, 179. Berkes states that there were also some people who left the country because of the Hat Law. Berkes, *Türkiye'de*, 485. A local newspaper from Ordu reported in January 1926 that the municipality should help poor children and street porters buy hats. Kemal Zeki Gençosman, *Altın Yıllar* (Istanbul: Hür Yayınları, 1981), 117. Even state officials found it difficult to afford a hat so the government accommodated them with a one-year loan called the 'hat advance'. Aktaş, *Tanzimat'tan*, 183.

73. Tunçay, *T.C.'nde Tek-Parti*, 151.

74. Chehabi, 'Dress Codes', 217.

public discussions that ensued focused on men's clothing, but they had wider repercussions concerning the importance of the modernization of the attire of the nation and thus had direct implications for women's clothing. Mustafa Kemal himself touched upon the issue of women's veiling during the very same visit to Kastamonu when he introduced the hat. In fact, this was one of the very few occasions where he rather explicitly referred to the forms of veiling from which he believed women should abstain. In one of his speeches during that visit, he stated that women could uncover their faces and look out at the world around them; he went on to say there was no harm in this if women were inculcated with a sense of religious and national morality.[75] In another speech, he mentioned that he had seen some women who were trying to cover their faces with a piece of cloth or the *peştamal* and turning their backs or sitting on the ground when they came across men in the street. He characterized such acts as strange, primitive and a source of ridicule for the Turkish nation. He said: 'Gentlemen, would the mothers and daughters of a civilized nation assume such an absurd and vulgar pose? This is a situation that ridicules our nation. It has to be corrected immediately.'[76]

Thus, the Hat Law of 1925, while only touching upon men's headgear, created a general atmosphere in which clothing change became a signifier for the modernization of the new republic, and women's dress was not an exception in this regard. The distinction between 'civilized' and 'uncivilized' forms of clothing came to occupy public discourses, and the issue of modern women's clothing began to appear more frequently in the press. It was only to be expected that women's veiling would become an issue given this atmosphere, which had taken on the tone of a national campaign for modern clothing; a firm link between the reform of men's headgear and women's veils was thus established. Mustafa Kemal's speech against the face veil that he gave during his visit to Kastamonu helped reinforce this link and forge the notion that, like the fez, women's veiling was also not approved of by the new regime, despite the fact that no clear agenda of reform or official measures regarding this issue had been put into practice.[77] Some opponents of the law used this perceived link between the abolition of the fez and the removal of the veil to mobilize people against the Hat Law. In some of the organized reactions to the hat reform, protestors claimed in their propaganda that women would subsequently be forced to uncover their faces.[78] In Kayseri, for

---

75. Caporal, *Kemalizmde*, 647.

76. Quoted in Arat, 'Turkish Women', 61. For the whole speech in Turkish, see *Atatürk'ün Söylev*, 227.

77. Later in the 1930s, Tekin Alp would also write in his famous book *Kemalizm* that Atatürk's speech against the face veil proved enough for many women to remove their *peçe* and adopt modern hats in the 1920s. He would claim that 'the fact that the *peçe* and the fez were removed almost at the same time was an indication for women's march towards liberty together with men'. Tekin Alp, *Kemalizm* (Istanbul: Cumhuriyet Gazete ve Matbaası, 1936), 123.

78. Aybars, *İstiklal Mahkemeleri*, 407.

example, a rumour that the government would soon outlaw the veil played a role in reactions against the Hat Law.[79] Oral historical testimonies also indicate that there were rumours in Istanbul that the *çarşaf* had been prohibited and that Atatürk had ordered women to stop wearing it, just like men had been ordered to stop wearing their fez and turban.[80] A telegraph from a group of women schoolteachers in Sivas which was directly sent to Prime Minister İsmet Pasha (İnönü) in February 1926 perhaps best illustrates how the link between the introduction of the hat and the removal of the veil was perceived and experienced at the local level. The women teachers complained about some rumours being spread by men in Sivas who had claimed that the hat would be abolished soon and women would have to wear the *çarşaf* again. The teachers asked the prime minister to see to it that the necessary measures be taken concerning these rumours and ensure that those who had spread them be held to account.[81]

The hat reform and the way it was applied had serious repercussions among ordinary people concerning women's veiling as well. Many women had removed their *peçe* and *çarşaf* because of such rumours and because of the encouraging atmosphere created by the hat reform in the modernization of clothing. Afet İnan, for example, argues that it became possible for the women students in the Faculty of Medicine to remove their *çarşaf* only after the inculcations of Mustafa Kemal in his speeches on modern clothing in 1925 and after the enactment of the Hat Law.[82] On Republic Day in October 1925, following the launch of the hat reform during Mustafa Kemal's visit, newspapers reported that everybody, including women teachers, had participated in the celebrations in Ankara with modern hats on their heads. One of those teachers, Mevhide Atıfet Hanım, had criticized the *peçe* and the *çarşaf* after she argued that Turkish women had become equal with men in the republic: 'The new enlightened mothers of the future are not so naïve a people that they would search for honour, virtue and grace under the *peçe*, under the *çarşaf*. They are confident that honour and purity are to be found in spirit, in manners, deep in essence.'[83] The change in women's clothing towards the end of 1925 was so

---

79. Chehabi, 'Dress Codes', 215; Brockett, 'Collective Action', 49.

80. Akkent and Frager, *Başörtü*, 189.

81. Presidency of State Archives of the Republic of Turkey, Republican Period (*T.C. Devlet Arşivleri Başkanlığı Cumhuriyet Arşivi* – hereafter BCA) 030.10/104.679.4, 16 February 1926. Having received the copy of the telegraph and the order of the prime minister to take the necessary measures, the minister of the interior informed the prime minister a few days later that according to the report of the governor of Sivas, such rumours had been spread by a certain Nergiszade Boyacı Ahmed and a legal investigation into him was undertaken. There was also an official request to transfer his case to the Independence Tribunal. The minister of the interior also ensured the prime minister that all the relevant authorities had been informed accordingly; they had been directed to prevent similar events from happening and to hand people who were involved in similar activities over to the legal authorities.

82. Quoted in Aktaş, *Tanzimat'tan*, 191.

83. Quoted in Gençosman, *Altın Yıllar*, 114.

visible, at least in the major cities, that the foreign press also celebrated this as the liberation of women and how they were becoming the symbols of modern Turkish life under the new regime.[84]

Likewise, the Hat Law could function as a reference point for those who wanted to initiate a similar change in the way women dressed. In fact, as shall be seen in the following section, the first anti-veiling campaigns emerged after the implementation of the hat reform, and some local administrators who organized these campaigns invoked the hat reform as a source of inspiration and legitimacy. It can be argued that the speech about women's dress that Mustafa Kemal delivered within the context of the hat reform probably served to encourage some sectors of the local elite who wanted to lead a change in women's dress similar to the one in men's clothing. The fact that the anti-veiling campaigns of the 1920s primarily targeted the *peçe* should not appear as a coincidence since Mustafa Kemal's speech could be read as his direct criticism of the segregation of women and, particularly, the covering of their face – and thus, the use of the *peçe*. As vanguards of the revolution, some state officials and members of the provincial elite saw themselves in the position of leading the way in their localities for the modernization of women's clothing as well.

On the other hand, the fact that women's veiling was not subject to regulation as part of the official clothing reform of the regime created an ambiguous and ambivalent situation that shaped the anti-veiling campaigns in the years to come. In other words, the Hat Law perhaps left a more significant mark on the transformation of women's clothing in terms of the method that should be followed in such a reform process. The decision of the regime not to outlaw the veil is significant for understanding the anti-veiling campaigns in the mid-1920s and afterwards, given the determination of the new regime to modernize clothing (as it was reflected in the Hat Law) and the means it had secured to do so. As stressed by Lewis, '[E]ven the great reformer, buttressed as he was by the Law for the Maintenance of Order and the "independence tribunals," did not venture to legislate against the veil.'[85] The second half of the 1920s was in fact a time of very important and radical reforms in Turkey. Thus, a law banning the *peçe* and the *çarşaf* would not be unthinkable. However, it was deliberately avoided, and not even suggested until the mid-1930s. The determined way the Hat Law was applied and the reactions it provoked perhaps formed one crucial element shaping the attitude of the Kemalist regime on the reform of women's clothing, preventing it from outlawing veiling out of fear that it might cause a social reaction even stronger than the one the Hat Law received.[86] This point was in fact underlined by some contemporary observers of the reforms in Turkey. Toynbee, for example, refers to the accounts of Western travellers in Central and East Central Turkey

---

84. There were fifteen news reports about Turkish women between June and December in 1925 in the *New York Times* alone. Zihnioğlu, *Kadınsız İnkılap*, 167; fn. 35.

85. Lewis, *The Emergence*, 271.

86. For a similar argument, see Aktaş, *Tanzimat'tan*, 189.

in 1925 and 1926, and quotes them, arguing that 'to enforce the emancipation of women in rural districts by the same drastic methods which they had employed in forcing hats upon the men would raise a storm'.[87]

Therefore, one can argue that the enormous reaction the Hat Law received was one important factor underlying the decision of the Kemalist regime not to outlaw veiling. However, it is also important to note here that this was not the only reason. Falih Rıfkı Atay, a member of Mustafa Kemal's close circle of friends, for example, argued that the president was convinced that women's emancipation would be realized gradually as a result of education and social transformation rather than as a by-product of a law or regulation. He claims that Mustafa Kemal knew from the very beginning that the issue of honour was as central as religion for Turkish society and acted accordingly; this was why there was no article related to women's clothing in the Hat Law.[88] He also claims that although he tried to promote modern life in the cities, Mustafa Kemal did not force peasant women to change and this was perhaps the only issue for which he favoured an evolutionary approach.[89] Having analysed the reports sent from various consulates in the provinces regarding the social position of women, the British Ambassador in Istanbul, Sir George R. Clark, also reported in 1927 along the same lines:

[I]t is worthy of note that the rulers of modern Turkey have had the wisdom or prudence to allow a considerable measure of liberty to those elements which continue to think the veil and the customs of Islam a necessity. Doubtless they trust to the schools to inculcate in the new generation ideas that will bring in the projected reforms automatically.[90]

If one reason for the Kemalist decision to not take a radical stance on women's dress was the prudence of the leading elite, the other one was related to the patriarchal concern the regime shared as it tried to modernize gender relations. The emphasis on the necessity of remaking the nation's women along modern lines existed side by side with an equally strong emphasis on protecting women's morality, pointing to a process which is characterized by Zehra Arat as the replacement of Islamic patriarchy with a modern one.[91] In other words, reforms

---

87. Toynbee, *Survey*, 77, fn. 1. Toynbee also noted that 'while among the menfolk in the villages the working of the new Western leaven was already perceptible, the traditional subordination and effacement of the womenfolk showed no sign of change'.

88. Falih Rıfkı Atay, *Niçin Kurtulmamak* (Istanbul: Varlık, 1953), 81.

89. Atay, *Çankaya*, 412.

90. Despatch N. 384 from Sir G. Clerk to Sir Austen Chamberlain, FO 371/12320, 20 June 1927.

91. Zehra F. Arat, 'Kemalizm ve Türk Kadını', in *75 Yılda Kadınlar ve Erkekler*, ed. Ayşe Berktay Hacımirzaoğlu (Istanbul: Tarih Vakfı Yayınları, 1998), 51–70. See also Kandiyoti, 'Emancipated'; Arat, 'The Project'; Saktanber, 'Kemalist Kadın'.

were within the 'modern-yet-modest' formulation, the patriarchal consensus between the elite and non-elite male actors.[92] This implied a strategy of initiating a change in women's clothing without so much undermining existing hierarchies and moral codes. The motivation behind understanding unveiling as the removal of the *peçe* and the *çarşaf*, without, for example, attacking covering of the hair as such, can be best understood within this framework. However, contrary to what has been generally emphasized in the literature,[93] neither the prudence of the regime nor its patriarchal concerns led to a total abandonment of the idea of regulating women's veiling through official decisions. Such decisions were indeed made in the 1920s to ban the *peçe* and the *çarşaf*, albeit only at the local level and only with the efforts of the provincial elite without central coordination and the strength of a law, or even a general decision or regulation originating from the centre. This was precisely what was expected from the local administrators and state officials; they were expected to lead the way and try to make the ideals of modernization a reality in their localities.[94]

Anti-veiling campaigns in the 1920s: The first wave

On 29 October 1925, the second anniversary of the foundation of the Republic of Turkey, the head of the Turkish Hearth (*Türk Ocağı*) and the Teachers' Union in the province of Trabzon, Mustafa Reşit Bey, addressed the crowd gathered for the celebration of this national holiday.[95] Decorated with laurel leaves and flags, like the other major buildings in the city, the Turkish Hearth was the centre of the celebrations in Trabzon town square, and Mustafa Reşit Bey made his speech from the balcony of the building. Underlining the merits of the republican regime compared to its predecessor, which he characterized as the 'corrupt' Ottoman regime, he finished his speech with the following statements:

> The civilized world has known us as an uncivilized people in bizarre clothing, in baggy trousers and big turbans. But in fact, these are the lands of the most civilized and dignified people in the world. Foreigners would certainly see the true essence of this dignified nation in our contemporary clothing. A thousand thanks and gratitude to the Republic that would carry us to prosperity with

---

92. Afsaneh Najmabadi, 'Hazards of Modernity and Morality: Women, State and Ideology in Contemporary Iran', in *Women, Islam and the State*, ed. Deniz Kandiyoti (Philadelphia: Temple University Press), 48–76; Berktay, 'Cumhuriyet'in'.

93. See, for example, Tunçay, *T.C.'nde Tek-Parti*, 150–1.

94. Mustafa Kemal in fact touched upon the necessity of a vanguard role played by state officials as regards the issue of the modernization of clothing during his visit to Kastamonu and also afterwards during the course of the hat reform. Goloğlu, *Türkiye Cumhuriyeti*, 161.

95. The Turkish Hearths (*Türk Ocakları*) was an association founded in 1912 to promote Turkish nationalism.

the blessings and prosperity of the motherland, and to the great saviour who rescued it. Long live the nation; long live the revolution; long live the Republic![96]

Having been born in Trabzon in 1892, educated in Istanbul as a biology teacher, and served as a teacher and mid-level bureaucrat in the Ministry of Education and the General Inspectorships with different capacities in different places throughout his career, Mustafa Reşit Bey was typical of the republican local elite in the provinces. His reference to clothing as the final mark of his speech for the Republic Day in October 1925 was in fact no coincidence. The hat had very recently been introduced as the modern male headgear by Mustafa Kemal, and a bill to ban all headgear other than the hat countrywide had been proposed to parliament only two weeks earlier, turning the issue of the modernization of clothing into one of the most topical issues in the country. It was thus within such a context that Mustafa Reşit Bey talked of the backwardness of the old style of clothing in his speech and tried to promote the idea in Trabzon that modern clothing would fit the Turkish nation and represent its 'civilized essence'.

The efforts of the provincial elite in Trabzon to promote modern clothing, in fact, went beyond the support they had given to the regime's legal reform to change men's headgear. On 2 October 1925, members of the Turkish Hearth in Trabzon decided at a mixed-gender meeting that women members should remove their *peçes* and *çarşafs*, wear overcoats and hats, and participate in social life.[97] They also decided that male members should wear hats, following the example of Mustafa Kemal. As the earliest example of an anti-veiling campaign in the 1920s,[98] this decision made by the Trabzon Turkish Hearth was seen by its members as a natural result of the role of the Turkish Hearth in guiding the people of Trabzon in their adaptation to modern ways and being good supporters and promoters of the ideals of the revolution.[99] Members also decided to advise the city's women accordingly

---

96. Mustafa Reşit Tarakçıoğlu, *Trabzon'un Yakın Tarihi*, reprinted in Hikmet Öksüz and Veysel Usta, *Mustafa Reşit Tarakçıoğlu, Hayatı, Hatıratı ve Trabzon'un Yakın Tarihi* (Trabzon: Serander, 2008), 199.

97. Ibid., 200.

98. An earlier attempt to eliminate gender segregation should be mentioned here. In December 1924, the governor of Istanbul issued a circular that removed the curtains dividing men's and women's sections on trams, trains and boats. Caporal, *Kemalizmde*, 650. Then in 1925, gender segregation was completely abolished on these vehicles. Zihnioğlu, *Kadınsız İnkılap*, 167.

99. Even before the establishment of the republic, there had been some local elites in Trabzon who supported the idea of adopting Western clothing. See Tirebolulu Hüseyin Arpaslan, *Trabzon İli Laz mı Türk mü?*, Giresun, 1339[1923], quoted in Çapa, 'Giyim Kuşamda'. Some ulema and local notables were trying to counter such arguments and prevent the women of Trabzon from following Istanbul women in the modernization of clothing by sending petitions to state authorities. Ebubekir Hazım Tepeyran, *Belgelerle Kurtuluş Savaşı Anıları* (Istanbul: Çağdaş Yayınları, 1982), 91–3.

in private meetings and conversations, and to encourage them to participate in public life.

This local initiative to change women's clothing in Trabzon was followed by similar attempts in a number of other cities. The mayor of Eskişehir issued a statement in December 1925 calling for the women of the city to remove their *peştamal*. The statement was issued only a few days after the enactment of the Hat Law and was clearly motivated by it:

> My dear townsmen who lead the way in the struggle for civilization as they did in the struggle for liberation.
>
> At a time when the last law has spread the hat throughout the Turkish nation, the time has also come to bring the *peştamal* veil, which is very uncomely, into line with civilized clothes and civilized views; thus this *peştamal* veil, which is a very primitive and uncivilized form of dress, has to end. Instead, dresses worn now by a fraction of our women have to prevail. The *peştamal* veils, which look especially grim because of their colours, have to be dyed with simpler and more dignified colours, and transformed into civilized clothing by changing their form. The municipality asks and requests this from our respected people and is confident that this change will be pursued by the beginning of January.[100]

The 'request' of the mayor of Eskişehir shows not only how strongly the link between the hat reform and the change of women's clothing was felt at the local level, but also the willingness of the local elite to reach a compromise on existing practices. No penalty was mentioned in the statement in the case of non-compliance. Although a total removal of the *peştamal* was the ideal, the mayor was ready to settle for a few civilizing adaptations if women were unable to do away with it completely. *Peştamal* were too colourful to look civilized, according to the mayor; they gave the women of Eskişehir a rural and backward appearance at a time of national revival for civilized dress. It is also interesting to note that the mayor referred to a group of women from Eskişehir whose clothing were to set an example for other women. Although the mayor didn't specify a particular kind of attire, he probably meant the way some teachers or other state officials dressed in Eskişehir at the time.

Later developments in Eskişehir demonstrate that this initial statement made by the mayor was ineffective and did not bring about the expected change in women's clothing. Having noted this, the city council of Eskişehir issued a decree banning the *peçe*, the *peştamal* and the *bohça*s women carry while going to the public baths.[101] However, it seems that this decree was not or could not be implemented

---

100. Çapa, 'Giyim Kuşamda', 24.

101. A *bohça* is a kind of bag created by tying up the crosswise ends of a square cloth. It is often used in villages and by the poor and thus has rural connotations. As we understand from the ban, some women in Eskişehir were carrying their clothes and goods to the public bath with *bohça*s, and this must have been a concern for the local authorities because of the rural or 'primitive' image they created in the city.

very effectively. Then, in January 1927, the provincial council of Eskişehir (*Vilayet Genel Meclisi*) issued a regulation along the same lines:

> Article 1- It has been decided by the city council to ban in the city centre the *peçe* and the *peştamal* used by some women and to prohibit the *bohça* that women carry when they go to the public bath. If there are still people who refuse to comply with the decision, the relevant article of the Law on the General Administration of Provinces will be implemented; that is, based on the minutes handed over by the Committee of Provincial Administration [*Vilayet İdare Heyeti*], they will be fined from five to twenty-five liras.
>
> Article 2- In the district capitals of the province, this decision will be applied two months after its declaration.
>
> Article 3- In the villages of the province, this decision will be put into practice six months after its declaration.[102]

All the headmen (*muhtar*) would be informed of the decision of the provincial council by the police in the neighbourhoods in the provincial centre and by the gendarme in the district capitals and villages of the province. The headmen would be responsible for notifying the public accordingly by visiting each house, door by door. The police, the gendarme and the municipal police sergeants (*belediye çavuşları*) would be responsible for implementing the decision. Yakut argues that the decision of the provincial council proved quite effective in the province of Eskişehir, especially in the provincial centre.[103]

In the meantime, the scope of the anti-veiling campaign in Trabzon surpassed that of the decision made by the members of the Turkish Hearth. A group of members of the Turkish Hearth and the Teachers' Union, organized as 'guidance committees' (*irşad heyetleri*), began visiting the districts of the province and the villages, informing people about the reforms of the new regime and its views on civilization and modern clothing.[104] There were also news items and articles in local newspapers promoting modern dress. Some members of the Trabzon Provincial Council submitted a proposal in December 1926 to ban the *peçe* and to reform women's dress, thereby transforming it into a modern and national form:

> The Turkish republic is based on Turkish culture, and its reference is our great Gazi [Mustafa Kemal]. The whole society is a follower of this great guide. Our province is a port of the Orient, its door opening to the West. It is the

---

102. Yakut, 'Tek Parti', 27.

103. Ibid., 28. Yakut also mentions that similar anti-veiling campaigns were organized in Bursa and Ordu in the 1920s, but he does not provide any details about the time and content of these campaigns.

104. Guidance committees were inculcating the notion, for example, that the hat was not contrary to Islam. Their work was, of course, not limited to propaganda directed at modern clothing, but also advised against speaking in Greek and encouraged saving money. See Öksüz and Usta, *Mustafa Reşit*.

strongest holder of Turkish existence. Therefore, it is a requirement of public interest to make a decision about contemporary women's clothing, which is a product of a foreign culture and lacks a national character. We propose a reform of this primitive and non-national clothing, the banning of the *peçe*, and the transformation of the clothing of women, who comprise half of our society, into a national and civilized state. We request an urgent debate on this proposal.[105]

The proposal submitted to the provincial council was discussed at a meeting at the Trabzon branch of the Republican People's Party before it was discussed and voted on in the council, which indicates the support and involvement of the local party members in the process.[106] The proposal was accepted unanimously, and the *peçe* was prohibited in Trabzon on 11 December 1926.[107] As the British Consul in Trabzon reports, the edict of the *vilayet* was 'threatening the refractory and their nearest male relations with sundry fines and varying terms of imprisonment'.[108] The province of Rize soon followed Trabzon; a similar decision banning the *peçe* in the city was made by the provincial council in January 1927.[109]

In some of the provinces, the decisions of the local authorities to ban the *peçe* and the *çarşaf* seemed to have been influenced by the comments of the Prime Minister İsmet Pasha, during his visits to these cities. In Aydın, the provincial council decided to prohibit the *peçe*, the *çarşaf* and the *peştamal*, together with some men's clothing, like the *zeybek* attire, which was particular to the region, at the beginning of 1927 following the visit of the prime minister. The governor of Aydın later informed the prime minister about the decision of the council in a letter in which he referred to the 'wish' İsmet Pasha had expressed during his visit concerning the transformation of the clothing of the people of Aydın into a civilized state:

To the Prime Minister of the Republic of Turkey, His Excellency İsmet Pasha

2.2.1927, Aydın

My honourable pasha,

At its first meeting on the first day of the new year, the general council of the province issued a decision, the copy of which is attached, that the clothing of the

---

105. Çapa, 'Giyim Kuşamda', 27. Another proposal was submitted to the provincial council to reform men's clothing and to ban baggy trousers and provincial shirts (*mintan*), which, it was argued in the proposal, were making those who wear them look 'primitive' and 'semi-savage'. The proposal was accepted and peasant men were given six months to adopt 'civilized' village clothes. Some district municipalities also issued similar regulations. Ibid.
106. Yahut, 'Tek Parti', 27.
107. Çapa, 'Giyim Kuşamda', 27.
108. Report from Consul Knight to Sir. G. Clerk in Constantinople, FO 371/12320, 12 May 1927. Caporal claims that the police were ordered to take those who continued veiling to the nearest police station. Caporal, *Kemalizmde*, 648–9.
109. Ibid.

people of Aydın, especially that of the women, which you noticed during your visit to Aydın last year, should be transformed into a civilized state. I am proud to inform you that I am striving toward the fulfilment of your wish, and with this opportunity, I request you accept my sincerest respects.

The Governor of Aydın[110]

As the letter of the governor shows, the anti-veiling campaign in Aydın was inspired by the visit of the prime minister and his ideas regarding the clothing of the people in the province. There is no mention in the letter of an order given by the prime minister to ban the veil, or a directive to issue a decision through the provincial council. Thus it remains unclear whether he ordered the governor to initiate a direct ban. However, it is certain that the perceived need to 'civilize' the clothing of the people of the province, or at least the prime minister's concern that the style of dressing common in the city was 'uncivilized', had been voiced during the conversations between the prime minister and the governor. This demonstrates the role played by the elites' desire to modernize women's clothing and their encouragement of it in the initiation of the anti-veiling campaigns, particularly in motivating the local administrators to realize these campaigns so as to gain the approval of Ankara. As had been the case in Aydın, the *peçe* was banned by the provincial council of Muğla, and the ban was reconfirmed at its meeting following the visit of prime minister.[111]

Driven by encouragement from Ankara and the motivation of the provincial administrators, the perceived need for the modernization of women's clothing began to be voiced in many cities, and local newspapers were central in this campaign. In the anti-veiling campaigns of the 1920s, the issue of women's veiling was approached not only as part of the modernization of Turkish society in general, but also as part of the struggle for women's equal rights. The idea that women had been emancipated by the new regime was prevalent and this was further strengthened by the momentum created by the campaign of the Women's Union for women's political rights[112] and especially by the total secularization of

---

110. BCA 030.10/53.346.6. *Zeybek*s were the irregular militia in the Aegean region of the Ottoman Empire who fought against the Greek occupation during the Turkish national struggle. The *zeybek* style of dress was banned in Aydın most probably because it was seen as backward and rural, just like the *peştamal* veil, by the political elite.

111. BCA 490.01/17.88.1. It is unclear in the document when the meeting occurred but as can be gleaned from some references, it was most probably in 1926.

112. In many Anatolian cities, the Turkish Hearths were centres that campaigned for women's political rights, a movement that was initiated by the Turkish Women's Union right after they were established in 1924. The Trabzon Turkish Hearth, for example, also actively supported the campaign by organizing meetings where female members supported the cause for women's right to vote and be elected. Such meetings also provided opportunities for women to appear in public in 'modern' clothing. Caporal, *Kemalizmde*, 690–1. See also, Öksüz and Usta, *Mustafa Reşit*.

the Civil Code in 1926. This provided further support for local efforts to modernize women's dress. In 1928, a local newspaper in the province of Ordu published an article which argued that Turkish women had been granted all the rights and freedoms they needed through the revolution and that the *peçe* and the *çarşaf* were inappropriate for the new status of Turkish women.[113] The author argued that enlightened Turkish women had understood this fact and went on to say that they had freed themselves from the meaningless and feudal influence of the *peçe* and the *çarşaf*. In short, contemporary civilization would not tolerate women wearing such kinds of clothing. In those 'historical days', as the author suggested, Turkish women had the right to dress in a modern manner and there was no need for a directive to come from the centre for that to happen.

As can be seen in the last example, the general discourse of these early anti-veiling campaigns in the second half of the 1920s revolved around the distinction between civilized and uncivilized ways of dressing. The logic employed by the political elite, both in the centre and in the provinces, was similar to what fuelled opposition to the fez, which had been characterized as Oriental, non-Turkish and traditional. The *peçe*, *çarşaf* and *peştamal* were viewed as rural, backward and uncivilized. The survival of traditional women's clothes at a time when a national celebration of modernization and women's rights was underway was seen by many Kemalist elites in the provinces, men and women alike, as a contradiction, as something dissonant with the spirit of the times. The abandonment of the *peçe* and the *çarşaf* was seen as being an indispensable part of women's emancipation and confirmation of their 'civilized' status under the republican regime.

The impacts of the efforts and campaigns of the local elite in the 1920s, however, remained limited. Although Mustafa Reşit Bey expressed confidence in his memoirs that the new reforms had not been received negatively by the people of Trabzon, his hometown, and that even the most difficult of those changes, such as the abandonment of gender segregation and women's seclusion, had been adopted quite easily,[114] reality told a different story. Writing about the political situation in Turkey around the same time that the ban was put into practice in Trabzon, Toynbee reported on the failure of the anti-veiling campaigns in 1927: 'At the time of writing, the Government had been attempting to make the abandonment of the veil obligatory in the Vilayet of Trebizond and in certain other districts, but had been compelled to abandon this experiment owing to the strength of the opposition which it encountered.'[115] Having noted that Trabzon had a reputation for being one of the most 'reactionary' cities in Turkey, the British Consul in Trabzon explained the continuation of the old veiling habits by underlining the strategies women used to get around the banning of the *peçe*. According to the consul, the inhabitants of Trabzon were 'somewhat easy-going' compared to the other cities

---

113. Çapa, 'Giyim Kuşamda', 24–5.
114. Öksüz and Usta, *Mustafa Reşit*, 196–7.
115. Toynbee, *Survey*, 77, fnt.1.

such as Rize and Erzurum, and this was reflected in the way they reacted to the anti-veiling campaign initiated by the local government.[116] Women were almost completely absent in the public life of Trabzon except as teachers and students, but it appears that, according to the account of the consul, in the few instances they appeared in public, women in Trabzon wore the *çarşaf* in such a way that the *peçe* was not necessary:

> At all events, being confronted in the present instance with a mere conciliar decree lacking the force of law, they [women of Trabzon] and their men-folk devised a compromise which, from their point of view, proved a complete success. The 'petché,' or short black veil which fell over the face, was duly discarded, while the 'charshaf,' as not being a veil in the sense of the decree, was retained in all its amplitude, and serves to protect the features to the exact extent desired by the wearer. Modesty being as much a distinguishing mark of the Trebizond women as jealousy is of their husbands, the situation has, to all intents and purposes, remained the same as before the promulgation of the edict, and with this state of affairs the local authorities have to be satisfied, at least for the present. The few female faces to be seen in the streets are, with very few exceptions, those of either school-mistresses or schoolgirls, who, having been the objects of special legislation, are, of course, in a category apart. The latter, growing up without the traditional restrictions of dress or manners will doubtless never adopt those of their mothers, except possibly in the case of a very few old-fashioned families where the tradition of filial piety is still strong.[117]

It seems that while the banning of the *peçe* in Trabzon had some impact, it did not result in substantial transformation of women's clothing or a decline in the practice of veiling itself. As the British Consul noted, the main difference that

---

116. Needless to say, such characterizations of Trabzon as 'reactionary' or 'easy-going' were subjective readings of the British consul. In fact, as a port city, Trabzon was still quite cosmopolitan in the early twentieth century. However, the ethnic composition of the city changed dramatically after the deportations of the Armenians in 1915 and the mass expulsion of the Greeks brought about by the compulsory population exchange between Greece and Turkey as part of the Treaty of Lausanne in 1923. See Michael Meeker, 'The Black Sea Turks: Some Aspects of Their Ethnic and Cultural Background', *International Journal of Middle East Studies* 2, no. 4 (October 1971): 318–45; Renée Hirschon, ed. *Crossing the Aegean: An Appraisal of the 1923 Compulsory Population Exchange between Greece and Turkey* (Oxford: Berghahn Books, 2003).

117. Report from Consul Knight to Sir G. Clerk in Constantinople, FO 371/12320, 12 May 1927. Consul Knight also reported that there were no women professionals in Trabzon except for schoolteachers, a few staff members in the women's wards of hospitals and two women clerks at the Trabzon post-office. He noted, however, that women were to be seen everywhere in the countryside, working the land. In the cigarette factory in Samsun, there were also women workers.

could be seen was generational and it was brought about by modern education and schooling. In another report on the progress of modernization in his consular district, the consul wrote that European-style entertainment and social gatherings were quite the exception in Trabzon, and at gatherings like balls, only the wives of officials and officers or schoolgirls could be seen, and the very few Turkish women who danced belonged to the latter group. Despite this very limited progress in eliminating gender segregation and modernizing women's clothing in Trabzon, he nevertheless noted that the situation of women in Trabzon was still better compared to what it was in other eastern cities, where women's veiling continued unabated:

> In my despatch No. 3 of the 12th May I had the honour to report on the almost total absence of modernization with regard to the position of women, and in this respect Trebizond, backward though it be, is ahead of the other eastern vilayets, where, at least in the towns, the face is still hidden by the 'petché' as completely as if the Ghazi had never been heard of.[118]

In other cities as well the change in women's clothing was only really visible in the dress of state officials and women from high-class families. The British Consul in Mersin's consular region, for example, reported in 1927 that although his district was 'old-fashioned and fanatical' in general, there was steady progress in the emancipation of women:

> The new type of woman now so familiar in Constantinople, turbaned or hatted and dressed in the modes of Paris, most of whom set a distinctly rapid pace, is making her appearance in Adana and Mersin in the shape of wives and daughters of imported officials or manufacturers and notables who had been abroad. Officials on the spot are also dutifully modernizing their womenfolk.

He noted that there was a livelier social life in comparison to Trabzon, at least in the city centres of Mersin and Adana, and mentioned the existence of mixed-gender public places and gatherings among the higher classes for which the harem would seem to have been a remnant of the past. Girls had begun to walk about town by themselves in Mersin, more Turkish women had started to appear at public balls, and more women had learned how to dance, with the daughter of the governor leading the way in this regard.[119] The countrywomen had never

---

118. Report from Consul Knight to Sir G. Clerk in Constantinople, FO 371/12320, 12 June 1927.

119. Report from Consul Chafy to Sir G. Clerk in Constantinople, FO371/12320, 21 May 1927. The consul notes in his report that the governor was quite vexed that women would or could not dance at the first public ball in the town and he told the consul personally that his daughter would be the first to dance at the next ball. A professional Hungarian dancer was teaching dancing at homes in both Mersin and Adana.

worn the veil anyway, and girls who had begun to go to school adopted modern manners in clothing, as in the case of Trabzon, which would, according to the consul, contribute to the abandonment of the veil in the future despite the fact that it was worn by many women: 'A large number of townswomen of the *bourgeoisie* class are still heavily veiled or half-veiled, and I understand that the Ghazi is wise enough not to impose any unveiling order in these parts. But the veil is, I think, dying a natural death. Girls growing up will simply not wear it'.[120]

Such observations of foreign diplomats point to a geographical difference in terms of the pace or scope of the change as well.[121] Having read all the reports, the British Ambassador in Istanbul also claimed that larger towns near the sea or railway system were ahead of those in the interior of the country and the countryside in terms of taking up European manners, clothing, social gatherings and entertainment.[122] In Izmir, for example, which was one of the most cosmopolitan cities in Turkey, the elite enjoyed a lively social life and there was increasing interest in modern sports, theatre and dancing. The acting British Consul underlined the distinctive character of social gatherings as follows:

> The real change lies not so much in the closer association of the Turk and the European as in the admission of his women-folk to the revels. Today the shortest skirts and the most powdered faces are to be seen on the Turkish lady at these gatherings. It is only at the gaming tables that she has not yet made her appearance in public.[123]

According to his observation, the veil (meaning the face veil) had practically disappeared in Izmir, although it was still possible to see some older women wearing it in villages or in remote and poorer suburbs, like Buca and Bornova, which points

---

120. Ibid. See also the Report from Consul Chafy to Sir G. Clerk in Constantinople, FO 371/12320, 27 May 1927.

121. For a detailed discussion of the influence of geographical differences in explaining the multiple transitions of late Ottoman societies to modernity, see Cem Emrence, *Remapping the Ottoman Middle East: Modernity, Imperial Bureaucracy and the Islamic State* (London: I.B. Tauris, 2011).

122. Despatch N. 380 from Sir G. Clerk to Sir Austen Chamberlain, FO 371/12320, 20 July 1927. For the British diplomats, the existence of Europeans or non-Muslims living in a town influenced the pace of change as regards women's clothing. The British Consulate in Edirne (Adrianople), for example, reported along the same lines as the consul of Mersin district that a slow but sure progress in women's status was occurring in the city and that the veil had become rare since 'the Jewesses of the town (of whom there are many) are always there to set at least a Levantine, if not a European, standard of dress and behavior'. The Report from Consular Officer, FO 371/12320, 25 May 1927.

123. Copy of the Report from Acting Consul in Smyrna, in Despatch N. 380 from Sir G. Clerk, FO 371/12320.

to an uneven change, even within a particular province.[124] Although people from the upper classes and the younger generation in particular were prepared to adopt European clothing, it appears that ordinary women had removed the face veil but were more reluctant to completely change their clothing, even in a city like Izmir: 'Modern European headgear is as yet practically unknown to the Turkish women of Smyrna. As a general rule the Turkish costume is little changed except for the omission of the veil. It appears to go against the grain for the Turkish woman to do away with the symbol of the distinction between Moslem and the non-Moslem.'[125]

In short, it seems that despite all the campaigns and propaganda that were carried out, the change in women's dress in the 1920s was limited to the elite or educated segments of the population. In fact, even among some elites there was still resistance to 'modern' ways, especially regarding women's clothing and public presence. One of the most prominent speakers of the Kemalist regime, Falih Rıfkı, expressed this reluctance in 1929 as an impact of the yet uneradicated 'Oriental' mind and past:

In the houses in which we were born, in the schools in which we studied, in the thoughts, feelings, and customs by which we were raised, in our clothing, our common understandings, and the way that we carry ourselves, from top to bottom, everything has changed. Neither a man nor a generation can emotionally absorb the widespread chaos that has taken place in the past eight to ten years, no matter how much he had every intention of doing so. The wound of being Oriental has encrusted us. There yet exists a scab on our skin. With a vigorous scrubbing of this scab, it can again be infected. We are half humans. Our correct ideas are still fighting against our wrong feelings. We still have a considerable number of brave revolutionaries who won't let their wives emerge from the *kafes*. The *sarık* that we cast off winds itself around our feet and trips us.[126]

---

124. The acting consul also reports, for example, that a large number of women were veiled in the province of Aydın when he visited there the previous holiday, but that the authorities had not interfered: 'It appears that there had been considerable traffic in undesirable women in certain cabarets and clubs of Aidin, and the more conservative portion of the population objected to the scenes which took place there. In Sokia [Söke, a district of the province of Aydın], on the other hand, the large garden belonging to the resident manager for the Macandrews and Forbes Company had been recently lent for a garden party for charitable purposes. The whole population of Sohia attended and none of the women were veiled'. Copy of the Report from Acting Consul in Smyrna, in Despatch N. 384 from Sir G. Clerk, FO 371/12320.

125. Ibid.

126. Falih Rıfkı (Atay), 'Bizim Çocuğumuz', *Çocuk Haftası* 1, 1929, quoted in Libal, 'From Face Veil'. *Kafes* is a lattice or a window grill used in Ottoman/Turkish house architecture to conceal windows for privacy. A *sarık* is a traditional male headgear, usually known as the Turkish-style turban and composed of a cloth wrapped around the fez or the traditional cap, *kavuk*.

Likewise, speaking on Republic Day in October 1928 at the Istanbul branch of the Women's Union, İffet Halim Hanım pointed to the slow pace of development in the modernization of women's clothing even in a city like Istanbul:

Our men have put on the hat and understood its benefits in a very short time. It was hoped that after them, our women would also feel the same necessity especially in a place like Istanbul, which is one of the most civilized cities of Turkey. However, unfortunately, the last couple of years have been wasted as a period of stagnancy. An outside eye would see us dressed in complete confusion. Some of us wear overcoats, some of us cover our heads with turbans, some with tulle, and a small number of us wear hats. We can no longer hesitate to choose a way of dressing that is equivalent to the way men dress. Those who, I do not know why, continue to hide their faces and still cover their heads should sincerely admit that they do not recognize how much harm they do to themselves because of this unnecessary insistence.[127]

Nevertheless, although the anti-veiling campaigns of the 1920s were limited in number and remained local initiatives, they were significant and unprecedented since the provincial elite attempted to directly intervene in women's clothing. Ideologically, they stemmed from a much older debate that had started in the late Ottoman Empire and stigmatized the *peçe* and the *çarşaf* as uncivilized clothing. In fact, the initial changes in women's dress along these lines had already begun before the establishment of the republic, and locally organized associations such as the Turkish Hearths (*Türk Ocakları*) had already created spaces in the provinces for women's greater public participation and for the struggle against gender segregation.[128] The anti-veiling campaigns of the 1920s can thus be seen as a continuation of a line of thought in Ottoman/Turkish history that had linked modernization and social development with women's emancipation and with changes in their clothing. Yet, they were also novel in that they were clearly motivated by the Hat Law of 1925 in terms of timing and as a source of legitimacy. Even though the law only concerned men's headgear, it triggered a public debate on 'civilized' ways of dressing as well as women's clothing and the importance of modernizing the outlook of the Turkish nation. Local elites' attempts to change women's manner of dressing in some provinces had emerged as part of this general momentum. The uncompromising manner with which the Hat Law was put into practice by the Kemalist regime and the reactions it received led to a tendency to deal with women's clothing not by enacting laws or imposing central decisions but through propaganda, example and, most importantly, by trusting the modernist visions and ambitions of the local elite. In this sense, although limited to a few provinces, the early examples of the anti-veiling campaigns of the 1920s created a path that would be followed later.

---

127. Gençosman, *Altın Yıllar*, 117–18.
128. Füsun Üstel, *İmparatorluktan Ulus-Devlete Türk Milliyetçiliği: Türk Ocakları (1912–1931)* (Istanbul: İletişim, 1997), 137–40.

In provinces where there was an outright ban, the campaigns were more limited at first, as seen in the statement of the mayor of Eskişehir and the decision made by the Trabzon Turkish Hearth. However, they gradually accelerated and were reinforced by the decisions of the local administrative bodies when that initial attempt was unsuccessful. The decisions to ban veiling in the 1920s were mainly made by provincial councils, which were probably thought to have a more effective legal capacity compared to municipalities because of the Law on the General Administration of Provinces (*İdare-i Umumiye-i Vilâyat Kanunu*). It appears that the early campaigns of the 1920s were more focused on the removal of the *peçe* and the elimination of rural forms of clothing particular to each province. The aim was to change women's clothing primarily in the provincial centres, despite the fact that some of the decisions were planned to be carried out in the district capitals and villages as well, as in the case of Eskişehir. However, this first wave of anti-veiling campaigns did not become a countrywide phenomenon. Even in places where they were initiated, they proved to be largely ineffective. The fact that similar bans were issued in the 1930s by the provincial authorities of the same cities that had initiated a campaign in the 1920s can be seen as an indication of the limited and weak impact of the earlier attempts. The main wave of anti-veiling campaigns would begin in the 1930s, when the Kemalist single-party regime became increasingly authoritarian in every domain following its consolidation of power.

Chapter 2

ANTI-VEILING CAMPAIGNS IN THE 1930s:
THE MAIN WAVE

Turkey in the 1930s

Many scholars of early republican Turkey see a change in the character of the Kemalist regime beginning in the 1930s. Mete Tunçay, argues, for example, that until 1931, the new regime was undergoing a process of formation.[1] In his periodization, the year 1931 marks the consolidation of the authoritarian single-party system in Turkey, with the period between 1931 and 1945 being relatively stronger and more compact in political terms. As he maintains, the consolidation of the regime in 1931 was realized and implicitly declared at the 'third' congress of the RPP in 1931,[2] where the main characteristics and principles of the regime were formulated. These principles, namely republicanism, nationalism, populism, secularism, statism and revolutionism, constituted the official state ideology known as the Six Arrows.[3] The 1931 RPP congress and the party programme issued there were the manifestations of the policies that would shape Turkey in the 1930s.

In fact, in 1929 the extraordinary measures taken after the Kurdish/Islamic rebellion of 1925 had come to an end and the government decided to abolish the Law on the Maintenance of Order (*Takrir-i Sükûn Kanunu*). Prime Minister İsmet Pasha explained this decision in his speech at the party meeting by referring to their confidence that a legal and administrative system that would prevent oppositional

---

1. Tunçay, *T.C.'nde Tek-Parti*.

2. This was in fact the second congress of the party. The first congress was held in 1927, but the RPP referred to this congress as the second congress 'because it retrospectively adopted the congress in Sivas in 1919 as its first, thus emphasizing (false) identification of the RPP with the national liberation movement and monopolizing its heritage'. Erik J. Zürcher, *Turkey: A Modern History*, 3rd ed. (London: I.B. Tauris, 2004), 175.

3. The first four principles were agreed to at the previous congress in 1927. The last two, statism and revolutionism, were added during the congress in 1931. For a detailed discussion of these principles, see Taha Parla, *Türkiye'de Siyasal Kültürün Resmî Kaynakları, v. 3: Kemalist Tek-Parti İdeolojisi ve CHP'nin Altı Ok'u* (Istanbul: İletişim, 1992); Taha Parla and Andrew Davison, *Corporatist Ideology in Kemalist Turkey: Progress or Order?* (Syracuse: Syracuse University Press, 2004).

forces from mobilizing against the regime had been successfully established during the four years the law was in force.[4] He argued that the government had succeeded in creating a new type of state based on an understanding of republican citizenship and the separation of religion and state.

Considering İsmet Pasha's speech, which referred to the end of emergency rule and the beginning of a new era in 1929, the periodization offered by Tunçay might seem contradictory at first. However, after publicly maintaining that it had abolished all opposition and succeeded in creating a strong, established order, the Kemalist regime suffered two unexpected blows. The first one was a brief experiment in 1930 with a multi-party system, which turned into a test of confidence and legitimacy for the regime. Established in August 1930 with the encouragement of Mustafa Kemal, the Free Republican Party (FRP) became unexpectedly popular as an opposition party, especially among the middle and lower segments of society, reflecting their discontent with some of the Kemalist reforms and policies instigated up until then.[5] As a second attempt to initiate a transition to a multi-party system,[6] the FRP was rather successful in the local elections against the RPP, which represented the regime with Atatürk as its immutable president. The FRP's party meeting in Izmir turned into a protest against the government. The success of the FRP alarmed the regime and drew its attention once again to its inability to spread its ideals to the public at large. Faced with increasing social support for the FRP, which tended to get out of the state's control, the ruling elite turned their back on the opposition party shortly after its establishment. The party was closed just three months after it was launched. Immediately following its closure, Mustafa Kemal began a three-month tour around the country to take the nation's pulse. This gave him the opportunity to observe more closely the scale of and the reasons for the social discontent which had risen to the surface. The tour also gave him the chance to formulate a new road map to institute a stronger regime.

The second shock was an incident that occurred in Menemen, a small town in the province of Izmir on the west coast of the country. In December 1930, a small group of people in Menemen who referred to themselves the army of the Caliphate attempted to declare an Islamic order in opposition to the republican administration.[7] The

---

4. 'Başvekil Pş. Hazretlerinin Nutku', *Hakimiyeti Milliye*, 5 March 1929.

5. For more on the Free Republican Party, see Walter F. Weiker, *Political Tutelage and Democracy in Turkey: The Free Party and Its Aftermath* (Leiden: Brill, 1973); Cem Emrence, *99 Günlük Muhalefet Serbest Cumhuriyet Fırkası* (Istanbul: İletişim, 2006); Cemil Koçak, *Belgelerle İktidar ve Serbest Cumhuriyet Fırkası* (Istanbul: İletişim, 2006).

6. The establishment of the Progressive Republican Party in 1924 by a group of political elites critical of the Kemalist circle was the regime's first experience with a multi-party system. For more, see Erik J. Zürcher, *Political Opposition in the Early Turkish Republic: The Progressive Republican Party* (Leiden: Brill, 1991).

7. For a critical analysis of the incident, see Umut Azak, 'A Reaction to Authoritarian Modernization in Turkey: The Menemen Incident and the Creation and Contestation of a Myth, 1930–31', in *The State and the Subaltern: Modernization, Society and the State in Turkey and Iran*, ed. Touraj Atabaki (London: I.B. Tauris, 2007), 143–58.

incident was quickly suppressed, but the rioters beheaded a young officer who tried to stop them. Even more traumatic for the regime was the indifference or reluctance of the people of Menemen to intervene. Mustafa Kemal interpreted this reluctance as tacit support or approval on the part of at least some segments of the population: 'The approval shown by some members of the community of Menemen for the savageness displayed by the reactionaries (*mürteciler*) is a source of shame for all patriots and the supporters of republicanism'.[8] This reaction to the Menemen incident was also the result of its crucial difference from the other rebellions that had previously occurred. The incident had occurred in a town in the west of Turkey, which was supposedly more developed in terms of urban and economic parameters than those in the east and therefore it was thought that it should have been well-integrated into the Kemalist regime and easily controlled by it.

This event had such an impact on the political elite that it initiated a discussion similar to the one raised after the Sheikh Said rebellion in 1925. In addition to the ineffectiveness of the reforms that had been carried out thus far, some elite even criticized some of the Westernized practices of the new era, such as beauty contests, which only served to alienate the majority of the people from the principles of the state.[9] The political elite's perception of the event also revealed its awareness of the discontent that existed in society. The president demanded an investigation into the political roots of the event and ordered strict control over the press, in addition to the harsh suppression of the rebellions and the forced migration of the people in the region who were accused of being involved in the uprising.[10]

The reactions that the regime faced in 1930 and the increasing discontent in society were as much the result of the economic failure brought on by the Great Depression as they were of the national policies and extraordinary measures applied in the second half of the 1920s. In fact, Cem Emrence argues that the effects of the economic crisis on Turkey were one of the primary reasons for the founding of the FRP.[11] With a largely agricultural economy based on the export of agricultural goods, Turkey was hit hard by the crisis, which was felt severely by both the peasantry in the countryside and the merchants and workers in the cities. 'Rising social discontent became the undisputed reality', Emrence suggests, which then led the president to try to channel this increasing opposition to a new political party that would work under his control. The programme of the opposition party focused on economic issues, taking up a liberal agenda to counter the effects of the crisis. With the FRP's elimination from the political

---

8. *Vatan*, 28 December 1930, quoted in Tunçay, *T.C.'nde Tek-Parti*, 293.

9. Nurşen Mazıcı, 'Menemen Olayı'nın Sosyo-kültürel ve Sosyo-ekonomik Analizi', *Toplum ve Bilim* 90 (Fall 2001): 131–46.

10. Tunçay, *T.C.'nde Tek-Parti*, 294.

11. Cem Emrence, 'Politics of Discontent in the Midst of the Great Depression: The Free Republican Party of Turkey (1930)', *New Perspectives on Turkey* 23 (Fall 2000): 31–52.

scene, Turkey turned towards statism and state-led industrialization as a reaction to the Great Depression.[12]

This turn towards more state control in the economy had a spillover effect on other aspects of the political and social spheres. Önen and Reyhan, for example, argue that the Provincial Law of 1929, which brought about a centralist structure in public administration, was directly linked to the economic policy of statism.[13] Zürcher also argues that having maintained a leading role in the economy, the Turkish state increased its power in every regard, which marked a different phase in the history of the Kemalist regime beginning in the 1930s. The elimination of all civil society organizations and their incorporation into the party structure, as well as the merger of the state and party in 1936, were the main components of the political repression that characterized the second phase of Kemalism, and this political repression was linked to the economic policies that emerged as a reaction to the effects of the Great Depression. The crisis of 1929 deepened social discontent and paved the way for a mutual loss of trust between the political elite and the majority of the population, and this was aggravated by the traumatic events of 1930 – the FRP experience and the Menemen incident. Thus, 'the authoritarian state that had been in being since 1925 felt a need for total control of every aspect of social life' in the 1930s.[14]

Çağaptay also characterizes the 1930s in a similar way, as 'High Kemalism' or 'Kemalism par excellence', by focusing on ideological components rather than the effects of the Great Depression and the statist policies following it.[15] According to Çağaptay, Turkey had focused on recovering from a decade of continuous warfare and major political restructuring in the 1920s. It was only after the establishment of a secular republic that Kemalism turned its attention to matters of ideology and became a more nationalist and authoritarian regime. Bozarslan also differentiates the 1930s from the previous phases of Kemalism by referring to the way it assumed a relatively compact form as an 'autonomous' ideology with the formulation of the Six Arrows.[16] He argues that compared to the 'Janus-like' Kemalism of the

---

12. Zürcher suggests that this turn was also shaped by the 1931 party congress, where the people around Prime Minister İsmet Pasha, who advocated a strict definition of statism, won out against those who favoured a more liberal interpretation, such as Celal Bey (Bayar), the head of the Business Bank (*İş Bankası*). Erik J. Zürcher, 'Turkey in the First World Crisis: From Authoritarianism to Totalitarianism', in *Routes into the Abyss: Coping with Crises in the 1930s*, eds. Helmut Konrad and Wolfgang Waderthaner (Oxford: Berghahn Books, 2013), 127–38.

13. Nizam Önen and Cenk Reyhan, *Mülkten Ülkeye: Türkiye'de Taşra İdaresinin Dönüşümü (1839–1929)* (Istanbul: İletişim, 2011), 540.

14. Zürcher, 'Turkey in the First', 2013.

15. Soner Çağaptay, 'Reconfiguring the Turkish Nation in the 1930s', *Nationalism and Ethnic Politics* 8, no. 2 (Summer 2002): 67–82.

16. Hamit Bozarslan, 'Kemalism, Westernization and Anti-liberalism', in *Turkey beyond Nationalism: Towards Post-Nationalist Identities*, ed. Hans-Lukas Kieser (London: I.B. Tauris, 2006), 28–34.

1920s, 'which was at the same time nationalist and the bearer of a project of civilization', the Kemalism of the 1930s was transformed into the ideology of a nationalist revolution, creating 'an openly and self-consciously anti-liberal and anti-democratic regime'.

Many of the changes that took place in the 1930s can indeed be seen as reflecting such a turn towards a more authoritarian regime. One was the increasing role of the RPP as a major instrument for spreading the ideology of the regime and mobilizing society. Of course, the party existed before the 1930s but it was much less active and held less political clout because of the extraordinary powers granted to the cabinet through the Law on the Maintenance of Order between 1925 and 1929.[17] It became much more active in the first half of the 1930s, especially under Recep Peker, the secretary-general of the party between 1931 and 1936. It also became closely identified with the state apparatus. In the new programme of the party that was agreed upon at the congress in May 1935, the party and the government were described as two complementary organizations. According to the new programme, the government was born out of the party and together they constituted a union.[18] The merger was implemented by a circular issued by Prime Minister İnönü in June 1936.[19] According to the circular, the minister of the interior would become the general secretary of the party, the governors of provinces would be the heads of the local branches of the RPP, and inspector-generals would also monitor party branches and the activities in the region where they served. Although it has been characterized as a merger of the state and the party, it can indeed be seen as a process through which the state took over the party: All those who were in charge at the time as the heads of party branches in the provinces were removed from office by the circular and the current governors took over their duties. The secretary general of the party, Recep Peker, was removed from his position three days before the circular was issued. This merger of the state and the party was completed by the incorporation of the Six Arrows into the constitution in 1937, thus making the party's principles the main principles of the state.[20]

As part of these policies of centralization and increasing state control, the number of general inspectorships, which were the institutions in charge of controlling the affairs of the provinces and organizing the operations of all governmental departments in the general inspection zone, also increased in the 1930s.[21] The

---

17. Erik J. Zürcher, 'The Ottoman Legacy of the Kemalist Republic', in *The State and the Subaltern: Modernization, Society and the State in Turkey and Iran*, ed. Touraj Atabaki (London: I.B. Tauris, 2007), 95–110.

18. *C.H.P. Dördüncü Büyük Kurultayı Görüşmeleri Tutulgası, 9–16 Mayıs 1935* (Ankara: Ulus Basımevi, 1935), 99–105.

19. Cemil Koçak, 'Siyasal Tarih (1923–1950)', in *Türkiye Tarihi 4: Çağdaş Türkiye 1908–1980*, ed. Sina Akşin (Istanbul: Cem Yayınevi, 1997), 84–173.

20. Ibid., 116.

21. For more on the general inspectorships, see Cemil Koçak, *Umûmî Müfettişlikler (1927–1952)* (Istanbul: İletişim, 2003); M. Bülent Varlık, ed. *Umumi Müfettişler Toplantı Tutanakları – 1936* (Istanbul: Dipnot, 2010).

First General Inspectorship (*Birinci Umûmî Müfettişlik*) was established in 1927 in the Kurdish provinces of southeast Turkey following the Sheikh Said rebellion. The second one was formed in February 1934 for the region of Thrace, followed by the Third General Inspectorship in 1935 which was in charge of the eastern and north-eastern provinces. As part of the policy of merging the state apparatus and the party, general inspectors became the highest-ranking inspectors of all the branches of the party organization, and thus the inspectorships and the RPP were in close contact. Moreover, in addition to their primary role (maintaining security and state control in their inspection zones), general inspectorships were also expected to create 'civilized' cities. According to the law, general inspectors were responsible for monitoring and supporting the development of their inspection zones, not only in terms of the economy, infrastructure or public health, but also in terms of social, cultural and civilizational progress.[22] Such generally defined responsibilities would sometimes lead to their heavy involvement in attempts to change social life in their regions. As will be discussed in the next chapter, some general inspectors played an active role in the implementation of anti-veiling campaigns within this framework.

In addition to the RPP and general inspectorships, one other institution that is particularly important for understanding the policies and nature of the Kemalist regime in the 1930s is the People's Houses (*Halkevleri*). Established in 1932 (right after the abolition of the Turkish Hearths) as a cultural organization organically linked to the RPP, the People's Houses aimed primarily at educating the masses and mobilizing people at the local level in accordance with the ideals of the new regime.[23] They were designed to be major centres for meeting and socializing, and they were expected to lead the social and cultural life in their localities through their activities and publications, extending all the way to villages by organizing village committees and People's Chambers. The People's Houses were responsible for creating an atmosphere where people from the countryside could become familiar with elements of modern life, ranging from theatre to dancing. It is therefore not surprising that they were heavily involved in initiatives for cultural change, including anti-veiling campaigns. In fact, as will be discussed in detail in the following two chapters, these three important institutions and their administrators – the RPP local branches, the inspector-generals and the People's Houses – played a critical role, together with the municipalities, as the actors of the anti-veiling campaigns in the periphery and as milieus in which the dynamics of the campaigns were shaped.

In addition to having undergone institutional changes, Turkey of the 1930s was also characterized by a wave of reforms, targeting especially cultural and social modernization. Western weights and measures were adopted in 1931. In 1932, it was required that the call to prayer (*ezan*) and some other elements of worship such as

---

22. Koçak, *Umûmî Müfettişlikler*, 303–7.
23. For a comprehensive account of the People's Houses and their role in the domestication of Kemalist reforms, see Lamprou, *Nation Building*.

sermons be carried out it Turkish.[24] The music reform (modernization of Turkish music) and the language reform (purification of Turkish and elimination of words with Persian and Arabic origin), which were referred to as 'revolutions' at the time they were put into practice (*Musiki İnkılâbı* and *Dil İnkılâbı*), were among the most radical of Kemalist reforms in the 1930s aiming at cultural modernization.[25] Both the Society for the Study of Turkish History, established in April 1931, and the Society for the Study of Turkish Language, founded in June 1932, played an active role in developing research and theories in support of Turkish nationalism, and these were not mere academic studies but were included in the school curriculum as part of ideological indoctrination.

The year 1934 was particularly significant in terms of the intensity of changes and the reforms that were introduced. The Settlement Law, which entailed the resettlement of thousands of people on the basis of the state's alleged security concerns, was enacted in June;[26] the Surname Law, which made the acquisition of family names mandatory for all citizens, was issued in July;[27] the law on the removal of appellations and titles like *efendi* and pasha, and the abolition of all civilian ranks, decorations and medals was passed in November. Towards the end of the year, women were granted the right to vote and be elected in parliamentary elections, which was celebrated in public discourse as the last and most important breakthrough in women's emancipation.[28] Promulgated in December, the Clothing Law (*Kisve Kanunu*) prohibited members of the clergy from wearing religious garments outside of services.[29] The law applied to all religions and applied to

---

24. For more the Turkification of the language of worship, see Dücane Cündioğlu, *Türkçe Kur'an ve Cumhuriyet İdeolojisi* (Istanbul: Kitabevi, 1998); Dücane Cündioğlu, *Bir Siyasi Proje Olarak Türkçe İbadet I* (Istanbul: Kitabevi, 1999); Umut Azak, *Islam and Secularism in Turkey: Kemalism, Religion, and the Nation State* (London: I.B. Tauris, 2010).

25. On the music reform, see Orhan Tekelioğlu, 'Modernizing Reforms and Turkish Music in the 1930s', *Turkish Studies* 2, no. 1 (2001): 93–108. On the language reform, see Geoffrey Lewis, *The Turkish Language Reform: A Catastrophic Success* (Oxford: Oxford University Press, 2000).

26. The law had an assimilative aim, seeking to impose Turkish language and culture on non-Turkish groups, particularly Kurds. Erol Ülker, 'Assimilation, Security and Geographical Nationalization in Interwar Turkey: The Settlement Law of 1934', *European Journal of Turkish Studies* 7 (2008), https://doi.org/10.4000/ejts.822.

27. On the Surname Law, see Türköz, *Naming and Nation-Building*; Emmanuel Szurek, '"Yan, Of, Ef, Viç, İç, İs, Dis, Pulos ... ": the Surname Reform, the "Non-Muslims," and the Politics of Uncertainty in Post-genocidal Turkey', in *Arabic and Its Alternatives: Religious Minorities and Their Languages in the Emerging Nation States of the Middle East (1920–1950)*, eds. Heleen Murre-van den Berg, Karène Sanchez Summerer and Tijmen Baarda (Leiden: Brill, 2020), 77–110.

28. In the parliamentary elections of 1935, eighteen women deputies were elected to parliament.

29. Although often referred to as *Kisve Kanunu*, the long title of the law was Law Prohibiting the Wearing of Certain Garments (*Bazı Kisvelerin Giyilemeyeceğine Dair Kanun*).

Jewish and Christian clergy members as well. Writing in December 1934, right after the enactment of the Clothing Law and during the heyday of the language and music reform, the American ambassador reported his observations of societal reactions to this sequence of reforms in the following way: 'Society, meaning the totality of the Turkish population and the foreign element in the country as well, is more bewildered than ever by this latest addition to the astonishing succession of "movements" put under way within the last few weeks'.[30] The acceleration of the reforms in 1934 was also reflected at the local level. In an article published by an Adana-based newspaper, a columnist characterized the last months of 1934 as the fastest and most worthy days of the 'major Turkish transformation'.[31]

This astonishing series of changes marked the attempt of the state to extend its control over society and increase its interventions in the everyday life of its citizens in an unprecedented manner. They aimed at a more definitive break with the Ottoman past and with all habits and norms coded as traditional, uncivilized, false or backward. This was a time when visual expressions of modernization, such as clothing, gained particular significance, reflecting the 'progress' brought about by the Kemalist regime. As Bozdoğan notes, 'what was unique to the Kemalist program in the 1930s was the inordinate time and energy invested in changing the forms of things and the official production, supervision, and dissemination of a distinctly republican *visual* culture of modernity'.[32] Placed in this larger context, the anti-veiling campaigns can thus be seen as part of larger attempts at cultural modernization in the 1930s, a project which gained one of its most symbolic manifestations in discussions around women's modernization and emancipation.

Modernizing women: Un/veiling in the 1930s

On 14 June 1930, a French journalist's visit to Istanbul and his article discussing Turkish women's progress made the headlines of the national newspaper *Cumhuriyet*.[33] Reprinting the photographs used by the journalist, photographs showing Turkish women in their 'old' clothing, *Cumhuriyet* quoted what the article had to say about how Turkish women had become modern in a very short time after the establishment of the republic. The indication of this change was the total disappearance of the *peçe* and the *çarşaf*, except for some elderly women in remote corners of Istanbul and Ankara, and the increased presence of women in the public sphere. *Cumhuriyet*'s coverage celebrated the French journalist's observation that 'the East was totally erased' in Turkey; the claim was made that Turkish women

---

30. Correspondence from Robert P. Skinner to the Secretary of the State in Washington, DC, United States National Archives and Records Administration (hereafter NARA) Record Group (hereafter RG) 84 Box. 350: 10/15/3 vol. 703, 5 December 1934.

31. A. Remzi Yüreğir, 'Hızlı Günler', *Yeni Adana*, 10 December 1934.

32. Sibel Bozdoğan, *Modernism and Nation Building: Turkish Architectural Culture in the Early Republic* (Seattle: University of Washington Press, 2001), 59.

33. 'Türk Kadını Hakkında Bir Makale', *Cumhuriyet*, 14 June 1930.

had been freed from the shackles of religion, and they were now living, dressing and marrying exactly like their sisters in the West.

It was quite common in Turkish newspapers of the 1930s, national and provincial alike, to publish articles from Western newspapers praising the progress of Turkey.[34] The opinions of European observers concerning Turkey, in particular their approval and acclaim, were a litmus test used to assess the degree of modernization achieved and the success of the republic. European dress codes and habits were a constant reference point. It was a matter of pride when an article published in a Dutch newspaper characterized the dress of the people of Ankara as 'clean, orderly and European'.[35] The way Westerners perceived the appearance of Turkish women was especially important. Since 'no single item of clothing has had more influence on Western images of Middle Eastern women than the veil',[36] its removal would be the most powerful symbol of social change, both for Western observers and in the eyes of the Kemalists. In other words, changing the image of Turkish women by emancipating them from the 'chains' of the *peçe* and the *çarşaf* and bringing women into the public sphere were seen as being the best ways to distance the new republic from its Ottoman past, and not only create a break with it but also triumph over it. Among the upper classes, 'you look like a foreigner' was the biggest compliment a woman could receive.[37]

Although these motivations were already guiding Kemalist policies and discourses concerning women in the 1920s, the stigmatization of the *peçe* and the *çarşaf* as uncivilized attire grew and more explicitly expressed in public in the 1930s. The propaganda posters of the RPP in the 1930s reflected this stigmatization through images of women; there was a contrast between the *peçe* and the *çarşaf* on the one hand, symbolizing the old and backward, and their removal and adoption of modern clothes on the other, symbolizing the new and modern.[38] As Bozdoğan underlines:

> Among the most canonical photographs of the Kemalist *inkılap* [revolution] are those of unveiled women in educational and professional settings – as students, artists, lawyers, doctors, even aviators. There were also photographs of women in the public spaces of parks, sports events, fairs, and national holidays. Images of modern women as inhabitants of modern spaces were preferred propaganda statements.[39]

In various mediums of popular culture – films, novels, advertisements, women's journals and lifestyle magazines – an ideal image of the new Turkish woman in

---

34. For examples of such articles published in provincial newspapers, see 'Türk Kadınının Vaziyeti', *Yeni Asır*, 30 July 1934; 'Türk Mücizesi', *Hakkın Sesi*, 7 November 1935; 'Türkiye Cumhuriyeti Milli Bayramı', *Kars*, 26 November 1934.

35. 'Bir Hollanda Gazetesinin Memleketimiz Hakkındaki İntibaaları', *Anadolu*, 6 September 1934.

36. Graham-Brown, *Images of Women*, 134.

37. Taşçıoğlu, *Türk Osmanlı*, 74.

38. For an example, see Lilo Linke, *Allah Dethroned: A Journey through Modern Turkey* (London: Constable & Co LTD, 1937), 215.

39. Bozdoğan, *Modernism*, 82.

modern attire and with a modern outlook was promoted and the removal of the *peçe* and the *çarşaf* was identified with incorporating modern norms into one's life, with being civilized and becoming part of the new Turkey as modern citizens.[40]

In addition to women's public visibility and participation in professional life alongside men, certain idealized characteristics of Turkish women, such as beauty and good manners, were particularly celebrated as part of their role as representatives of Turkey's modernization. One important way that such characteristics were promoted in the 1930s was national beauty contests, the first of which was organized in 1929 by the newspaper *Cumhuriyet*. Having beauty contests would be an indication that Turkey was as civilized as the other countries that were sending their beauty queens to international beauty competitions and that Turkish women were as beautiful and modern as their counterparts in the West.[41] These contests were also an opportunity to stage a new image of Turkish women dressed in modern clothing without veils. In fact, many news reports and commentaries published about these contests, in and outside of Turkey, did not fail to make reference to the removal of the veil. When she returned to Turkey from an international competition in Paris, the Turkish beauty queen of 1931, Naşide Saffet Hanım, said in an interview that the most frequent question she received was whether Turkish women were wearing the *peçe* or if they dressed like her. She had assured the international public that Turkey had now adopted European manners and that the *peçe* had been removed.[42] When Miss Turkey, Keriman Halis Hanım, won the international contest and became Miss World in 1932, this was celebrated as a 'national victory' and as the most effective propaganda campaign that Turkey could ever launch at the global level; the whole world had the chance to learn about the new Turkish woman and centuries of harem legends and images of the *peçe* and the *çarşaf* were finally erased.[43] Beauty contests and such propaganda campaigns were concerned with sending the Turkish public a message as much as they were with conveying the 'right' image in the West. As Shissler suggests, 'Turkish beauty queens really did embody a social agenda just by existing.'[44] One primary element of this agenda in the country was to normalize women's new image and defame the *peçe* and the *çarşaf* as uncivilized attire responsible for Turkey's backwardness, while also promoting the adoption of modern clothing.

---

40. For example, see Camilla Trud Nereid, 'Domesticating Modernity: The Turkish Magazine *Yedigün*, 1933–39', *Journal of Contemporary History* 47, no. 3 (2012): 483–504.

41. A. Holly Shissler, 'Beauty Is Nothing to Be Ashamed of: Beauty Contests as Tools of Women's Liberation in Early Republican Turkey', *Comparative Studies of South Asia, Africa and the Middle East* 24, no. 1 (2004): 107–22.

42. 'Türk Güzelinin Zaferi', *Cumhuriyet*, 8 April 1931.

43. See, for example, 'Anlatalım!', *Cumhuriyet*, 14 February 1932. For Yunus Nadi's article which draws parallels between the victory of the Turkish national struggle against the Greeks on 30 August 1922 and Keriman Halis's election as Miss World, see 'Büyük Zaferin Zaferleri Silsilesinden … ', *Cumhuriyet*, 31 August 1932.

44. Shissler, 'Beauty', 120.

The emphasis on women's outward appearance in the 1930s was also related to women's increasing political mobilization. It is not a coincidence that the importance of women's roles in social and political life was underlined in the party programme issued at the general RPP congress in 1931.[45] With the decision to allow women's participation in local elections in 1930, women's membership in the party began to be considered a critical issue by the regime's leadership. As one party document indicates, initially women's applications for membership in local party branches were subject to the approval of the party centre. The process was simplified in 1930 and the approval of local branches was seen as being enough for women's acceptance into the party.[46] It is crucial to emphasize, however, that the target of the party was those women who were not state officials, since officials were not allowed to be the members of the party according to the Law on State Officials (*Memurin Kanunu*).[47]

Despite these initial efforts, however, the level of women's participation in the party as well as in organizations like the People's Houses was still considered to be low. Women's acquisition of the right to participate in parliamentary elections in 1934 and the upcoming national elections in 1935 were seen as being particularly appropriate occasions to reverse this situation. The party centre repeatedly sent directives to its local branches urging them to increase women's membership in the party; it was characterized as being vital for the success of party activities to secure women's active participation.[48] Such directives were also published in provincial newspapers.[49] Some local branches of the RPP were trying to mobilize women for party membership by organizing meetings at which women could learn about the party's principles and programme. The RPP Administration in the province of Kars, for example, published in the provincial newspaper an announcement explaining that according to the party's regulations, party members were not allowed to vote for non-member candidates; thus, women had to be party members in order to be elected as second voters.[50] They organized a meeting specifically for women at the local party branch to explain the party programme and to make it easier for women to join the party. In the announcement, the local party administration informed the women of the city that the first phase of the general elections (to elect second voters) was fast approaching and 'it was

---

45. Zihnioğlu, *Kadınsız İnkılap*, 221.

46. BCA 490.01/1.4.10 and BCA 490.01/1.4.20.

47. Women who were state officials but applied to be members of the party were thus denied membership. It was also mentioned, however, that they were seen as 'natural' members of the party anyway. BCA 490.01/1.4.10, 2 September 1930.

48. For example, see *Cumhuriyet Half Fırkası Genel Kâtipliğinin Fırka Teşkilâtına Umumî Tebligatından Halkevlerini ilgilendiren kısım, cilt 5, Temmuz 1934 den Birincikânun 1934 sonuna kadar* (Ankara: Ulus Matbabası, 1935), 55.

49. See, for example, 'Hanımlara bir Salık', *Antalya*, 13 December 1934; 'Kadınların Saylavlığı, Fırka Genel Kâtibi Bay Recep Peker'in Tamimi', *Yeni Asır*, 14 December 1934; 'C.H.F. ve Kadınlar', *Antalya*, 20 December 1934; 'Kadınlar', *Yeni Adana*, 23 December 1934.

50. 'C.H.F. İdare Heyeti Reisliğinden', *Kars*, 17 December 1934.

in women's own interest' to participate in the party meeting. A similar meeting was organized in Izmir by women themselves; more women began to become members of the party and the People's House in order to show their gratitude for their newly acquired rights.[51] Women's compliance with these calls and applications for membership to the party in various cities were also frequently reported in the provincial newspapers, most likely in order to contribute to the further political mobilization of women.[52] Some even claimed that the number of women becoming party members was about to exceed the number of male party members in certain cities.[53] Women's active involvement as delegates at local party congresses and their election as members of local administrative councils were also publicly celebrated in newspapers.[54]

Women's membership in the party and other political institutions and their political mobilization would almost automatically necessitate their removal of the *peçe* and the *çarşaf*; stigmatized as backward, uncivilized and non-Turkish, such veils were the ideological opposite of all the norms that the Kemalist regime was trying to promote. However, despite all the propaganda and efforts made, the real picture was quite different from the article penned by the French journalist mentioned at the beginning of this section. The 'East' was in fact not erased; the *peçe* still existed, and the *çarşaf* was fairly common in Turkey in the mid-1930s. Towards the end of 1934, Mahmut Yesari, a well-known novelist and playwright of the time, complained in a column in *Yedigün* that women were still veiled in some parts of Turkey.[55] That is the reason why a second wave of anti-veiling campaigns would be organized but in a much more militant way compared to the campaigns of the 1920s.

The main wave: Why in 1934?

Because they were organized and implemented at the local level, without a central decree or legislation marking their beginning or a closely monitored plan coordinating them throughout the country, it is difficult to pinpoint exactly when another wave of anti-veiling campaigns began in the 1930s. The earliest example located within the scope of the research upon which this book is based is the

---

51. 'İzmir kadınları üye yazılıyor', *Yeni Adana*, 12 December 1934; 'İzmir kadınları fırkaya üye oluyorlar', *Halk*, 13 December 1934.

52. See 'Cumhuriyet Halk Fırkasının başardığı ve başaracağı işler … ', *Yeni Adana*, 17 December 1934; 'Fırkamız Bayanlarımız', *Antalya*, 3 January 1935; 'Gümüşhanede kadınlar C.H. Fırkasına giriyorlar', *Kars*, 24 January 1935; 'Giresunda fırkaya giren kadın üyeler', *Halk*, 21 January 1935.

53. See 'Gümüşhane bayanları istekle fırkaya yazılıyor', *Halk*, 21 January 1935; 'Gümüşhanede Kadınlar', *Kars*, 24 January 1935.

54. See 'Halk Fırkasının ocak ve nahiye kongreleri bitti', *Yeni Adana*, 1 January 1935; 'Samsun vilayet umumi meclisinde kadınlar da bulunacak', *Halk*, 21 January 1935.

55. Nereid, 'Domesticating', 502.

banning of the *çarşaf* in Safranbolu, then a district of the province of Zonguldak, in August 1933.[56] While it is possible that there were campaigns against the use of the *peçe* and the *çarşaf* or direct bans on wearing them in a number of places before, it seems that a visible sequence of anti-veiling campaigns began in mid-1934, reaching its peak in 1935. As mentioned above, there were numerous reforms in 1934, but there is no simple explanation for why the main wave of anti-veiling campaigns started in 1934. It seems that particularly significant in terms of its timing was women's acquisition of their political rights on 5 December 1934. Although there were anti-veiling campaigns before that date, they increased dramatically in number afterwards, and anti-veiling campaigns spread all around the country in 1935. They often occurred with reference to the prior reforms that had been carried out to elevate women's social status, especially regarding their acquisition of political rights.

In Turkey, women's struggle to gain full political rights had begun long before the 1930s. As mentioned in the previous chapter, the pioneering organization in this regard during the republican period was the Turkish Women's Union, which was established in 1924 primarily with the aim of achieving that goal.[57] While the idea of granting women political rights had surfaced several times inside and outside parliament before 1930, particularly during the debates on the changes in the electoral law and in the constitution, the women's movement was able to make its first concrete achievement with the passing of the new Municipal Law of 1930. With this law, women were granted the right to vote and be elected in local elections. In 1934, a change to the constitution granted women the right to vote for members of parliament and be elected as well. On the day the changes were passed in parliament, Prime Minister İsmet İnönü delivered a speech in which he characterized this reform as one of the greatest achievements of the Kemalist revolution as it would forever be known as a revolution of women's liberation.[58] According to İnönü, Turkish women, who had acquired their social rights through the Civil Code of 1926, finally had the chance to complement them with political rights, which opened to them the door of public life. In other words, the idea was that the granting of these rights would increase women's participation not only in political life, but also in every sphere of public life, implying that women would join the work force and would appear in public in a variety of roles in greater numbers. In fact, as discussed in the previous section, following the law granting women political rights, there was a campaign to increase women's membership in the party. In addition to the party's efforts, there was also an increase in the organization of special women's sections of the local branches of many associations in the provinces and in the establishment of new associations by women themselves. The idea that this reform would increase women's participation in public life was

---

56. 'Safranboluda çarşaf menedildi', *Cumhuriyet*, 21 August 1933.

57. For a detailed discussion, see Zihnioğlu, *Kadınsız İnkılap*.

58. *T.B.M.M. Zabıt Ceridesi*, term IV, 5th legislative year, vol. 25, meeting 12, 5 December 1934.

also promoted in local newspapers.[59] In many provinces, women held meetings to celebrate their new rights and to send messages of gratitude to the president, the prime minister, the RPP and parliament.[60]

Women's right to vote and be elected was seen as the final and most important step in the new regime's effort to modernize women. The fact that women lacked those rights in many European countries was often invoked as a means of highlighting the progressive nature of this move. Many interpretations of this development, both at the national and local level, emphasized its (supposed and expected) effect of changing Turkish women's 'backward' image symbolized by veiling. News articles published in major newspapers on the day of women's acquisition of political rights, for example, hinted at a direct connection between women's political rights and the removal of the *peçe* and the *çarşaf* in terms of the advancement of women's social status, often by using the very same statements and analogies. 'From now on', *Cumhuriyet* would write, 'it would be possible to see Turkish women in the *çarşaf*, under the *peçe* and behind the *kafes* only in the pages of history.'[61] Indeed, this very phrase would be repeated numerous times in various sources and would later be attributed to Mustafa Kemal himself, referring to one of his speeches after the bill granting women political rights was passed:

> This decision provides Turkish women with a place in social and political life that is above all nations. From now on, in order to see Turkish women in the *çarşaf*, under the *peçe* and behind the *kafes*, it would be necessary to look at history. Turkish women have acquired their civilized place at home and have shown success in business life. Turkish women, whose first experience with political life was at the local elections, have now acquired their greatest right with the right to vote and be elected [to parliament]. This right, which is lacking in many civilized nations, is now in the hands of Turkish women and they will use it with confidence and merit.[62]

This connection between the modernization of women's clothing and their political rights was constantly emphasized in the local newspapers as well. An article published in a Trabzon newspaper shows how this link was reinforced at the local level: 'The news agency reported on the removal of the *peçe* and the *çarşaf* in Muğla. Does the women's right to vote and be elected to the parliament ... not mean

---

59. For example, see 'Kadınlarda Saylav Seçilecekler', *Halk*, 6 December 1934.

60. See 'Trabzon Kadınları Sevinçlerini Büyüklerimize Bildirdiler', *Halk*, 10 December 1934; 'Türk Kadınlığının Unutmam'lığı', *Halk*, 10 December 1934; 'Kadınların Bayramı', *Halk*, 10 December 1934; 'Urla Kadınlarının Sevinci', *Halk*, 24 December 1934.

61. 'Bugünkü Meclis İçtimaı', *Cumhuriyet*, 5 December 1934. See also 'C.H.F. Grup Kararları', *Yeni Asır*, 6 December 1934; 'Atatürk Ulusal Savaşında Kadından Saylav Yapacağını Söylemişti', *Yeni Asır*, 16 December 1934.

62. Perihan Naci Eldeniz, 'Atatürk ve Türk Kadını', *Belleten* XX, no. 80 (1956), 741; also quoted in Caporal, *Kemalizmde*, 700.

the abolition of the *peçe* and the *çarşaf* anyway?'[63] Another article in a Kars-based newspaper celebrated women's political rights as a sign of the universal character of the Turkish revolution; these rights would rescue Turkish women from the age of imprisonment symbolized by the *peçe*, the *çarşaf* and the *kafes*.[64] Likewise, in a report on the yearly performance of the local party administration of Antalya, which was read at the local party congress, the head of the Antalya party branch pointed to the particular significance of the upcoming national elections because of women's participation and their liberation from centuries-old segregation symbolized by the *peçe* and the *çarşaf*: 'The Turkish revolution found the Turkish woman behind the *kafes* at home, in the *peçe* and the *çarşaf* in the streets and in a servile situation in the family. But now, the Turkish woman is among us, equipped with rights that her sisters lack in the most civilized countries'.[65] Evidently, there was a widespread assumption on the part of the Kemalist elite, at the centre and in the periphery, that women's acquisition of political rights would bring about their increasing participation in public life and, therefore, modernization of their clothing. In other words, they assumed that there was a direct link between women's visibility and the removal of the *peçe* and the *çarşaf*, since they were the ultimate symbols of women's seclusion and the very obstacle to their visibility. With this line of thinking, women's participation in the public sphere wearing *peçe* and *çarşaf* implied a contradiction; having gained all their rights, modern Turkish women would thus be modern in dress as well.

A contemporary observer also hinted at a link between the granting of women's political rights and the removal of the *peçe* and the *çarşaf*. In fact, while reporting about the change in the election law to include women's suffrage, the American ambassador argued that this change also included an article aiming at the elimination of the veil. Skinner mentioned in his correspondence that he had enquired into the matter at the *Vilayet* (the governor's office) and found out that an article added to the election law about determining the identity of voters was concerned with women wearing the face veil. The ambassador interpreted this as being a legal regulation concerning the use of the *peçe*:

> I now have the honor to enclose herewith translations of the laws in this regard, as published in the Official Gazette. Article 3 of Law No. 2598 states: 'The ballot of those voters whose person and identity is not discernible at the moment of the casting of the vote shall not be accepted.' Inquiry by the Embassy at the Vilayet indicates that this provision aims at the discouraging of the wearing of the veil by women in general and during the elections in particular. Thus, the granting of votes to women is used as another weapon towards the Government's objective of abolishing the veil and the other relics of the Ottoman tradition. Previously

---

63. Cevat Alap, 'Ayinesi iştir kişinin lafa bakılmaz', *İkbal*, 13 December 1934.

64. 'Kadınlarımızın saylav seçimi', *Kars*, 24 December 1934.

65. Report of the administrative board presented at the RPP 1934 Congress of the Province of Antalya, BCA 490.1/618.28.1, 11 December 1934.

the Republican régime has discouraged the use of the veil, but this is the first time that a positive legal measure in this regard has been taken.[66]

The wording of the article, as it was correctly translated by the ambassador, did not include any direct reference to the face veil or elimination of the face veil.[67] However, Skinner could be right in suspecting that adding this new article to the election law could hardly be a coincidence. In other words, the spirit of the law might have entailed a concern about the veil, even if its wording did not. Ever since the era of Abdülhamid II, there were concerns that the veil could be used to conceal one's identity; so it is likely that this article was shaped by the fear that the veil would be used for a similar purpose during elections. It is debatable, however, whether this can be read as issuing a legal measure against the *peçe* as the American ambassador does.

Women themselves also made a similar association between the acquisition of political rights and unveiling. As will be discussed in Chapter 4 in more detail, during gatherings that women organized in various cities to celebrate their political rights, the removal of the *peçe* and the *çarşaf* was mentioned as being part of women's efforts to be worthy of this reform.[68] A petition sent from the *Trabzon İdman Yurdu*, a local youth and sports club in Trabzon, to the city council requesting a ban on the *peçe* and the *çarşaf* also justified this request by referring to women's new rights. Reporting from Trabzon, the local newspaper stated that at the meeting of the club, 'it was decided that it is not right for Turkish women to continue wearing the *çarşaf* and the *peçe* at a time when they vote and are elected as deputies and as members of the municipal and provincial councils.'[69]

Another possible connection as regards the timing of the anti-veiling campaigns can be made with the fact that Turkey hosted the 12th Congress of the International Alliance of Women for Suffrage and Equal Citizenship (IAW) in Istanbul in April 1935. This was an important opportunity for the Kemalist regime to display the progress it had achieved in the modernization of Turkish women. As Libal suggests, the congress may have created additional impetus for women's suffrage, since 'having women in parliament when the IAW Congress convened in Istanbul a few months later would contribute to Turkey's image as a "progressive"

---

66. From Robert P. Skinner to the secretary of the state in Washington, DC, NARA RG 84. Box. 350: 10/15/3 vol. 702, 20 December 1934.

67. *İntihabı Mebusan Kanununun Bazı Maddelerinin Değiştirilmesine ve Kanuna bir Madde İlâvesine Dair Kanun*, Law no. 2598, 11 December 1934.

68. See, for example, 'Türk Kadınlığının Kıvancı', *Yeni Asır*, 9 December 1934; 'Atatürk kadınlarımıza değerli işler dileyor, her tarafta kadınlar kıvanç içinde', *Yeni Asır*, 11 December 1934.

69. 'Trabzon Kadınları da Çarşafları Atıyorlar', *Yeni Asır*, 16 February 1935. Some local newspapers based in Trabzon reported that the petition was put out by the Trabzon Home for Adolescents (*Trabzon Erginler Yurdu*). 'Kadın Peçe ve Çarşaflarının kaldırılması hakkında erginler yurdu belediye meclisine muracaat ediyor', *Halk*, 11 February 1935; 'Trabzon Gençliği', *İkbal*, 13 February 1935.

and "modern" country'.[70] In fact, the American ambassador also drew a connection between the granting of suffrage to women and the holding of the IAW Congress:

> It is not at all improbable that impetus was given to these concessions by the fact that on April 18th, next, the Twelfth Congress of the International Alliance of Women for Suffrage and Equal Citizenship will meet at Istanbul. Turkey is fond of modernization and of making a good show, and women's suffrage and eligibility to the Assembly is in step with occidental ideas and should make a favorable impression on the proposed International Congress of Women in Istanbul. Color is lent to these conjectures by the speech of the Prime Minister in which he said that the ballot and eligibility to the chamber were not given to women as favors but as just rights.[71]

Likewise, the congress may have also strengthened the aim of removing the *peçe* and the *çarşaf*, or at least decreasing their use as much as possible, given that unveiling was also an equally strong symbol of women's emancipation that could be displayed to the delegates coming from all around the world. References to Turkish women's 'liberation' from the veil could be seen in photos, publications and reporting about the congress and in the reports and press releases of the IAW.[72] In her speech at the congress, the head of the Turkish Women's Union, Latife Bekir Hanım, would thank Mustafa Kemal for 'rescuing' women and for giving them their political rights through a reference to unveiling: 'In Turkey, women were called on by Atatürk to remove the *çarşaf* and to take their place next to men.'[73] Actually, Atatürk did not make such a public call but statements such as Latife Bekir's would certainly play a role in reinforcing the idea that he called upon women to remove their *peçe* and *çarşaf* and would thus contribute to the effectiveness of the anti-veiling campaigns.

Scope, content and discourse

It is difficult to determine in exactly how many cities and towns anti-veiling campaigns were initiated. However, it can safely be argued that anti-veiling campaigns were quite widespread in Turkey in the second half of the 1930s. There were also local attempts to eliminate certain types of male clothing, such as

---

70. Kathryn Libal, 'Staging Turkish Women's Emancipation: Istanbul, 1935', *Journal of Middle East Women's Studies* 4, no. 1 (Winter 2008): 31–52. Libal indicates that an official IAW account claims that the president of the IAW met the mayor of Istanbul before the congress and mentioned women's suffrage in Turkey, and then this conversation was relayed to Mustafa Kemal.

71. Correspondence from Robert P. Skinner to the secretary of the state in Washington, DC, NARA RG. 84 Box. 350: 10/15/3 vol. 702, 11 December 1934.

72. Libal, 'From Face Veil'.

73. Caporal, *Kemalizmde*, 695.

traditional baggy trousers (*şalvar*), and such efforts were also initiated in the mid-1930s. However, they remained quite few in number and involved only a limited number of provinces.[74] The anti-veiling campaigns, on the other hand, were a countrywide phenomenon. Moreover, the existence of an anti-veiling campaign did not seem to be related to a particular ethnic or religious background, or any other characteristic of the social composition of the city in which it was initiated. Thus it was possible to come upon an anti-veiling campaign in just about any city, from important province capitals to the smallest district capitals. To the extent that can be gleaned from local newspapers and archival documents, a large number of anti-veiling campaigns resulted in the declaration of outright bans. Although a few of these bans were issued by provincial councils under the leadership of governors, an overwhelming majority of them were carried out through city councils as part of the legal capacity of municipalities.[75] In either case, implementation of the bans was mainly in hands of the municipal police (*zabıta*), and as will be discussed in the next chapters in more detail, women who continued to wear the banned veils had to pay fines in some instances.

The content of the bans and the actors involved varied from city to city. Some cities only banned the *çarşaf*; others, both the *peçe* and the *çarşaf*; in yet others, the ban also included the *peştamal* and other local varieties of veils. In Antalya and Erzincan, for example, the ban also included the *kafes* in addition to the *peçe* and the *çarşaf*. The campaigns that included the removal of the *kafes* indicate that the eradication of gender segregation and the elimination of all barriers to women's visibility were among the primary motivations behind the anti-veiling campaigns. In Rize, the city council even asked women to stop carrying umbrellas, which they were using to conceal themselves.[76] In most of the decisions, women were given a certain period to adapt to the new norms and they were advised to replace their *çarşaf* with an overcoat. This period of time differed in each city, but the general tendency was to grant a few weeks for the removal of the *peçe* and a longer period of time, from three to six months, for the removal of the *çarşaf*. This was probably because the *peçe* was considered to be easier to deal with, since women did not need to replace it with another piece of clothing, unlike the *çarşaf*. It was perhaps

---

74. There was a municipal ban on men's traditional baggy trousers, *şalvar*, in Adana, for example. 'Caket pantalon', *Akşam*, 10 November 1934; 'Adanada yasak edilen kıyafetler', *Cumhuriyet*, 13 December 1934; 'Ulusumuza yakışan kılık', *Ak Günler*, 5 January 1935. It is important to note that the ban on men's *şalvar* was initiated earlier than the ban on the *peçe* and the *çarşaf* in Adana. In Maraş, the baggy trousers men wore, known as *karadon* in the region, and *aba* (kind of a shirt without arms) were banned by the municipal council. The decision was made simultaneously with the ban on the *peçe* and the *çarşaf*. See the letter from the RPP Maraş Administration to RPP Secretariat General, BCA 490.01/17.88.1, 5 November 1935.

75. In Erzincan, for example, the ban was implemented by a decree issued by the provincial council.

76. See 'Rizede peçeler ve çarşaflar kalkıyor', *Yeni Asır*, 1 March 1935.

also related to the fact that uncovering women's faces was considered to be a more urgent task.

The process leading to a decision to ban the *peçe* and the *çarşaf* most often began as an initiative launched by a group of local elites belonging to a certain local institution, supported by a propaganda campaign in the local newspapers, and, in most cases, eventually followed with an outright ban. In Aydın, for example, People's House members began discussing the removal of the *peştamal* veil in early 1934, while the actual ban came a year later.[77] This was not just the case in Aydın, however; in many other cities People's Houses and their members played a particularly significant role in the organization of the campaigns. In March 1935 in Siirt, a decision was made at a meeting of the People's House to remove the *peçe*.[78] In the case of Diyarbakır, for which we lack information concerning whether or not an outright ban on the *peçe* or the *çarşaf* was in fact carried out, an anti-veiling campaign was also launched through the efforts of the members of the People's House, who, it seems, were all men, as suggested by reports in the news. They organized a meeting where they decided to be the first to ask their family members to stop wearing the *peçe* and *çarşaf* so they could be the vanguards of the campaign.[79] In some cities, People's Houses were the settings of meetings held with other local institutions to discuss the banning of the *peçe* and *çarşaf*. In Çankırı, for example, 'all institutions', including the local party branch, had organized a joint meeting at the People's House and decided to ban the *peçe* and the *çarşaf* in the city.[80]

It should be emphasized that in Istanbul and Ankara, the two major cities of the country, anti-veiling campaigns were not carried out, at least not publicly, by either the city council or on the initiative of any local institutions. Ankara, the capital of the new republic, was a stage upon which to display the modern face of Turkish society. Thus, the removal of the *peçe* and the *çarşaf* was perhaps considered a given. Similarly, in Istanbul, issuing a ban on the *peçe* and the *çarşaf* would have undermined the image of the city as the country's most cosmopolitan and developed city.[81] In fact, there are indications that propaganda was considered sufficient to initiate a change in women's clothing in these cities. At least, this was what was declared by the authorities publicly. The lack of such bans in Istanbul,

---

77. 'Aydında peştemalı kaldırmağa çalışıyorlar', *Cumhuriyet*, 14 April 1934.

78. 'Siirtte peçelerin kaldırılmasına karar verildi', *Halk*, 25 March 1935.

79. 'D. Bekir Halkevi üyeleri kendi ailelelerinin çarşaf ve peçelerini kaldırdılar', *Halk*, 24 December 1934; 'Diyarbekir kadınları da çarşafı atıyorlar', *Cumhuriyet*, 29 December 1934.

80. 'Çankırı'da peçe çarşafların atılması kararlaştırıldı', *Yeni Asır*, 1 January 1935; 'Memleketin her tarafında çarşaf ve peçeler kaldırılıyor', *Halk*, 3 January 1935.

81. Interestingly, however, there was a campaign and a subsequent ban on the *kafes* in Istanbul. For a detailed discussion on the campaigns against the *kafes*, see Sevgi Adak, 'Women, the *Kafes* and the City. Gendering Urban Transformation in Early Turkish Republic', in *Nation, Body and Visuality in the Post-Ottoman Urban Space. Turkish and Yugoslav Cities in the Interwar Period*, eds. Nataša Mišković and Karl Kaser (Oxford: Berghahn, forthcoming).

for instance, became an issue in some newspapers. Rumours emerged that the *peçe* and the *çarşaf* would also be banned in Istanbul, like in many Anatolian cities, but the governor of the city declared that there was no need for a ban for the enlightened and progressive people of Istanbul; in other words, it was expected that the women would remove their *peçe* and *çarşaf* by themselves.[82]

The case of Izmir, on the other hand, was more complicated. Together with Istanbul and Ankara, it can be considered to be part of the 'centre' in terms of its socio-economic composition and relatively more cosmopolitan population. In fact, since there was no visible anti-veiling campaign in the city, it must have been seen as such by the local administrators as well as by the regime. However, a letter sent by the Governor of Izmir, Fazlı Güleç, to the Ministry of the Interior in 1937 indicates that there indeed was a propaganda campaign behind the scenes to convince women who were wearing the *çarşaf* in the city to stop doing so. In other words, without harming the image of Izmir as a modern city by openly organizing an anti-veiling campaign (and thus admitting that the *peçe* and the *çarşaf* were an issue), the governor had preferred to solve the issue by ensuring that no reporting about it would appear in the newspapers.[83]

Although local decisions to ban the *peçe* and the *çarşaf* may have varied in terms of scope and the mechanisms used, one can talk about overarching elements or reference points that were generally employed in the propaganda of almost all the local campaigns against veils. One of these references was the removal of any sign of the 'old regime'. In many of the decisions banning the *peçe* and the *çarşaf*, and also in the commentaries and news reports about anti-veiling campaigns, such forms of clothing were stigmatized as the remnants of the old regime, the old mentality and the Ottoman past. In fact, this was a manifestation of a more general strategy of the new regime to rely on binary oppositions and comparisons with the Ottoman past. As Libal notes, 'The early republican regime relied upon discursive constructions of Ottoman backwardness to legitimize the new national leadership and construct a new Turkish citizen subject,' and this could be widely seen in discussions on women's clothing as well.[84] In one of the articles published in the Trabzon-based newspaper *Halk* calling upon women to remove their *peçe* and *çarşaf*, the author characterized the *peçe* and the *çarşaf* as the only remaining elements that continued to humiliate the Turkish nation; they were the 'black

---

82. 'İstanbulda da çarşaf çıkarılacak', *Cumhuriyet*, 4 September 1935. A news report published in a Trabzon newspaper mentioned that there were police centres in some neighbourhoods of Istanbul which warned (*tenkid*) women who were living in their area of control against going out with the *çarşaf*. I could not find another source mentioning such a practice, however. See 'İstanbul münevver kadınları bu garip örtüyü kendiliğinden atacakdır', *Halk*, 16 September 1935.

83. See the letter from the Governor of İzmir Fazlı Güleç, to the Minister of the Interior Şükrü Kaya, Ministry of the Interior of the Republic of Turkey, Directorate General of Security Archives (*Emniyet Genel Müdürlüğü Arşivi* – hereafter EGM) 13216-7/1, 24 November 1937.

84. Libal, 'From Face Veil', 49.

stamp of the palace and the sultanate' on the blameless and clean forehead of a generation that was capable of proving its capacity to reach the highest point in civilized social life.[85] In another article, the same author equated women's use of the *peçe* and the *çarşaf* with men's use of the fez; like the fez, the *peçe* and the *çarşaf* were also Ottoman vestiges, and therefore it was absurd to insist on wearing such clothing in contemporary civilized times.[86]

Another frequent motivation mentioned in the anti-veiling campaigns was the cleansing of the public sphere of anything that was coded as a sign of backwardness and the result of 'uncivilized' modes of thinking and behaviour. The *peçe* and the *çarşaf* had been seen as signs of backwardness ever since they became an issue of debate, but this discourse reached an unprecedented level during the anti-veiling campaigns of the mid-1930s. In other words, equating the *peçe* and the *çarşaf* with backwardness, and therefore with being uncivilized, was perhaps the most frequent reference point in the anti-veiling campaigns. At a meeting held by a group of women in the province of Muğla in December 1934, for example, the women decided to remove their *çarşaf* by declaring that it was 'a sign of backwardness' (*gerilik alameti*).[87] In their petition to the city council to issue a ban on the *peçe* and the *çarşaf*, members of the youth and sports clubs in Trabzon, led by the Trabzon Home for Adolescents (*Erginler Yurdu*), argued that such old types of clothing were not compatible with the new advanced lifestyle of the Turkish nation and contrary to the progressive step forward Turkish women had just started to take.[88] In another article published by a newspaper based in Trabzon, the *peçe* and the *çarşaf* were characterized as the clothing of people who believe in fairies, ghosts and fortune telling and therefore they were incompatible with the revolution and the republic Atatürk had entrusted to the Turkish youth.[89]

Discourses on the *peçe* and *çarşaf* were not solely concerned with their symbolic considerations, however. It was emphasized that there were also some practical reasons and health concerns that would make the removal of the *peçe* and the *çarşaf* beneficial for women. For example, it was argued that it would be easier for women to walk around in the city without them. Women who removed their veils would also be exposed to sunlight and thus get a proper amount of vitamin D. Such health concerns were in fact used as the primary reasons for unveiling in some cities. In Sungurlu, for example, a district of the province of Çorum, the District Health Council (*Sağlık Kurulu*) was directly involved in the decision-making process at the municipality during the anti-veiling campaign.[90] The anti-veiling

---

85. Cemal Rıza, 'Peçe ve Çarşaf', *Halk*, 31 October 1935. See also Cemal Rıza, 'Çarşaf', *Halk*, 12 November 1935.

86. 'Peçe ve çarşaf, şehrimizin sayın bayanlarına', *Halk*, 19 December 1935.

87. 'Muğla kadınları çarşafları kaldırıyor', *Halk*, 31 December 1934.

88. 'Kadın peçe çarşaflarının kaldırılması hakkında erginler yurdu belediye meclisine muracaat ediyor', *Halk*, 11 February 1935. See also, 'Belediye meclisi genclerin tekliflerini kabul etti. Bugün meclisde kat'i karar verilecek', *Halk*, 14 February, 1935.

89. 'Trabzon kadınları ve çarşaf', *İkbal*, 29 October 1934.

90. 'Sungurluda peçe ve çarşaflar kalktı', *Cumhuriyet*, 10 July 1935.

campaigns which included the banning of lattice windows also did so out of a deliberate concern for health.[91]

As much as it was identified with being new, modern, civilized and healthy, the removal of the *peçe* and the *çarşaf* was also seen as a sign of a return to the national. In other words, there was also a deliberate effort in the discourses used during the anti-veiling campaigns to promote the idea that the *peçe* and the *çarşaf* were alien to the essence of Turkish culture. Thus the modern was always reconciled with the national; the *peçe* and the *çarşaf* were not *millî* (national), while the modern clothing that was supposed to replace them was, and perfectly so. Moreover, it was also quite frequently emphasized in the press that such veils were not Islamic either. This point was important not only as a means of challenging resistance to the anti-veiling campaigns for religious reasons, but also as a way of responding to a more general and perhaps stronger perception that linked the practice of veiling with morality. In fact, a counter discourse was utilized to break this link. It was argued that the *peçe* and the *çarşaf* in fact highlighted women's sexuality by covering their faces and bodies. Thus, it was argued that they could not be seen as a means of protecting women's chastity, and the claim was made that their use had never helped to eliminate such social ills as adultery, prostitution or sexual harassment. Some even argued that the *peçe* and the *çarşaf* were contrary to 'national morality' and in fact enabled such ills to survive.[92] The claim was put forward that people who sought morality and chastity in the *peçe* and the *çarşaf* should see the immoral acts that were in fact being concealed by such veils.[93] In this way, the 'true' moral order would be established once veils were removed; the anti-veiling campaigns would thus not be seen as running counter to the male-dominated social structure.

The legal framework

As mentioned above, in most of the anti-veiling campaigns in the 1930s, the bans on the *peçe* and the *çarşaf* were issued by municipalities, in particular as the result of decisions made by city councils. This marked a major difference from the anti-veiling campaigns of the 1920s, which were predominantly organized by provincial councils led by governors. As was noted in the previous chapter, the provincial council of Eskişehir, for example, banned the *peçe* and the *çarşaf* through the Law on the General Administration of Provinces (*İdare-i Umumiye-i Vilâyat Kanunu*). Enacted in 1913 as the Temporal Law on the General Administration of Provinces (*İdare-i Umumiye-i Vilâyat Kanunu Muvakkati*), it remained in force after the establishment of the republic and increased the power of provincial administrations.[94] The principle of decentralization and the separation of functions

---

91. See 'Çarşaf ve peçeden sonra kafes!', *Hakkın Sesi*, 28 January 1935.
92. See Yusuf Ziya, 'Çarşaf', *Cumhuriyet*, 28 June 1932; 'Kafesler Kalkacak', *Hakkın Sesi*, 11 February 1935.
93. See 'Çarşaf', *Hakkın Sesi*, 30 July 1934.
94. Önen and Reyhan, *Mülkten Ülkeye*, 311–44.

in provincial administration were in fact confirmed by the Ottoman Constitution of 1876. However, there was also a growing tendency on the part of the Committee of Union and Progress to create a more centralized system. The law issued in 1913 brought about a twofold system of provincial administration: 'One general, as components of the national apparatus of government, the other special or local, as decentralized administrative entities, with a recognized legal personality.'[95] While maintaining the power of the central authorities, it granted more freedom to local administrators on certain matters and for that reason the law has been interpreted in the literature as a decentralizing move.[96] Although governors continued to be the most significant local actors in the republican era, municipalities begun to play a more active role, especially in the 1930s. The increasingly prominent role the municipalities played in the anti-veiling campaigns should be seen as part of this general trend and the strengthened position of the municipalities should be seen as an instrument of attempts to bring about modernization.

Until 1930, municipal administration was mainly based on Ottoman municipal laws and regulations, which did not constitute an effective institutional tradition. Municipalities in the Ottoman Empire were weak in terms of both financial capacity and their position vis-à-vis other administrative structures, such as the governors or the *vakıf* system (charitable foundations).[97] Perhaps the case of Istanbul was slightly different, since the municipal system, known as the *Şehremaneti* (*Préfecture*), was subject to a different legislation and therefore it was relatively more effective. This legal structure changed over time, with major transformations occurring during the Second Constitutional Period after 1908. Equally important were the changes in practice, namely in the actual workings of the municipalities despite the fact that the legal framework remained intact. As Serçe has noted, based on the case of the Izmir Municipality between 1908 and 1913, practices that were in fact against or outside the scope of the law could become the norm, which made the legacy of the Ottoman municipal administration more complicated than the legal regulations reveal on paper.[98]

The importance that the new Kemalist regime attached to the municipalities first became apparent in a number of legal regulations enacted in the first years of the republic. Tekeli characterizes this period (1923–30) as a time of preparation for the restructuring of the municipal administration that occurred in the 1930s, despite the fact that these early attempts remained loose and superficial.[99] The

---

95. Lewis, *The Emergence*, 391.

96. Önen and Reyhan, however, suggest that this law reflects the strategic policy of the Unionists which sought to empower local administrations to an extent that would not detract from political centralization. Önen and Reyhan, *Mülkten Ülkeye*, 342.

97. For more, see İlber Ortaylı, *Tanzimattan Cumhuriyete Yerel Yönetim Geleneği* (Istanbul: Hil Yayın, 1985).

98. Erkan Serçe, *Tanzimat'tan Cumhuriyet'e İzmir'de Belediye (1868–1945)* (Izmir: Dokuz Eylül Yayınları, 1998), 15.

99. İlhan Tekeli, *Cumhuriyetin Belediyecilik Öyküsü (1923–1990)* (Istanbul: Tarih Vakfı Yurt Yayınları, 2009), 32–42.

first regulation, issued in February 1924, concerned municipal taxes, and as such it reflected the aim to make municipalities more active by increasing their financial resources.[100] Also in February 1924, the Ankara Şehremaneti (*Préfecture*) was established; it was modelled on the Istanbul Şehremaneti with the goal of encouraging the urban development of the new capital. In March 1924, the Village Law (*Köy Kanunu*) was issued; this law was also concerned with reorganizing the municipal administration and focused on clarifying administrative divisions.[101] A few other legal regulations issued in the 1920s increased the capacity of the municipalities vis-à-vis other institutions, such as the *vakıf* administration. Introduction of the Civil Code in 1926 was one of these regulations which crystallized the ideal of 'modern life' and thus had a major impact on the decisions and workings of the municipalities.[102]

Perhaps the most crucial change in this period was the law regarding the punitive power of the municipalities (*Umur-u Belediyeye Müteallik Ahkam-ı Cezaiye Kanunu*)[103] which was issued in April 1924 and supported later by articles regarding municipal sanctions in the new Criminal Law of 1926.[104] The law was presented to parliament as a pressing need, since the decisions made by municipalities were ineffective because they were unable to mete out punishment.[105] As Tekeli points out, empowering the municipalities with the right to impose penalties marked a major shift in terms of municipal administration.[106] The law made it possible for municipalities to impose fines in cases of non-compliance with municipal decisions and as a result of the law they could prohibit artisans and merchants from engaging in crafts and trade for up to fifteen days. The punitive measures meted out by municipalities were final, and they were also able to imprison people who did not pay their fines.[107] In 1927, through an amendment

---

100. *Belediye Vergi ve Resimleri Kanunu*, Law no. 423, 26 February 1924. However, soon after this, some of the financial sources allocated to municipal administrations were again transferred to the central authorities. Tekeli, *Cumhuriyetin*, 38.

101. Önen and Reyhan, *Mülkten Ülkeye*, 461.

102. Tekeli, *Cumhuriyetin*, 41

103. *Umur-u Belediyeye Müteallik Ahkam-ı Cezaiye Hakkında Kanun*, Law no. 486, 16 April 1924.

104. Tekeli, *Cumhuriyetin*, 39; M. Ali Gökaçtı, *Dünyada ve Türkiye'de Belediyecilik* (Istanbul: Ozan Yayıncılık, 1996), 122.

105. For such arguments, see the parliamentary debate on the bill, *T.B.M.M. Zabıt Ceridesi*, term II, 2nd legislative year, vol. 8/1, meeting no. 38, 15 April 1924 and meeting no. 39, 16 April 1924.

106. Tekeli claims that this significantly increased the power of the municipalities over *esnaf* organizations (guilds), which were the centres of Unionist opposition to the Kemalist regime in the early years of the republic. Tekeli, *Cumhuriyetin*, 36–9.

107. The fines ranged from a hundred *kuruş* to twenty liras and were to be issued by the city councils based on documentation provided by the municipal police (*zabıta*). Municipalities could impose one day of imprisonment for every one lira that was owed.

to the law persons fined by municipalities were given the right of appeal.[108] The bolstering of the municipalities with punitive power contributed to their role in the anti-veiling campaigns only in the 1930s, however, since it was only after the strengthening of the municipal administration with a new legal framework in 1930 that municipalities could become more active actors at the local level.

The new Municipal Law was introduced in April 1930.[109] The law was modelled on French and German municipal laws[110] and aimed at the reorganization of local administration in line with the aims of the new regime in terms of social modernization and economic development. As Tekeli notes, the Municipal Law of 1930 marked a turning point regarding the approach of the new regime to municipal administration. This understanding was particularly shaped by the principle of populism (*halkçılık*), which entailed acting 'for the people despite the people' (*halka rağmen, halk için*); municipalities would henceforth become the agents that would create civilized life in modern cities, even if this necessitated acting against the will of the people.[111] In other words, for the leaders of the republic, municipalities were not only concerned with building infrastructure for urban development; they were also promoters and implementers of modern visions of security, order, hygiene, culture and identity. This understanding had found expression in the inauguration speech Mustafa Kemal Atatürk gave for the legislative year in November 1935:

> One of our primary aims is that Turkish lands, in all our cities and reaching far to the villages, will become a landscape of prosperity and development (*bayındırlık*). Any place that is home to a Turk will be an exemplary place for health, cleanliness, beauty and modern culture. In addition to state institutions, I want the municipalities, which are directly in charge of these tasks, to work with this view and thinking.[112]

It should be mentioned that although the Municipal Law of 1930 aimed at strengthening the municipalities, it also was a sign of the increasingly authoritarian tendencies of the Kemalist regime, determined as it was to centralize the bureaucratic apparatus and enhance the control of the central authorities. In other words, the new law was not designed to expand the autonomy of local administrations with the aim of sharing political power. Municipal administration was an extension of the central administration, and as such, municipalities were to work under the coordination and control of Ankara. Because of these characteristics, Gökaçtı, for example, characterizes the Municipal Law of 1930

---

108. *Umuru belediyeye aid ahkâmı cezaiye hakkındaki 16 nisan 1340 tarih ve 486 numaralı kanunun altıncı ve yedince maddelerini muaddil kanun*, Law no. 959, 17 January 1927.

109. See *Belediye Kanunu*, Law no. 1580, 10 April 1930.

110. Gökaçtı, *Dünyada*, 127.

111. Tekeli, *Cumhuriyetin*, 51.

112. *T.B.M.M. Zabıt Ceridesi*, term V, 2nd legislative year, vol. 6, meeting 1, 1 November 1935.

as a reflection of the single-party regime's turn towards statism.[113] The law indeed aimed at both increasing the control and regulative power of the central authorities over municipal bodies and widening the scope of activity and financial capacities of these bodies so they could penetrate into and regulate daily life in the cities. It also was concerned with standardizing municipal administration all around the country. In fact, this attempt at standardization was secured not only by the new law, but also by the circulars issued for the municipalities by the Ministry of the Interior.[114] Through these control mechanisms, campaigns organized on certain matters could quite easily spread and become standard practice. The fact that Ankara was setting the example for the rest of the cities was also a factor contributing to efforts at standardization. These efforts of course rarely guaranteed that the same results would be achieved in every city; however, municipalities were envisioned as the bridges that linked the aim of achieving contemporary levels of civilization to the aim of creating civilized cities at the local level.

Limited by the laws issued by the central authorities as well as by its tight control, municipalities were nevertheless allowed a certain degree of freedom of action. As mentioned in the first article of the Municipal Law of 1930, they were defined as entities in charge of organizing and satisfying the common and civilized needs of the city and city dwellers at the local level. Expanding the scope of duties for the municipalities was one of the aims of the law, since the previous law regulating municipal administration was considered inappropriate for the modernizing efforts of the new regime and as an obstacle to progress.[115] The law was really quite specific about detailing the expanded duties. However, it was also inclusive in the sense that these duties were framed in general terms, such as ensuring the health, welfare and prosperity of city dwellers. They had the power to take action if the order, hygiene and peace of the city were under threat. The first and second items of Article 19 gave municipalities the power to enact measures to achieve these aims and they could implement orders and bans.

To make it possible for municipalities to carry out these newly assigned duties more effectively, the Municipal Law of 1930 also required all municipalities to implement a municipal police regulation (*zabıta talimatnamesi*). The municipal police would be responsible for the enforcement of all decisions made by municipalities, including municipal bans and fines. With an additional law issued in May 1930 which stipulated the punitive powers of municipalities, municipalities were able to issue warnings (*tenbihname*) through which city councils could announce decisions and bans and the amounts of fines that would be imposed in case of non-compliance.[116] In some of the anti-veiling campaigns, this law was used as a reference point to support the right of the municipalities to issue a ban. In Bergama, for example, a district in the province of Izmir, a committee formed by

---

113. Gökaçtı, *Dünyada*, 128.
114. Ibid., 137.
115. Tekeli *Cumhuriyetin*, 60.
116. Ibid., 87.

the city council prepared a new chapter for the municipal police regulation based on this law so they could include bans on the *peçe* and the *çarşaf* in the regulation and stipulate the fines to be imposed.[117] As can be seen in the case of anti-veiling campaigns, it seems that such an approach was used by municipalities as a means of establishing 'modern' urban life. A warning issued by the city council of Ankara, for example, prohibited hanging unaesthetic things on buildings or dumping garbage on empty plots of land.[118] Some of these warnings were shaped by circulars from Ankara. In April 1936, for example, Şükrü Kaya, the minister of the interior, sent a circular to all municipalities asking them to take measures to reduce street noise.[119]

The right to appeal municipal punishment, however, was an important factor limiting the effective implementation of municipal decisions in practice. To overcome this limitation, the punitive power of municipalities was increased further with an amendment in June 1934.[120] It became mandatory to present a reason for an appeal, and appeals which did not have a valid justification were to be rejected. In addition, mayors, deputy-mayors and department heads in the provinces, and mayors in district capitals, were given the power to issue fines (up to five lira in the provinces and three lira in the district capitals) when they themselves saw anything that ran contrary to municipal rulings. These punitive measures could not be objected to, and thus the amendment severely limited the right of appeal, especially for fines of relatively low amounts. By giving mayors and other high-level municipal administrators the right to impose sanctions without the need for a written record or the approval of a municipal committee (*belediye encümeni*), the new law expanded their powers considerably. Press reports concerning the new amendment also emphasized the increasing power of mayors in terms of imposing punitive measures.[121] A columnist writing for a provincial newspaper claimed that with the new regulation, it would be easier to ensure that people would perform their duties for the city and the public and municipalities would be able to fulfil their mission of satisfying the social and civil needs of cities more adequately.[122]

Thus, by the mid-1930s, first with the 1930 Municipal Law and then with subsequent laws strengthening their punitive powers, municipalities were empowered and granted a legal framework which made it possible for them to issue rulings and punishments that would regulate the behaviour of the people as part of their aim of creating 'civilized' urban life. Municipalities intervened in daily life through decisions concerning circumstances ranging from spitting in the streets to where to hang up clothes to dry. The anti-veiling campaigns initiated by

---

117. Thus, the bans became part of the municipal police regulation (*zabıta talimatnamesi*). See 'Bergama'da çarşaf, peçe ve kıvraklar kaldırılıyor', *Anadolu*, 6 December 1934.

118. Tekeli, *Cumhuriyetin*, 87.

119. Ibid., 88.

120. *Umuru belediyeye müteallik ahkâmı cezaiye hakkındaki kanunu muadil 19-V-1930 tarih ve 1608 sayılı kanunun bazı maddelerini değiştiren ve yeniden madde ekleyen kanun*, Law no. 2575, 15 July 1934.

121. For example, see 'Belediye cezası', *Son Posta*, 8 August 1934.

122. Rıza Atilâ, 'Belediye cezaları', *Yeni Mersin*, 23 June 1934.

city councils should thus be seen as part of the work of municipalities. The bans on the *peçe* and the *çarşaf* must have been considered a 'civilized need' at the local level, as it was formulated in the Municipal Law. It is crucial to underline, however, that the existence of this legal capacity did not ensure in practice the compliance of all municipalities in issuing rulings. In other words, the making of municipal decisions and regulations concerning the behaviour and daily conduct of people, albeit made easier with an authoritarian single-party regime in power, was very much dependent on the intentions of municipal administrators, from mayors to members of the city councils. In fact, the process leading up to municipal decisions like bans on the *peçe* and the *çarşaf* often involved administrators as well as groups and actors outside the municipal organization. Governors, administrators and members of local party branches, People's Houses, local sports clubs and associations could all play a role in initiating and shaping these campaigns. The implementation of the bans was an even more complicated issue, determined by the support as well as opposition of various social actors. This quite complex web of local dynamics would inevitably become even more complicated by the involvement of the central government, by the directives coming from Ankara. The anti-veiling campaigns of the 1930s should therefore be understood as shaped by the interplay between the local actors and the efforts of Ankara to control and coordinate the process in the provinces.

Between hesitation and intervention: Ankara on the anti-veiling campaigns

The major characteristic of the anti-veiling campaigns in the 1930s, as can be gleaned from the newspapers of the time, was that they were 'local'. It was obvious and publicly known that the regime leadership in Ankara favoured 'modern' clothing for both men and women in accordance with the modernization brought about by the new republic, but it was not clear whether the state – the president, the government, the party centre or parliament – would do something concrete about the fact that women still wore 'traditional' veils when they went outside, especially in the provinces. News about the banning of the *peçe* and the *çarşaf* in some cities appeared to be of local origin, stemming from the vanguard role of provincial administrators as well as the mobilization of local people to celebrate women's increasing social status, their political rights and the modernization of the country in general. The fact that news of anti-veiling campaigns from the provinces was celebrated in national newspapers that were practically semi-official publications of the ruling party was a sign of the support of the centre for these attempts. However, on the surface at least, there was no indication that the government was directly involved, nor were there traces of action by the central party administration.

Given the character of the Kemalist regime and the authoritarian single-party system it had established, it seems logical to assume at first that such major interventions in people's daily practices would not or could not be possible without the involvement of the central administration. In fact, if we take up the hegemonic state-centric interpretations of the current literature or a centre–periphery analysis emphasizing a coherent, monolithic centre, we would expect that anti-veiling campaigns began with an order from Ankara. I will argue that Ankara was indeed involved in the process, but the nature of this involvement was far more complicated than dominant approaches to analysing the Kemalist state would suggest; the way the central government and the party tried to control and coordinate the anti-veiling campaigns was more complex than sending well-formulated, consistent and concrete orders to the provincial administrators.

The first document indicating the Kemalist regime's involvement is a circular sent out by the Ministry of the Interior on 11 August 1934 in which the ministry informed provincial leaders that the issue of the *peçe*, the *çarşaf* and the *peştamal* should not be handled through decisions and laws, and on this important and sensitive matter, the goals should be achieved through encouragement (*teşvik*), inculcation (*telkin*) and propaganda.[123] The circular reveals that there were locally initiated attempts and plans concerning the removal of, or at least decreasing/ discouraging, the use of the *peçe*, the *çarşaf* and the *peştamal*; its goal was presumably to keep such efforts within certain limits. Indeed, as early as August 1933, for example, the newly appointed district governor of Safranbolu, then a district of the province of Zonguldak, had banned the use of the *çarşaf* in the district capital.[124] In Giresun in April 1934, the removal of the *peçe* in the city was proposed to the city council by a council member, a doctor named Nabi Bey, and the council had unanimously accepted his proposal and given the mayor the authority to announce it as a municipal ban.[125] Although not outright bans, it seems that anti-veiling campaigns had also already begun during the years 1933 and 1934 in other cities as well. Newspaper reports mention that women removed their *peçe* and *çarşaf* in Bursa and Kütahya, for example, but did not indicate how the initiative got started or who was involved in the campaigns.[126]

---

123. I have not seen the original circular sent out by the ministry, but its existence and content is mentioned in another circular sent by the ministry to the governor of Ordu. Copy of the Letter of the Minister of the Interior to the Province of Ordu dated 14 May 1937, EGM 13216-7/1, 18 June 1937. A letter sent by the governor of Çanakkale mentions a circular sent by Ankara dated 17 February 1934. If this is true, then there should be a circular that was sent by the Ministry of the Interior to the provinces even earlier than the one mentioned above. In my research I have not come across a document dated 17 February 1934. It is also possible that the date was written 17 February 1934 by mistake in the Çanakkale governor's letter (so 17.2.1934 rather than 17.12.1934) as it should refer to the circular dated 17 December 1934. From the Governor of Çanakkale to the Ministry of the Interior, EGM 13216-7/1, 21 March 1936.

124. 'Safranboluda çarşaf menedildi', *Cumhuriyet*, 21 August 1933.

125. 'Giresun'da peçe kalkıyor', *Cumhuriyet*, 24 April 1934.

126. 'Bursada artık çarşaf giymeyecekler', *Cumhuriyet*, 29 October 1933; 'Kütahya hanımları ve çarşaf', *Cumhuriyet*, 6 May 1934. A later report from Bursa in July 1934 indicated that local municipalities in the province had begun to implement their decisions regarding the banning of the *çarşaf* and *çarşaf*-like clothes, which means that there were local bans in Bursa even before the ministry sent out the initial circular. See 'Güzel bir karar', *Cumhuriyet*, 28 July 1934.

It seems that this first circular did not achieve its aims because the minister of the interior sent another directive to all provincial governors and general inspectors on 17 December 1934, immediately after the enactment of the law granting women their political rights.[127] As will be discussed in more detail in the next chapter, this directive was in fact motivated by a letter received by the ministry from the deputy governor of Antalya asking for the opinion of the central government on the matter of the use of the *peçe* and the *çarşaf*. It seems that the ministry deemed it important enough to issue a general directive and thus inform all governors and general inspectors about the matter instead of just replying to the deputy governor's letter.

The directive begins by saying that 'it has been understood from a letter' that efforts had been made to take various measures in some places to prevent women from going out with the *peçe* and the *çarşaf*, and in some cities, the idea of using the municipal police (*zabıta*) for this purpose had been considered by some local administrators. This opening sentence implies that in addition to the letter written the deputy governor of Antalya, there were probably other local administrators consulting the ministry and asking about the matter of creating a more forceful plan of action. Having mentioned the existence of such initiatives without reference to a particular city, the directive continues by calling on local administrators to be responsible and moderate in dealing with the issue. Seemingly content with the compliance of women with the state's modernization efforts in general and concerned that interventions in women's veiling could provoke reactions, the interior minister indicated that the governors should focus on propaganda activities and steer clear of taking extreme measures related to the reforms:

> At a time when our women are in fact abiding by the requirements of our revolution, it is necessary to avoid carrying this issue too far by taking measures that might provoke undesirable reactions. The requirements of the revolution should not be enforced by the municipal police force, but they should be accepted through well-administered inculcation. Therefore, it would be best to be content with the use of propaganda on the matter of the *peçe* and *çarşaf*.[128]

In addition to demonstrating that some anti-veiling campaigns did begin as local initiatives, these circulars sent out by the minister of the interior are also crucial for clarifying the initial position of the regime on the question of unveiling. It shows that the regime favoured a moderate and gradual transformation with the aim of avoiding 'undesirable reactions' regarding this sensitive issue. On the other hand, the directive quoted above can also be read as an invitation for the local administrators to promote propaganda for unveiling, and thus it clearly indicates

---

127. From the Minister of the Interior to all Provinces and General Inspectorships, EGM 13216-7/1, 17 December 1934.
128. Ibid.

the involvement, or at least the encouragement, of the centre regarding the anti-veiling campaigns. It also demonstrates, however, the will of the central authorities to limit the desire of some local administrators to be more radical in interpreting regime ideals and putting them into practice. Thus, it points to Ankara's ambiguous attitude and reflects disagreements about how to do away with the *peçe* and the *çarşaf* and promote 'modern' clothing instead.

These disagreements surfaced at the 4th General Congress of the RPP in May 1935. The idea of issuing a law banning the *peçe* and the *çarşaf* countrywide was suggested by the delegates of the provinces of Muğla and Sivas, and this triggered a debate about how to proceed. The commission that prepared a report on the suggestion took a negative position, maintaining that in the villages, where two-thirds of the population lived, the *peçe* and the *çarşaf* were not used, and in cities, where the rest of the population resided, such veils had gradually disappeared without legislation being needed. The veils, the commission claimed, had survived here and there only because of women's respect for their fathers and husbands. The question was then whether it was necessary to take measures, whether this 'rotten fruit had to be plucked from the branch' through government efforts. Some members of the commission supported the idea that the government should intervene, at least to eliminate the *peçe* by adding an article to the Police Law; it was argued that this was necessary to bring about change more quickly.[129] In the end, however, the commission unanimously decided that there was no need for legislation and that progress should be achieved through a 'shortcut action' of the party and party-government institutions (*parti ve parti hükümeti kurumlarının kestirme bir hareketiyle*). The Minister of the Interior Şükrü Kaya also supported the report of the commission and argued that the 'women's revolution' had been viewed as one of the most fundamental principles of the Turkish revolution and thus was followed closely by the government. Approval of the commission's proposal by the general congress would thus suit the government and be considered an important directive. Having discussed the report of the commission, the general congress then rejected the idea of resorting to general legislation on unveiling, only, however, by the end of an intense debate.

One of the delegates, Hakkı Tarık Us, a well-known journalist, author and deputy of the province of Giresun, agreed that the issue of the *peçe* and the *çarşaf* should be taken up by the government and the party, but he suggested that it should also be reconsidered in the light of the principles mentioned in the new party programme accepted two days earlier by the general congress. Here, Us was referring to the revolutionary spirit of the party programme. He added that parliament had already issued legislation requiring that the Ministry of Health organize Health Commissions in the provinces which had the power to place bans on the *kafes*. The question for Us was why legislation banning the *peçe* was seen as unnecessary

---

129. It is interesting to note that even those delegates who were in favour of a general ban made a distinction between the *çarşaf* and the *peçe*, as they considered the latter to be completely unacceptable while the former was more tolerable. *C.H.P. Dördüncü*, 144.

while there was a legal basis for banning the *kafes*. The *çarşaf* was a different matter, he argued, one that had economic aspects and perhaps involved women's concerns about fashion. Us also claimed that they needed precise legislation by pointing to the already existing public desire to eliminate this form of dress. He mentioned that the decisions that had been implemented by some provincial councils (such as in Trabzon in the 1920s and most recently in Adana) were indicators of this general need and desire; for him, the fact that the provincial councils had felt that it was necessity to issue such bans was proof of the spread of that need and desire in the country. Thus, he asserted that such local efforts had to be supported by a revolutionary (not evolutionary) party attitude and that the issue should not be left to the course of time. He argued that such a solution would also encourage provincial councils that had been hesitant to act since a lack of action would be unlawful.

Tarık Us's particular concern was the use of the *peçe* to conceal one's identity. As one of the members of the commission, this was why he proposed that they ban the *peçe* by adding an article to the Police Law.[130] A delegate from Yozgat, Yusuf Duygu, proposed that a general clothing law was necessary. He argued that if the issue was left to provincial councils and municipalities, some of them might not be willing to deal with it and they could use the lack of a law as an excuse for their reluctance to act.[131] Duygu's concern was more about the image such veils created in the eyes of foreigners. A female delegate from Niğde, Naciye Osman Kozbek, also supported the compulsory removal of the *peçe*. She argued that it was necessary since Turkish women had been given the right to work alongside men. In addition, she asserted that the *peçe* was a source of problem during elections because people could use it to conceal their identities and cast multiple votes.[132]

Some delegates, however, had opposed the idea of passing a law on unveiling. Aka Gündüz, for example, another prominent writer and journalist who was also a member of the commission who prepared the report on the proposal to legislate against the *peçe* and the *çarşaf*, claimed that the *peçe* and the *çarşaf* had nothing to do with the Turkish revolution, that the revolution had not been carried out for their sake. In response to Us's claim that they did represent an issue, Gündüz insisted that it was merely a matter for the municipal police (*zabıta meselesidir*) to handle and that taking up such a minor issue at the congress was petty and something not in line with the ideology of the Turkish revolution. Another delegate from İçel, Dr. Muhtar Berker, also argued that a law was unnecessary, but his reasons were

---

130. While Us was defending his position, there were other members of the congress who were supporting him by applauding. Ibid., 145–7.

131. Ibid., 149.

132. Ibid., 151. According to the reporting of a local newspaper in Konya, Kozbek was so disappointed the suggestion to issue a law banning the *peçe* was rejected by the congress that she left the meeting right after this decision. 'Bayan Kızdı, Kurultay Salonunu Terkedip Gitti', *Babalık*, 20 May 1935.

different. He claimed that not everything should be achieved through legislation and that the existing laws on provincial and local administration made it possible for the authorities to handle the issue.

The debate about the *peçe* and the *çarşaf* was brought to an end by the Minister of the Interior Şükrü Kaya. He stated that the congress was a platform for discussing important issues, not argue about whether a piece of black cloth should be removed by law or by administrative measures. Like Gündüz, Kaya also characterized the *peçe* and the *çarşaf* issue as a minor one not worthy of discussion. He said that such veils were foreign to Turkish culture, and in villages, where the majority of the population lived, women's faces were uncovered. He added that a law banning veils would depict Turkish women as being attached to a piece of cloth and thus would cast a negative image. Kaya was certain that as an issue of security, the *peçe* was already properly being handled. He stated that women did not vote wearing the *peçe* over their faces, and the faces of people in public places, and of all sellers at the markets, were uncovered. He believed that the *çarşaf*, on the other hand, had economic dimensions and that some women continued to wear it because of economic difficulties. Thus he claimed that a gradual approach would be more appropriate and that it should be left to the discretion of women, adding that the provinces should act based on their own necessities in their own ways. Instituting a law, he said, could put the party in a difficult position. Perhaps more persuasively, Kaya also added that if such a law were needed, the leader of the revolution would have issued it already, referring to the unwillingness of Mustafa Kemal to intervene in the matter.

Kaya's speech could be considered to be relatively moderate given that he suggested a gradual approach and underlined the importance of women's own decisions, as well as the actions of the provinces. However, there were also rather critical elements in his speech that may be seen as indications of a more active attitude regarding unveiling in government circles. In other words, in his speech, he also said things that could be interpreted as contradictory to his remarks on the need to follow a gradual approach. He first referred to the need for inculcation and urged the delegates of the congress to promise that they would practise and promote the removal of the *peçe* and the *çarşaf* in their own circles. Then he went on to say that the party and the People's Houses should 'enlighten' people on this matter. And finally, Kaya reassured the delegates that the government had received the message it needed to hear during the debate that had taken place at the congress and would act in accordance with that message, both administratively and politically. He added that the ideas discussed at the congress would inspire the government and the members of parliament, concluding his speech by saying that 'maybe the members of the party congress who will meet four years later will see this issue completely resolved'.

The debate reveals the existence of varying positions in the party. The central elite (deputies) as well as delegates coming from the provinces had diverse opinions about how to eliminate the *peçe* and the *çarşaf*. The point that work should be done to do away with veils, however, was clear and this had an impact on the tone of the directives sent out by Ankara after the congress. Two months later, on 22 July 1935, the minister of the interior sent a circular to all governors and inspectors general underlining very explicitly the desire of the Kemalist revolution to do away with the *peçe* and the *çarşaf* and to provide Turkish women with a civilized social status.[133] The language of the circular was harsher compared to his previous circulars; he characterized the *peçe* and the *çarşaf* as originating from 'foreign traditions' and that they had been 'wrapped around the head of the Turk by beastly lusts' (*hayvanca ihtirasların Türk başına doladığı*). A copy of the circular was also sent to the secretariat general of the presidency, the prime ministry and other ministries, the chief of general staff, the general gendarmerie commandership (*Umum Jandarma Komutanlığı*) and the directorate general of provincial administration, informing these institutions that the governors and the inspectors general were thereby instructed to take 'appropriate measures' (*münasip tedbirler*) and engage in propaganda to eliminate the *peçe* and *çarşaf* (*çarşaf ve peçenin ortadan kaldırılması için … telkinler yapılması*).

What 'appropriate measures' meant exactly was unclear in the circular, however, because, again, he indicated that while the Kemalist revolution was determined to do away with the *peçe* and the *çarşaf*, 'in the field of social policy, this reform was left to the civilized discretion of women and men'. Thanks to this 'discretion', the minister suggested, in the ten years since the establishment of the republic, impressive progress had been achieved. The critical point here is that while he emphasized that 'this reform was left to the discretion of people', he also mentioned the contributions expected of local administrators, referring to local attempts to remove the *peçe* and the *çarşaf* that had been made starting in the 1920s. The letter praised such efforts:

> In achieving this progress, the municipal and provincial councils have had significant influence. However, since these decisions [of the municipal and provincial councils] lacked the power of law, there have been delays in their application in some places. In fact, at the congress [of the RPP] this year, while discussing the *çarşaf* and the *peçe* issue, critiques were voiced indicating that the *peçe* survives as a bad tradition in some places. It was even suggested that we immediately handle this situation by enacting a law. But trusting the revolutionary and modernist character of the Turkish nation [*Türk milletinin devrimciliğine ve yenileşme hissine güvenerek*], the government suggested that this bad habit could be discouraged over time through propaganda and effort [*propaganda ve gayretlerle*]. Recent research and investigations reveal that the *peçe* and the *çarşaf* have started to disappear almost everywhere; in large cities like Ankara, Istanbul and Izmir, they disappeared completely, and in other places, partially. It is understood that people who go to the big cities from such places [where the *peçe* and *çarşaf* still partially survive] all remove their *çarşaf* and *peçe*, but they embrace them when they return to their hometowns because

---

133. From the Minister of the Interior to General Inspectorships and provinces, EGM 13216-7/1, 22 July 1935.

they fall into tradition and are swayed by gossip. It is clear that this revolution will be completed with a few encouraging steps.[134]

Again not clarifying about what these 'encouraging steps' should be, the minister suggested that state officials must take the lead: 'If everyone [every official] influences his family members and his immediate circle, this issue will then be solved naturally.' Once again, Ankara emphasized that state officials were its 'natural hands' in the provinces.[135] While the state pointed out that it trusted in the personal influence of state officials in their surroundings, the circular did not prescribe 'appropriate' ways of carrying out propaganda. However, it also did not ignore the impact the local decisions of municipal and provincial councils had had in the past. Thus, it left local administrators with a rather ambiguous order. Those who wanted to take an active approach and push for a decision could do so if they wished, and those who opted to trust in state officials as models for the public at large could find justification for their lack of action.

The only point where the circular urges provincial administrators to be more cautious about the use of the *peçe* and the *çarşaf* and directly intervene was in cases where such veils created a security concern, i.e., if they were used with the aim of concealing someone's identity.[136] The minister stated that women selling goods at marketplaces with the *peçe* over their faces, as could be seen in Istanbul, should be warned first through the use of appropriate language, and he said that if they continue to wear the *peçe*, then they could be banned from selling their goods. He also noted that the police should be vigilant about dangerous people, both men and women, in large cities, and make sure that women wearing the *peçe* are not allowed in public places such as steamships, trams, coffee houses and night clubs (*gazino*).[137]

---

134. The hand-written draft is not very different from the final circular except for a few insignificant wording changes. There is only one sentence in the draft that is not included in the final version. It is an unfinished sentence crossed out by the minister himself. It reads: 'In sum, this *peçe* and *çarşaf* issue [should be handled in a?] way worthy of the revolution.' The original Turkish version is as follows: 'Hülâsa, bu *peçe* ve *çarşaf* meselesinin devrime layık bir şekil ... '

135. For a party document characterizing state officials as the 'natural hands' of the RPP (*fırkanın tabii uzuvları*) see, Memur Bayanların Fırkaya Kaydedilemeyeceği, BCA 490.01/1.4.10, 2 September 1930.

136. This in fact contradicts what Kaya had argued at the general party congress. He had stated that the security element of the issue had already been handled, but as can be seen in the circular, he still felt a need or was prompted to send directives to the local authorities to take action.

137. In particular, there were concerns about thefts being carried out by people wearing veils because that had been done in the Ottoman period as well. In fact, men wearing the *çarşaf* when they go to meet their lovers or go to a brothel has been a popular theme in comedy movies in Turkey, even in those depicting Turkey of the 1970s. Attempts at theft with the use of the *peçe* and the *çarşaf* did occur on many occasions, and those incidences seem to have been used in propaganda against the *peçe* and the *çarşaf* during the anti-veiling campaigns as well. See for example, 'Bir Çarşaflı Kadının Hırsızlığı', *Antalya*, 10 January 1935; 'Çarşaflı Hırsız Tutuldu', *Babalık*, 6 March 1935; 'Mersin'i Soymak İstediler', *Yeni Mersin*, 2 July 1934.

Following this letter, one and a half months later on 9 September 1935 the general secretary of the RPP sent a circular to local party administrators.[138] He informed them about the circular sent by the minister of the interior to the provincial governors and asked them to assist the governors on the issue of the *peçe* and the *çarşaf*. This was an attempt by the party to secure the coordination of local party administrators with the governors and thus achieve unified effort in the provinces. The general secretary also asked the local branches to inform the party centre about the situation. Interestingly, on the same day that the party secretariat sent the circular, the Ministry of the Interior sent its original circular (dated 22 July) to the governor of Denizli again to make sure that he received it.[139]

These circulars certainly paved the way for the acceleration of the anti-veiling campaigns and were read by some local administrators as Ankara's call for action on the issue of unveiling. As can be seen in the responses of some local party branches, the circular sent to the governors by the Ministry of the Interior (on 22 July 1935) had already set the local elite into action before the arrival of the circular of the party (on 9 September 1935), and it prompted joint meetings of the high staff of the governorships with local party administrators and, in some cases, with municipal administrators.[140] In fact, even before the Ministry of the Interior circular sent on 22 July, the impact of the debate on the *peçe* and the *çarşaf* at the party congress in May had already been felt at the local level. Local newspapers informed their readers about the discussions held at the party congress, including the one about the *peçe* and the *çarşaf*.[141] Thus, the general public in the provinces learned that the issue of unveiling appeared to be a concern in Ankara but that the idea of handling the issue with legislation was rejected. In addition, since

138. See the letters from the RPP Yozgat, Muğla, Trabzon and Sinop local party administrations to the RPP Secretariat General, contained in BCA 490.01/17.88.1. I have not seen the original letter sent by the general secretary of the party, but the response letters of some local party administrators mention that they had received such a circular.

139. Apparently, when the circular of the ministry was first sent to the governor of Denizli as a letter to his name, the post office in Denizli forwarded it to the governorship of Samsun, since the governor of Denizli had just been appointed as the governor of Samsun. Having received the circular coming from Denizli post office, the governor of Samsun had informed the ministry that he received the circular, but not as the governor of Denizli but Samsun. Thus the ministry sent another copy to the new governor of Denizli on 9 September 1935. A copy of the relevant correspondence is contained in EGM 13216-7/1. Whether the fact that this mistake was corrected on the same day the RPP general secretary sent a circular to all local branches was a coincidence is an open question. It is possible that this issue continued to be a topic of correspondence between the Ministry of the Interior and the RPP Headquarters between 22 July (the date of the circular of the ministry) and 9 September (the date of the circular of the party centre).

140. See, for example, the letter from the RPP Yozgat Administration to the RPP Secretariat General, BCA 490.01/17.88.1, 13 November 1935.

141. For example, see 'Kurultay ne yaptı?', *Ak Günler*, 3 June 1935; 'Büyük Kurultayın Toplantısında', *Babalık*, 19 May 1935.

the minister of the interior had asked the members of the congress to promise that they would first urge the women in their own families and circles to stop wearing veils, the delegates of some provinces suddenly found themselves under a great deal of pressure. *İkbal*, a Trabzon-based newspaper, mentioned the request that Şükrü Kaya had put to the delegates while reporting about the congress. An editorial addressed all the delegates of Trabzon by name to remind them of the promise they had made to the minister of the interior. The author pointed out that they had thereby promised to fight for women's liberation from veils and it would bring shame on them if they failed to do so.[142]

The delegates of some provinces had actually already created an initiative for unveiling right after the congress without waiting for the circulars. In other words, the influence of the debates at the congress in Ankara was felt at the local level, especially among the local elite, through the delegates who had attended. The delegates of Sinop, for example, had informed all party members in the province about the debates at a party meeting held after they returned from Ankara.[143] Having listened to the impressions of their delegates about the party congress, some members of the local party branch suggested that the *çarşaf* should be banned in Sinop. At a general meeting held at the local party branch one day before the arrival of the circular dated 9 September, representatives from the party, the governorship and the municipality came to an agreement that the *çarşaf* should be replaced with overcoats.

Therefore, it should be emphasized that although the circulars issued by the Ministry of the Interior and the General Secretariat of the RPP (dated 22 July and 9 September 1935, respectively) were quite instrumental and resulted in an acceleration in the spread of anti-veiling campaigns in the periphery, the circulars were sent to the local authorities *after* the *peçe* and the *çarşaf* had already been banned in some cities, and in some others, *after* an anti-veiling campaign (although without an outright ban yet) had already been initiated. Even the initial circulars sent by the interior minister in 1934, which were less imperious compared to the ones sent after the party congress, came *after* the initiation of campaigns in a number of cities. In other words, local initiative had been playing a significant role right from the very beginning. The central administration, especially the Ministry of the Interior and the RPP General Secretariat, encouraged these local attempts to change women's clothing, but the parameters and content of this change were not so obvious. On the one hand, the *peçe* and the *çarşaf* were clearly stigmatized as being backward and undesirable in official communiqués signed by some very high-ranking administrators; on the other hand, Ankara was quite cautious about intervening in women's veiling. This ambiguity was reflected in its communications with provincial administrators and party branches; thus, Ankara's involvement in the process was at times ambivalent, sometimes even inconsistent. In effect, it accelerated gradually, and never reached a level that completely determined the

---

142. Cevat Alap, 'Görgüler Duygular', *İkbal*, 30 May 1935.

143. From the RPP Sinop Administration to the RPP Secretariat General, BCA 490.01/17.88.1, 30 September 1935.

process at the local level. Left vague and sometimes even incoherent in terms of the policy guidance of the central authorities, the anti-veiling campaigns were shaped mainly by local actors and circumstances. In particular, the role and attitude of the local elite were critical in shaping the practices carried out under the banner of the campaigns. However, Ankara also did not hesitate to intervene in the course of the campaigns more actively on certain occasions, especially when some local administrators acted overzealously or indifferently, as well as in cases of opposition and resistance in certain cities.

Chapter 3

THE LOCAL ELITE, SOCIAL OPPOSITION AND RESISTANCE

The local elite in the Turkish context

Despite the fact that Turkish modernization under the Kemalist regime has attracted enormous attention and is frequently analysed in comparative studies on authoritarian modernization as an important case, the question of how the regime was working in practice, not only through the visible high politics of Ankara but also in the provinces, has been left largely unexplored until quite recently. In classical analyses, early republican Turkey is classified as an exclusionary single-party regime which built its power on the already existing divisions in society.[1] That division was based on the schism between the Westernized, educated urban classes and the conservative peasant masses. Atatürk's own speeches, which characterized the party as 'a school for the education of the common people', have been seen as representing the basis of this approach.[2] In certain versions of this analysis, early Kemalist Turkey has been characterized as operating a tutelary system which built itself upon this rift in society.[3] Duverger's classical analysis of single-party systems and particularly his discussion on the difference of the Turkish case from the fascist and communist single-party regimes have been quite influential in the common characterization of the Kemalist regime as a tutelary one.[4]

---

1. For example, see the relevant chapters in Samuel P. Huntington and Clement H. Moore, eds. *Authoritarian Politics in Modern Society: The Dynamics of Established One-Party Systems* (New York: Basic Books, 1970). See also Frederick W. Frey, 'Political Development, Power and Communications in Turkey', in *Communications and Political Development*, ed. Lucian W. Pye (Princeton: Princeton University Press, 1967), 298–316.

2. See Sabri Sayarı, 'Some Notes on the Beginning of Mass Political Participation in Turkey', in *Political Participation in Turkey: Historical Background and Present Problems*, eds. Engin D. Akarlı and Gabriel Ben-Dor (Istanbul: Boğaziçi University Publications, 1975), 121–33.

3. See, for example, Ergun Özbudun, 'The Nature of the Kemalist Political Regime', in *Atatürk: Founder of a Modern State*, eds. Ali Kazancıgil and Ergun Özbudun (London: Hurst&Company, 1997), 79–102.

4. Maurice Duverger, *Political Parties* (London: Methuen, 1951).

One of the shortcomings of such analyses and the subsequent versions that built on the 'Westernized elite vs the people' framework is the neglect of the local as an important dimension of social and political change. In other words, the local, which has usually been referred as the 'periphery', has been associated with the masses, the peasantry and the 'traditional' segments of society, and thus it is often seen as a passive and comparatively much less significant part of any analysis. In this line of thinking, the local primarily became a significant factor in Turkish politics only through the transition to a multi-party system in 1946. Although the elections did make the participation of the citizens in politics possible through direct voting (and indeed the introduction of competitive politics was a major breakthrough), it would be misleading to argue that the local was ineffective and insignificant before the introduction of the multi-party system. In addition, as noted in the introduction of the book, the idea that authoritarian single-party regimes should be studied first and foremost by looking at central politics has been rightly criticized based on new theoretical and empirical research on the state and state–society relations.

The neglect of the local is particularly visible in the lack of analyses in the literature on local elites. As regards the political elite in Turkey, the emphasis is almost exclusively on the elite in the 'centre', on the people taking part in high politics and the bureaucracy in Ankara. In his classic work *The Turkish Political Elite*, Frederick W. Frey, for example, focuses on the profiles of the members of parliament between 1920 and 1957.[5] Frey explains this choice by referring to the focal position of parliament; because there was a high degree of governmental integration in Turkey. In this analysis, the impact of the local could thus be felt through its influence upon deputies, and this is how Frey conceptualized localism, measured by looking at the ties of the deputies to the province they represented.[6] He acknowledges that local pressure on the deputies existed even during the single-party era, but he does not discuss in any detail how this pressure worked or what role local actors played in this period. Localism's main impact came with the transition to a multi-party system: 'The opening up of the tutelary developmental system and the inauguration of a Western, multi-party parliamentary structure emphatically increased the representation of local forces, that is, of *local elites*.'[7] In a more recent study, Ahmet Demirel revives Frey's analyses and provides a more detailed profile of the members of the parliament during the single-party era based on new sources.[8] Since Demirel's focus is also on the central elite and the elections, the local is included to the extent that it could have an influence on parliament, which is again measured by localism. In addition to arguing that localism decreased from the 1920s to the 1930s, which signifies a weaker link between parliament and the local, Demirel also mentions an effort by the regime

---

5. Frederick W. Frey, *The Turkish Political Elite* (Cambridge, MA: The M.I.T. Press, 1965).

6. For the period Frey studies (1920–1957), the overall degree of localism seems to be limited, since only 58 per cent of the deputies were born in the provinces they represented. Ibid., 93–4.

7. Ibid., 397. Emphasis added.

8. Ahmet Demirel, *Tek Partinin İktidarı: Türkiye'de Seçimler ve Siyaset (1923–1946)* (Istanbul: İletişim, 2013).

to nevertheless symbolically include those segments of society which were not part of the political elite and, by doing so, to limit the increasing tendency in parliament towards bureaucratization.[9]

This tendency to focus exclusively on the political elite in the capital has led scholars to overlook the role of local actors and dynamics in the implementation and interpretation of the policies formulated in Ankara. Since the 1950s, the emphasis of modernization theory on the bureaucracy and the elite as the agents of social change has shaped major studies on Turkey and been influential for subsequent analyses despite the critiques the theory has received. In works that see a strong state tradition in Ottoman/Turkish political formation, the central elites are characterized as an undifferentiated group who saw the state as being vital for holding the community together, while also being intolerant and suspicious of the periphery.[10] With this line of thinking, the dichotomy of 'strong state vs. weak civil society' shaped the Ottoman/Turkish polity and the bureaucratic elite obtained almost unchallenged power under the Kemalist republic.[11] In some formulations of this reading, it is not only the state that emerges as a concept that is above any other actor or notion in political culture; the Ottoman/Turkish state is also seen as being unique among its contemporaries in many aspects.[12]

Perhaps the most hegemonic framework in Turkish studies in the last forty years, the centre–periphery approach, which was first formulated by Şerif Mardin, follows a similar line of analysis through an emphasis on the centre–periphery rift as the main point of rupture and confrontation between state elites and society.[13] However, it is not state-centric in the sense that it incorporates cultural and social dynamics into the analysis and attributes relatively more power and autonomy to the periphery, to the people excluded by state ideology: societal actors.[14] In Mardin's analysis, the centre–periphery axis deeply rooted in the Ottoman social and economic structure was merged with another source of social conflict with the beginning of modernization. This resulted in an intra-elite conflict at first, dividing the elite into pro-Western and traditionalist/Islamist camps. As the modernist faction got stronger and dominated the state, Islam had become an element of the culture of the periphery and thus the centre–periphery rift came to coincide with the pro-Western vs. traditionalist–Islamist

---

9. For instance, in the 1931 elections, the RPP decided to nominate carefully selected 'ordinary' workers and peasants for membership in parliament and as a result thirteen peasants and ten workers were elected. Expected to be loyal and nationalist, these deputies were supposed to maintain their original occupations, their links with their hometowns and their 'authentic' attire. Ibid., 117–22.

10. See Heper, *The State*.

11. See Heper's discussion on bureaucratic transcendentalism. Ibid., 67–97.

12. For example, see Gabriel Ben-Dor and Engin D. Akarlı, 'Comparative Perspectives', in *Political Participation in Turkey: Historical Background and Present Problems*, eds. Engin D. Akarlı and Gabriel Ben-Dor (Istanbul: Boğaziçi University Publications, 1975), 157–62.

13. Mardin, 'Center-Periphery'.

14. Şerif Mardin, 'Projects as Methodology: Some Thoughts on Modern Turkish Social Science', in *Rethinking Modernity and National Identity in Turkey*, eds. Sibel Bozdoğan and Reşat Kasaba (Seattle: University of Washington Press, 1997), 64–80.

divide. This cultural alienation of the masses from the rulers, of the periphery from the centre, is a key component in centre–periphery analyses.[15]

One strategy that the state employed was to make some concessions to local notables to 'facilitate the expression of their interests' and thus acknowledge 'the right of notables to participate in single-party politics'.[16] In fact, works that note the importance of the local by devoting a few paragraphs to explaining the social base of the Kemalist regime have largely emphasized the role of local notables and their alliance with the central authority. In particular, the RPP has been described as 'having born out of an alliance between the central military-bureaucratic-intellectual élite and local notables'.[17] Özbudun suggests that this alliance continued throughout the single-party era despite the predominance of the state bourgeoisie and that 'local notables also wielded considerable influence particularly at the local level'.[18] Although the relationships between the state and local notables were far more complex,[19] this complexity was ignored at the expense of emphasizing the determining role of central policies. The assumption was that as long as this alliance with the local notables was intact, the regime could apply its policies and maintain its support. More importantly, such analyses reduce the local to 'local notables' upon whom other local agents were dependent, thus overlooking both the multiplicity of local actors and the complexity of local politics.

An increasing number of studies, however, have started to focus on the relationship between the central authorities, local elites and societal forces in the shaping of state policies at the local level. This increasing interest in the local has become particularly visible in analyses of the connection between state formation, nationalism and political violence, especially during the late Ottoman Empire and the transition to the Turkish republic. In *Sorrowful Shores*, Gingeras analyses the role of the central authorities not as an exclusive force but as one operating within the complexities of local society through the case of the South Marmara region between the Balkan Wars and the establishment of the Turkish republic in 1923.[20] Gingeras argues that even after the establishment of the Kemalist regime, there were limitations to Ankara's control over the provinces and that 'local officials and

---

15. Mardin, 'Center-Periphery', 175. See also Ergun Özbudun, *Türkiye'de Sosyal Değişme ve Siyasal Katılma* (Ankara: Ankara Üniversitesi Hukuk Fakültesi Yayınları, 1975), 19–46.

16. Engin Deniz Akarlı, 'The State as a Socio-Cultural Phenomenon and Political Participation in Turkey', in *Political Participation in Turkey: Historical Background and Present Problems*, eds. Engin D. Akarlı and Gabriel Ben-Dor (Istanbul: Boğaziçi University Publications, 1975), 135–55.

17. Özbudun, 'The Nature', 82.

18. Ibid., 84. Similarly, Tunçay also notes that the Kemalist elite agreed to the preservation of the privileged position of local notables as long as they did not oppose the modernization policies of the new regime. Tunçay, *T.C.'nde Tek-Parti*, 134.

19. See, for example, Martin Van Bruinessen, *Agha, Shaikh and State: The Social and Political Structures of Kurdistan* (London: Zed Books, 1992).

20. Ryan Gingeras, *Sorrowful Shores: Violence, Ethnicity, and the End of the Ottoman Empire, 1912–1923* (Oxford: Oxford University Press, 2009).

provincial populations continued to resist or negotiate the rules laid down by the centre'.[21] Üngör's analysis on population policies and nationalist homogenization in Eastern Turkey between 1913 and 1950 also reveals that local elites played a critical role in the interpretation and implementation of government legislation, and thus they determined the fate of the Armenians who were subjected to genocidal destruction.[22] His discussion of the Kurdish deportations between 1916 and 1934 also shows that the local elites played a significant role in the continuation of the social engineering policies in the region from the empire to the republic, since they remained largely intact.[23] Moreover, the local elite were not simply implementers of central policies but that 'they often take the initiative to propose suggestions'.[24]

Michael E. Meeker's ethnographical study of the Eastern Black Sea region is perhaps the most inspiring work on the unfolding of local political dynamics in the early republican era. He looks at the daily working of the local social structures beyond the questions of population engineering and violent episodes of nation-building, and maintains that they function as formative blocks of the state apparatus in the provinces. In Meeker's analysis, local elite networks, a complex of non-official elites that were prominent in the Ottoman imperial system, played an important role in the continuity between the empire and the republic. The local elite, Meeker notes, could oppose the official policies strengthening centralized government under the republic, and 'when such policies were nonetheless adopted, local elites proved adept at repenetrating and recolonizing the new state system'.[25] Meeker's focus, however, is mainly on the influential local families and thus he tends to use a narrower definition for the local elite, differentiating them from state officials and administration:

> … state officials of the Kemalist period followed a governmental practice of the imperial period, turning to leading individuals from large groupings for assistance even though this contradicted nationalist ideology and institutions. As a consequence, an imperial state society at the local level had gradually but efficiently reoriented itself to become a national state society at the local level. Leading individuals from large family groupings, the descendants of aghas from agha-families, now appeared as nationalist rather than ottomanist in behavior, speech, and dress.[26]

He argues that local elites came to dominate the public sphere during the *later* decades of the Turkish republic once the centralized and radical policies of the early

---

21. Ibid., 165.
22. Uğur Ümit Üngör, *The Making of Modern Turkey: Nation and State in Eastern Anatolia, 1913–1950* (Oxford: Oxford University Press, 2011).
23. Ibid., 167. Zürcher also shows that the new regime could rely on the existing organization of provincial administration at the lower echelons. Zürcher, 'The Ottoman Legacy'.
24. Üngör, *The Making*, 187.
25. Meeker, *A Nation*, xxi.
26. Ibid., 297.

decades had come to an end. This is why he talks about local elites *re*penetrating, *re*colonizing or *re*inhabiting the new state system *after* the period of revolutionary change during the 1920s and 30s.[27] While their legitimacy was undermined for a brief period during the heyday of the Kemalist revolution, the regional social oligarchy had revived itself following the transition to multi-party politics in the late 1940s.

Other scholars have drawn attention to the significance of 'mid-level elites' or 'mid-level professionals' in order to understand how the Kemalist ideology was translated into policies and how they were implemented. Childress, for example, suggests that these mid-level elites were the products of state policies, but they were also their producers. Her research on the members of the *Talim ve Terbiye Heyeti* (Council of Educational Policy), a committee that provided assistance to the Ministry of Education, reveals that their role was essential, since they designed, implemented and mediated the Kemalist experience.[28] Although such research is crucial to seeing that the 'Kemalist elite' in Ankara was not monolithic but multi-levelled and diverse in their vision, the focus is nevertheless exclusively on the educated elite, since the concept of mid-level elite is defined mainly based on people's levels of education and subsequent career paths. Even in works that also follow these elites in practice in the provinces, this focus on the educated segments of society, the doctors, teachers, journalists and so on, does not change.[29] In other words, the local elites in this usage are again limited, this time to civil servants and professionals.

In his study of People's Houses, Lamprou uses the concept of local elites in a broader manner.[30] He focuses on the Kayseri and Balıkesir People's Houses and looks at these institutions as places where various local actors competed, negotiated and domesticated the policies imposed by the centre.[31] Lamprou's analysis of local

---

27. Emphasis added. Studies on contemporary provincial elites, however, reveal that families that had been local notables since the Ottoman periods quickly adapted to the republican system and did not wait until the 1940s to penetrate the local administration. See Ayşe Durakbaşa, 'Taşra Burjuvazisinin Tarihsel Kökenleri', *Toplum ve Bilim* 118 (2010): 6–38; Meltem Karadağ, 'Taşra Kentlerinde Yaşam Tarzları Alanı: Kültür ve Ayrım', *Toplum ve Bilim* 118 (2010): 39–58.

28. Faith J. Childress, 'Taking Side Roads: Researching Mid-Level Elites as Turkish Social History', in *Towards a Social History of Modern Turkey: Essays in Theory and Practice*, ed. Gavin D. Brockett (Istanbul: Libra, 2011), 97–122.

29. Kathryn Libal, 'Specifying Turkish Modernity: Gender, Family and Nation-State Making in the Early Republic', in *Towards a Social History of Modern Turkey: Essays in Theory and Practice*, ed. Gavin D. Brockett (Istanbul: Libra, 2011), 81–96; Gavin D. Brockett, 'A View from the Periphery: The Provincial Press as a Source for Republican Turkish Social History', in *Towards a Social History of Modern Turkey: Essays in Theory and Practice*, ed. Gavin D. Brockett (Istanbul: Libra, 2011), 123–53.

30. Lamprou, *Nation Building*.

31. For a similar discussion on provincial RPP branches, see Metinsoy, 'Kemalizmin Taşrası'. See also Murat Turan, *CHP'nin Doğu'da Teşkilatlanması* (Istanbul: Libra, 2011).

power networks points to a more diverse group of elites composed of both locals and non-locals. He underlines that in the province centres, these urban elite were the people who staffed all significant political, financial and social institutions. On the one hand, he predominantly refers to the local notable families (landowners and merchants) as the key elites at the local level who usually occupied the local party leadership, the Municipal and Provincial assemblies, and the financial and cultural/social institutions (Chambers of Commerce and Industry, various associations) and acted as 'middlemen between state and population'.[32] On the other hand, Lamporu shows how well integrated these local notables were into the political system, vertically connected to the state elite in the centre, as well as to civil servants in the provinces. Moreover, there were professionals from notable families and local state officials, blurring the difference between the local and non-local, and referring even to a symbiosis of state and non-state actors in some instances.[33] The dynamics and structures of local societies, most notably the size and strength of the state apparatus and the availability of educational institutions, played an important role in the different composition of people occupying institutions in each setting. Thus, the differentiation between locals and 'outsiders' (appointed state officials), albeit important in many instances, did not necessarily need to be rigid; local institutions could easily turn into a power struggle between different local families and among local or non-local appointed state officials.

I follow a similar line of analysis and suggest that the local elite have to be analysed with a more inclusive approach. As discussed above, it is not easy to refer to a concise definition of the concept of local elite in the existing literature, since it has been overwhelmingly dominated by analyses of central elites and macro-level power relations, and the local has been predominantly understood as the role of local notables. However, I must unpack the concept here and explain the definition I have adopted in this book in order to underline more precisely the focus of analysis. I define the concept of local elites as a cluster of actors which is composed of members of the state and party administration at the provincial level, as well as local notables and the prominent members of all local institutions, from the People's Houses to sport clubs, professional organizations and associations, as well as local opinion leaders and leading contributors to local newspapers. Tekeli suggests that there was an interesting division of labour among institutions at the local level in the single-party era and that urban life and the Kemalist policies of the 1930s and 1940s can only be understood by simultaneously analysing these institutions and their members who were clustered around the party branch and municipality in each province.[34] I argue that this institutional diversity, as well as the diversity among the members of institutions, allowed for competition, conflict

---

32. Lamprou, *Nation Building*, 52.
33. Ibid., 69.
34. Tekeli, *Cumhuriyetin*, 52–3. Tekeli points that each institution was specialized and focused on one ideological aspect or targeted social aim, and it is critical to note that these duties were assigned to separate institutions apart from the party and state offices.

and negotiation, regardless of the strength of the ideological unity expected of them by the regime centre. Some of the people who worked at these local institutions were appointed officials but there was a considerable number of people who were locals and part of this local elite cluster. Simply put, they were the people, both men and women, who constituted educated and/or high-status groups at the local level, as they were assumed to be or were represented as the 'enlightened' segment of the population or leading members of the local communities. This cluster of local elites coincides with a network of power relations at the local level. It is very important to emphasize that they were far from being homogeneous politically; being a 'republican' or 'supporter of the regime' was in fact a much broader notion than is usually argued in the literature on the single-party era. The shape that regime ideals would take in practice at the local level was as much a product of the conflicts and negotiations between these local elites as they were of central policies. As such, the local elites played a critical, if not the most important, role in the shaping of the anti-veiling campaigns.

Negotiating Kemalism: The local elites in the anti-veiling campaigns

On 23 December 1934, only nineteen days after the enactment of the law granting women's political rights, Cevat Alap, a journalist for *İkbal* newspaper in the province of Trabzon, addressed the local authorities in his column.[35] As we learn from his article, the governor of Trabzon had recently issued a circular and advised all state officials not to process the petitions of women wearing the *peçe* and *çarşaf*. Alap requested that this decision to be turned into a general ban including all public places:

> This ban can gradually be expanded to the following: A woman cannot sit in the park wearing the *peçe* and the *çarşaf*, cannot enter Güzelhisar Park, cannot go to the movie theatre, and finally, cannot walk around in the market or bazaar. If we do not issue such a ban today, the revolution, the regime, will do so itself, perhaps not today or next year, but soon. The regime and the revolution, which have given women the right to elect and be elected, will completely eliminate the *peçe* and the *çarşaf*, which are now a sign of being uncivilized, through a law like the one on the attire of priests and hodjas.

It seems that for Alap, both granting women their political rights and the law regulating the clothing of the religious personnel, came one after the other in 1934, were influential signs that the state could intervene in the dress of women. His article was a call, a local voice, demanding the realization of regime ideals through a local initiative; he invited the local administrators to act before the central authorities made a concrete move. This was precisely what the regime expected from the local elites: to lead the way in social and cultural modernization. Local administrators,

---

35. Cevat Alap, 'Çarşaf, Peçe Artık Yok Olmalıdır', *İkbal*, 23 December 1934.

state officials and women in particular were critical in the eyes of Ankara as agents of change in the provinces. Many local elites had also envisioned themselves as such. For some of them, at least, men and women alike, there was no need for a directive to come from the centre for every effort made in the modernization process. Some of the local elites, however, were much less enthusiastic about unveiling, or they were hesitant, or even reluctant. This diversity in the attitudes of the local elite, as well as in their initiatives and strategies, and Ankara's response to those initiatives, are essential if we want to understand the complexity of the anti-veiling campaigns in Turkey in the 1930s.

The most apparent initiative of the local elites was the leading role they played in propaganda efforts. Such efforts were especially put into practice by using local newspapers. Given the difficulties the regime was facing in fully penetrating society through established institutions because of limited state capacity, local newspapers had took on an important function in the eyes of the authorities in convincing and leading the masses.[36] The provincial administrators also had very limited means at their disposal for propaganda apart from the newspapers; thus the local elite used them as a platform on which they tried to initiate and promote the anti-veiling campaigns at the local level. The propaganda activities of the local elite can be seen as being quite normal, since propaganda was the only concrete advice mentioned in the circulars coming from Ankara. But some local newspapers began to publish articles about the need for the elimination of the *peçe* and the *çarşaf* even before Ankara started sending out circulars on the issue.

One crucial characteristic of this propaganda was that although its pro-regime stance was obvious, there was nevertheless an effort to represent the desire for such a reform as a genuinely local one, voiced by the elites of the cities themselves. In other words, most of the local authors and journalists represented the abandonment of the *peçe* and the *çarşaf* as the natural end result of the modernization of Turkish society and they depicted themselves as the natural agents of that modernization. Formulated as 'we the new Turkish youth', 'the enlightened people of our city', 'the women of our city' or simply 'the people' (of Bursa, of Konya and so on), the self-representation of the local elite emphasizing the agency of the local had the aim of portraying the initiative as something expected from the historical position of the city as a 'vanguard' city and something they had to do to be worthy of the revolution or else they would fall behind the other cities in the fight to cast off women's veils. The idea of being a vanguard city was frequently invoked by local elites in mobilizing the public in various cities.[37] We can think of this as a dual competition at the local level: various members of local elites were fighting to be the leading agents of change in their cities, and there was a competition among cities to be the vanguard in the anti-veiling campaigns.

---

36. See, for example, 1935 Report of the Party Inspector Adnan Menderes, Deputy of Aydın, BCA 490.1/618.27.1, 2 December 1935.

37. For examples of this kind of propaganda, see 'Trabzon kadınları ve çarşaf', *İkbal*, 29 October 1934; 'Halk evinde dün akşamki toplantı', *Antalya*, 20 December 1934; 'Eni konu konuşmalar', *Halk*, 11 April 1935.

Likewise, the introduction of a campaign in a certain province capital soon came to affect the district capitals in that province, creating a snowball effect and an atmosphere of competition. The way campaigns were reported in provincial newspapers shows how this comparison among district capitals in a particular province put pressure on district administrations and demonstrates how they felt a need to follow the province capital or other district capitals in banning the *peçe* and the *çarşaf*. In 1933, *Yeni Mersin*, a newspaper published in the province of İçel, for example, reported on the inability of the district of Tarsus to launch a successful campaign against the *peçe* and the *çarşaf* despite the fact that there was a 'movement' in the district and general demand among the women.[38] It was reported that the desired results could not be achieved because ineffective modes of action were employed and the matter was not well followed up on. The support of the district governor and the municipality were mentioned in the article, suggesting that in Tarsus the issuance of a ban was a hollow formality. *Yeni Mersin* was 'hoping' that Tarsus would soon follow the example of Mersin, the province capital, and celebrated the fact that the *çarşaf* was already prohibited at parks and public places in the district capital. A female member of the Tarsus municipal council proposed that they issue a ban, yet this was brought onto the agenda of the council only at the beginning of 1935. *Yeni Mersin* again pushed for reforms so that the women of Tarsus could get rid of their 'ogre clothing' (*umacı kılık*)[39] and published commentaries inviting the members of the Tarsus municipal council not to buy into the arguments of those who claimed that the issue could be solved naturally over the course of time. Rıza Atilâ, a columnist writing for *Yeni Mersin*, implied that if there were any doubts concerning this issue in Tarsus, it would mean that Tarsus had failed to understand the great aims of the revolution.[40]

Although the efforts of some local elite to represent the anti-veiling campaigns as genuinely local endeavours were mainly propaganda, there were cases in which the initiative did in fact originate locally, especially concerning the right way to organize and implement an anti-veiling campaign. One example of such an initiative can be seen in a letter that the deputy governor of Antalya wrote to the minister of the interior towards the end of 1934 in which he expressed curiosity about the opinion of the government and the party as regards the proper way to eliminate the *peçe* and the *çarşaf*.[41] Pointing out that the Kemalist revolution had

---

38. 'Çarşaflar Tarsusta da kalkıyor', *Yeni Mersin*, 16 September 1934.
39. 'Tarsus Belediye M. toplantısı', *Yeni Mersin*, 4 February 1935.
40. Rıza Atilâ, 'Yeni Çağın Artığı', *Yeni Mersin*, 4 February 1935.
41. From the Deputy Governor of Antalya to the Ministry of the Interior, EGM 13216-7/1, 17 November 1934. The date of the letter appears as 17 November 1934 on the original document. However, it is highly likely that this was a mistake and it should be 17 December 1934, since in the reply letter of the ministry, the date of the letter by the deputy governor appears as 17 December. It is also logical that the ministry immediately replied to the letter of the deputy governor rather than waiting for a period of one month. From the Minister of the Interior to the Province of Antalya, EGM 13216-7/1, 17 December 1934.

attained yet another major achievement by granting women political rights, rights that they lacked even in the most civilized nations, he suggested that it would be inappropriate for Turkish women to welcome this achievement by wearing the *peçe* and the *çarşaf*. The deputy governor was convinced that such veils made Turkish women appear primitive to foreigners.[42] More importantly, he argued that it was already proven by 'years of struggle' that this issue could not be handled by mere inculcation. It is crucial here to note that the deputy governor's characterization of the struggle against the *peçe* and the *çarşaf* as a struggle lasting many years refers to a certain degree of continuation that existed at the local level between the earlier anti-veiling campaigns in the 1920s and the later ones in the mid-1930s. It also shows that while this struggle had been shaped by propaganda activities, this local administrator was convinced that there was a need for more effective measures. In fact, at the end of the letter, the deputy governor asked whether the government had already made clear plans or was planning to make a decision on the issue. If there was no such decision, he said that he would request permission to use the municipal police to prevent women wearing the *peçe* and the *çarşaf* from entering public places such as parks and theatres in Antalya. He suggested that since women had acquired political rights, now was a good time to issue a ban.

This letter was written before the circular issued by the minister on 17 December 1934 which urged governors not to use the police and to resort solely to propaganda and inculcation. It was in fact probably one of the reasons that the minister penned the circular. On the same day, in a circular sent to all governors and inspectors general, the minister also replied separately to the deputy governor's letter: 'It is not appropriate to use the municipal police to prevent women wearing the *peçe* and the *çarşaf* from entering places or walking around. One should attain this goal only through well-administered inculcation. Therefore, it is necessary to be content with the use of propaganda in this regard.'[43] Demonstrating the determined will of a local administrator to initiate a forceful campaign, the letter of the deputy governor of Antalya also points to the tendency of some local actors to solve the issue by taking stronger measures. Despite the warnings of the minister, this tendency continued to guide the actions of some local administrators. This was partly because the circular sent from the Ministry of the Interior was clear about the regime's position regarding the use of the *peçe* and the *çarşaf* but unclear about how to undertake efforts apart from propaganda and state officials' vanguard role. If these efforts failed or were found to be ineffective or insufficient, some local administrators saw themselves as being in a position to devise a stronger framework of action and go beyond mere propaganda. The case of the province of Ordu is another good example that reflects such tendencies.

---

42. It is interesting to note that the main concern of the deputy governor about the issue of veiling was the kind of image it represented in the eyes of the foreigners. As it was mentioned in the previous chapter, this was in fact a very widespread concern in public discussions throughout the anti-veiling campaigns.

43. From the Minister of the Interior to the Province of Antalya, EGM 13216-7/1, 17 December 1934.

In Ordu, the fight against the *peçe* and the *çarşaf* had begun in the 1920s.[44] However, these earlier attempts were ineffective and the issue resurfaced as a public concern when women acquired political rights in 1934. As can be seen in a number of documents, there were efforts, including a municipal ban, to eliminate the *peçe* and the *çarşaf* in the province during the course of 1935.[45] These efforts, it seems, also proved to be unsuccessful as the governor of Ordu informed the Ministry of the Interior on 5 March 1937[46] that he had felt a need to issue a declaration banning the *peçe, çarşaf* and *peştamal* in Ordu as of 23 April 1937:

> In a nation like ours that has taken its place among the advanced nations of the world, it is a national and civic duty for every citizen to acknowledge the civilized rights deserved by women, women who have acquired an elevated status and proven their political capacity. It has been possible for some time [in Ordu] to encounter the *peçe* and the *çarşaf*, which certainly do not fit the women of an advanced and civilized nation. In addition, it has also been seen that scarves and umbrellas have been used on unnecessary occasions. Especially the hamam *peştemals* present a revolting scene. The achievements of our generation today came about thanks to loyalty and obedience to principles and the regime, and the civilized Turkish regime does not favour such unsightly and strange clothes. Every citizen should know full well that those who do not follow the revolution and the regime will be seen as inclined towards reactionism (*irticaa meyyal*); indeed, they would be perceived as being impaired by this horrible will and tendency (*bu çirkin arzu ve temayül*). Men who use their civilized rights in an ideal fashion should respect the civilized rights of their wives; it is a national and legal duty and obligation for them to urge their wives to follow these [civilized rights/principles] (*riayete icbar eylemeleri*).[47]

In the declaration, it was also announced that the names and addresses of those who did not abide by the ban would be registered by the municipal police and police officers in the province capital and district capitals, and by the village governors and members of the council of elders in the villages. These names would be handed over to the highest state authority in every administrative unit and the individuals would be fined from 5 lira to 25 lira based on the Law on Provincial Administration. In addition, the petitions of women who wear veils would be refused at public offices and courts, and the officials who work at state offices were to report such cases to the relevant authority. The declaration also announced that

---

44. See Chapter 2.

45. The Ministry of the Interior received three anonymous letters complaining about these efforts in July 1935. From the Minister of the Interior to the Deputy Governor of Ordu, EGM 13216-7/1, 29 July 1935.

46. Copy of the Letter of the Governor of Ordu to the Ministry of the Interior, EGM 13216-7/1, 5 March 1937.

47. Copy of the Declaration on the *Peçe*, the *Çarşaf* and the *Peştamal* Ban by the Governor of Ordu, EGM 13216-7/1, 5 March 1937.

not only the workers themselves but also the owners of factories and companies would be held responsible for the clothing of their female workers. Since state offices were a symbol of civilization, the declaration also reminded state officials to be sensitive regarding the clothing of their wives and female relatives.

The declaration sent out by the governor of Ordu is one of the most comprehensive declarations in the struggle against the *peçe* and the *çarşaf*. By affecting the lives of a broad swathe of people, from workers at factories to women in the villages, the governor had attempted at a very ambitious plan of action. Particularly significant was the direct link he established between the wearing of the *peçe* and the *çarşaf* and the way it was reactionary; for him, the use of veils was a direct form of opposition to the regime. He was probably very proud of this comprehensive plan of action, and informed the Ministry of the Interior with the hope of demonstrating his devotion to the principles of the regime as a governor. On 28 April 1937, five days after the ban on the *peçe*, the *çarşaf* and the *peştamal* was put into practice in Ordu, the governor informed the ministry of the process and its immediate results.[48] In his letter, he reported that the ban had been put into effect under the close control of the municipal police, supported by the police and the gendarmerie forces. The ban, he noted, 'had been applied with complete success' and there remained no trace of the *peçe*, the *çarşaf* or the *peştamal* in Ordu. Proudly he reported that all women, including those in the district capitals and villages of the province, had removed those 'uncivilized clothes'.

Having received this last letter reporting the results of the ban, the ministry realized that they had not received the first letter to which the declaration of the governor of Ordu was attached. The ministry asked the governor to send a copy of the declaration in which he explained the contents of the ban.[49] Having read the copy of the declaration, the minister of the interior felt a need to warn the governor. He reminded the governor of the earlier circulars of the ministry urging local administrators to act responsibly and carefully on the issue of unveiling, and he warned him that he had no right to enforce a punishment based on the law mentioned in his declaration, the Law on Provincial Administration:

I) Your declaration on the ban on the *peçe*, the *çarşaf* and the *peştamal* has been analyzed. It is not right to exact a punishment based on the Law on Provincial Administration, nor is it right to refuse to process the petitions of women who come to state offices and courts wearing the *peçe*, *çarşaf* or the *peştamal*, as you announced in your declaration. It was clearly stipulated in circular no. 3613 dated 11.8.1934 and in a letter directly sent to the governors through the General Police Headquarters dated 22.7.1935 that the issue of the *peçe*, the *çarşaf* and the *peştamal* is primarily left to the discretion and manners of our women and that it should not be dealt with by issuing decrees and orders. Also, it was stipulated that you must act in a careful manner regarding this important and sensitive issue and that the targeted goals should be achieved through encouragement, inculcation

---

48. Correspondence from the Governor of Ordu, EGM 13216-7/1, 28 April 1937.
49. From the Minister of the Interior to the Governorship of Ordu, EGM 13216-7/1, no date.

and propaganda. It has also been noted that the families of state officials should lead the way on this issue through encouragement and propaganda.

II) In order to apply the punitive measures in Article 68 of the Law on Provincial Administration, it is necessary that your order be based on law; however, there is no law that mentions a ban on the *peçe* and the *çarşaf* either explicitly or implicitly. Since you are under a republican administration, every order and declaration should be based on law, and since the *peçe* and the *çarşaf* are not banned by law, it is completely against the spirit and aim of the law to punish those who wear these veils.

III) The second article of your declaration is also against the law because both the courts and other official departments are obliged to process the appeals of all citizens, regardless of their clothing. However, they can ask women whose faces are covered to reveal their faces so they can identify them. But they cannot refuse to process the petitions of women because they come to the offices wearing the *çarşaf* or the *peştamal*. If they do such an unlawful act, they will face an administrative investigation based on regulations.

IV) For the reasons explained above, I ask that the punitive measures mentioned in the declaration not be applied, and [the elimination of the veil] should be realized in a natural way, through measures suitable for local circumstances and through encouragement and propaganda.[50]

This letter clearly shows that Ankara was still very hesitant about directly intervening in women's veiling through bans and orders in May 1937. Most importantly, perhaps, was the reminder that there was no law banning these veils, and thus the governors had no right to issue a punishment based on the Law on the Provincial Administration or any other law. On the other hand, Ankara certainly knew that there were decisions and orders issued by city councils in other provinces and district capitals, and as far as it can be traced in official documents, it had shown no such forceful opposition against such decisions as it did against the declaration of the governor of Ordu. It seems that to issue a decision as part of the municipal bans based on the legal capacity of the municipalities to maintain order and attain urban development was acceptable or tolerable for Ankara, while an anti-veiling campaign as ambitious and comprehensive as the one organized in Ordu was not. It is also clear that even if a municipal decision or a ban was declared by a certain city council, Ankara was still reluctant to apply that decision or ban by issuing fines, and was certainly more alert if such decisions were put into practice by the local administrators by using the municipal police or the gendarmerie. In fact, all documents show that Ankara consistently warned the local authorities against the use of force in the unveiling issue. What the local authorities should understand from 'encouragement' or 'inculcation' and what measures or tactics

---

50. Copy of the Letter of the Minister of the Interior to the Province of Ordu dated 14.5.1937, EGM 13216-7/1, 18 June 1937.

should be used to make them a reality remained unclear, however. In other words, the local administrators were left with the knowledge that, on the one hand, this 'task of unveiling' should be realized, but on the other hand, it was not clear how this would be done.

In fact, even after the circular was sent out and contrary to the interior minister's orders, other local authorities did use the municipal police to impose bans on the *peçe* and the *çarşaf*. In a few instances, such as in Denizli and Bursa, women who continued to wear the *peçe* and the *çarşaf* had to pay fines for not obeying the municipal regulations.[51] In some of the notices published in local newspapers concerning the bans, women were warned of the possibility of municipal police intervention in cases of non-compliance.[52] In Bergama, a district of the province of Izmir, the city council announced that not only women who did not comply with the decision, but also shop keepers who employed women wearing the *peçe* and the *çarşaf*, and persons who harassed women wearing 'national' attire (meaning 'modern' and unveiled), would be fined.[53] In some cities, rulings made by city councils to ban the *peçe* and the *çarşaf* were put into practice by having the police and soldiers physically remove women's veils in the streets and by charging the police to patrol the main streets and make sure that women complied.[54]

Some local elites tried to complain to the authorities in Ankara about the way the anti-veiling campaign was being implemented in their cities. On 30 July 1935, the deputy governor of the province of Kastamonu sent a letter to the minister of the interior informing him about the anti-veiling campaign going on there.[55] The deputy governor reassured the ministry that the local authorities had paid the utmost attention to the elimination of uncivilized clothes like the *peçe* and the *çarşaf*, and he reported that at the last meeting of the city council, it was unanimously decided that such veils should be eliminated in the province. He also noted that the decision was immediately put into practice and the police were prepared and acting very carefully; the deputy governor said he was certain that this 'ugly tradition' would fade away in a very short period of time. Almost a month later, the ministry received another letter from a state official, the second commissioner

---

51. Hakkı Uyar, 'Tek Parti Döneminde Denizli'de Siyasal Hayat', in *Uluslararası Denizli ve Çevresi Tarih ve Kültür Sempozyumu: Bildiriler 1*, ed. Ayfer Özçelik et al. (Denizli: Pamukkale Üniversitesi Fen Edebiyat Fakültesi Tarih Bölümü Yayınları, 2006), 561–79. We do not know precisely how many women were fined in the province of Denizli in total. A news report in a Bursa newspaper mentions that more than a hundred women were fined in a few months by the city council. 'Çarşaflar Kalkıyor', *Hakkın Sesi*, 10 October 1935.

52. For an example from Trabzon, see 'Çarşafların yasağı hakkında Belediye Riyasetinden', *Halk*, 30 April 1936.

53. 'Bergama'da Çarşaf, Peçe ve Kıvraklar Kaldırılıyor', *Anadolu*, 6 December 1934.

54. For example, in Aydın such actions by the police were reported in letters of complaint. See the telegraph by Dokumacı Ahmet Şevki to President Atatürk, EGM 13216-7/1, 16 August 1935.

55. From the Deputy Governor of Kastamonu to the Ministry of the Interior, EGM 13216-7/1, 30 July 1935.

Tahsin, through the general directorate of security, complaining that in Tosya, a district of the province of Kastamonu, the gendarmerie had forcefully removed some women's *peçe* and *çarşaf* in the streets.[56] The letter stated that because of this, the people of the district were offended. Having received this complaint, the Ministry of the Interior asked both the governor of Kastamonu and the General Directorate of Gendarmerie to report on the issue.[57] The governor of Kastamonu replied by assuring the minister that the decision of the municipality of Tosya had been put into practice with the help of state officials and the enlightened citizens of the town, and that no action by the municipal police was needed and no complaint had been received. The city council of Tosya, the governor added, had made this decision regarding the *peçe* and the *çarşaf* based on the circular of the ministry on 22 July 1935. According to the governor, only some prostitutes who were registered with the municipal police and continued to wear the *peçe* and the *çarşaf* were called to the police station and warned to not to wear such uncivilized clothes; he made the claim that no 'honourable women' were harassed by the gendarmerie.[58]

Such cases suggest that Ankara was well aware of the actions of the local authorities and tried to limit them but could not get them fully under control. This may hint at the limited capacity of the regime to coordinate such campaigns. It may also suggest that, particularly in cases like the anti-veiling campaigns of the 1930s in which the policy guidelines of the central government were loose and ambiguous, disagreements both among the elite in Ankara and between Ankara and the provinces tended to come to the surface, creating an ambiguous situation in terms of how to turn a reform ideal into reality. Because of this ambiguity, some local administrators experienced difficulty in their attempts to promote unveiling while balancing the concerns mentioned by Ankara and the demands of locals. The governor of Sinop, for example, asked for the guidance of the minister of the interior because some members of the local RPP branch and the municipal council of Sinop were insisting on a council ruling to ban the *çarşaf*, while the governor was concerned that this would go against the instructions in the circulars coming from Ankara:

> Based on the circular of the high authority of the ministry, we have been trying to handle this issue through encouragement, inculcation and propaganda instead

---

56. From Second Commissioner Tahsin to the General Directorate of Security, EGM 13216-7/1, 21 August 1935.

57. From the Ministry of the Interior to the Governorship of Kastamonu, EGM 13216-7/1, 14 September 1935; To the General Directorate of Gendarmerie, EGM 13216-7/1, 24 September 1935. For another example of a complaint letter, sent from Ödemiş in 1937, a district of the province of Izmir, reporting on women who were mistreated by the gendarmerie for wearing the *çarşaf*, see Yılmaz, *Becoming Turkish*, 127–8. It is also stated in the letter that in Tire, another district centre close to Ödemiş, soldiers were tearing off and throwing away women's headscarves (*yazma*) that were 'no bigger than the palm of your hand'.

58. From the Governor of Kastamonu to the Ministry of the Interior, EGM 13216-7/1, 17 October 1935.

of issuing rulings and orders, and to bring it about as progress emerging from our women's own will; we have not abstained from working towards creating the opportunities for our women to adopt the style and form of clothing that women in large cities have already generally adopted. Although we have achieved some results, the *çarşaf* is still being used because of the impact of old traditions, and those local women who had come to the municipality wearing overcoats during the last elections have again begun wearing the *çarşaf*. Thus, some [members of the local party branch and the municipal council] are claiming that this issue should be handled by issuing a ruling and making the removal of the *çarşaf* compulsory, following the example of the ruling the Provincial Council had issued several years ago for the abandonment of the *peçe*. I am in need of – and ready for – your guidance regarding the situation and for the meeting of the Provincial Council.[59]

What seems clear is that the central government's lack of clear guidelines on how to eliminate the *peçe* and the *çarşaf* significantly increased the space of action for the local elite. They were in a position to choose the mechanisms by which people would be mobilized and how they would be 'convinced' or 'inculcated', and they were also free to decide on how new forms of dress and gender relations would be promoted. For example, the governor of Maraş organized a meeting for forty-three state officials from the province of Maraş and nearby provinces whose wives were wearing the *peçe* and the *çarşaf*.[60] He 'convinced' these state officials at the meeting to persuade their wives to stop wearing the *peçe* and the *çarşaf* and thus be good examples for the rest of the community. Ten days later, he organized a tea and dancing event at the People's House where forty-one of these state officials participated with their wives, who were wearing 'civilized' clothing without veils.[61] The news that the local state officials (*yerli memurlar*) of Maraş had kept their promise to the governor and attended the tea party with their unveiled wives even made it to the national newspapers.[62] As the case of Maraş shows, minor state officials who were locals of the cities in which they were living and working were under particular pressure from provincial administrators.

In some cases, the members of city councils, local party branches and People's Houses were coordinated in an effort to support unveiling. In Antalya, for example, mobilization against the *peçe* and the *çarşaf* had in fact increased even before the deputy governor of the city wrote to the interior ministry, and this was predominantly carried out with the involvement of the local party and People's

---

59. From the Governor of Sinop to the Ministry of the Interior, EGM 13216-7/1, 4 March 1935. I was unable to find anything concerning the reply of the ministry. However, the city council of Sinop banned the *çarşaf* in September 1935.

60. From the Governor of Maraş to the Ministry of the Interior, EGM 13216-7/1, 28 October 1935.

61. From the Governor of Maraş to the Ministry of the Interior, EGM 13216-7/1, 7 November 1935.

62. See 'Maraşta çarşaf ve peçe kalkıyor', *Cumhuriyet*, 9 November 1935.

House elites. The party branch organized a tea party on 13 September 1934, specifically with the aim of 'encouraging women to engage in social activities'.[63] At the tea party, the head of the party branch, Şerafettin Bey, gave a speech in which he explained the duties of the 'enlightened' women of Antalya, one of which was to eliminate the *peçe* and *çarşaf* mentality.[64] This first initiative was followed by a meeting at the Antalya People's House to discuss the *peçe* and the *çarşaf* issue.[65] Three days later, a committee was drawn up and tasked with doing away with the *peçe* and the *çarşaf* by the female members of the Antalya People's House.[66] In Siirt, after state officials decided to eliminate the *peçe*, women who stopped wearing the *peçe* were invited, along with their husbands, to a special movie screening organized by the People's House. In the province of Çankırı, efforts to create mixed-gender environments where unveiled women could participate materialized in the form of a New Year's celebration at the People's House; members of the House were expected to come with their wives and daughters without their *peçe* and *çarşaf*.[67] In Kayseri, a tea party was hosted by the mayor, Nazmi Toker, and the members of the city council were expected to participate with their wives.[68] In other cities as well, activities that were associated with 'modern' social life and aimed at increasing women's participation in public life were organized on a more regular basis.[69]

---

63. 'Bu akşamki çay', *Antalya*, 13 September 1934.

64. 'Fırkamızın çay gecesi', *Antalya*, 20 September 1934.

65. 'Halkevinde dün akşamki toplantı', *Antalya*, 20 December 1934.

66. 'Antalyada çarşaf ve peçelerle mücadele başladı', *YeniAsır*, 23 December 1934; 'Antalyada kafesler ve çarşaflar yasak edildi', *Yeni Asır*, 14 February 1935. The city council of Antalya banned the *peçe*, the *çarşaf* and the *kafes* on 12 February 1935. See 'Kent Kurultayının Bir Kararı', *Antalya*, 16 February 1935. According to the decision, all *kafes*s had to be removed by the end of February, while for the removal of the *peçe* and the *çarşaf*, women had time until the end of April. 'Antalya belediyesi de peçe, çarşafların kaldırılmasına karar verdi', *Halk*, 14 February 1935.

67. 'Çankırıda peçe çarşafların atılması kararlaştırıldı', *YeniAsır*, 1 January 1935. The governor of Çankırı was reporting in November 1935 that thanks to the decision of the municipal council, there remained no problem called the *peçe* and the *çarşaf* problem in Çankırı and all women had happily adopted 'civilized' clothes. From the Governor of Çankırı to the Ministry of the Interior, EGM 13216-7/1, 4 November 1935. However, four years later, the same governor would complain about conservatism and religious fanaticism for the inability of most of women of Çankırı to adopt modern clothing, except for the families of state officials. See Metinsoy, 'Everyday Resistance'.

68. 'Kayseride soysallık savaşı', *Cumhuriyet*, 3 December 1934. In Kayseri, the *peçe* and the *çarşaf* would be banned in the entire province of Kayseri in September 1935. 'Kayseri ve Çermikte de Çarşaf Kalktı', *Cumhuriyet*, 16 September 1935.

69. For example, in the province of Trabzon, the People's House decided to organize a tea party every two weeks starting from the beginning of December, 1934. 'Çaylı Dans', *Halk*, 10 December 1934. The members of the Trabzon sport clubs also decided to organize a special night where all members would attend with their family members. 'Erginler yurdunda', *Halk*, 19 March 1936.

Local elites also played a leading role in efforts to help women adapt to the new dress codes. In some cities, local institutions and associations, such as the local branches of the Turkish Red Crescent Society (*Kızılay*), provided poor families with overcoats.[70] In Trabzon, a special committee was formed with the collaboration of the People's House, the municipality, the Red Crescent, the RPP and the Chamber of Commerce for the same purpose.[71] In Maraş, the People's House distributed a hundred and fifty overcoats to poor women.[72] In Antalya, a similar committee was established under the authority of the provincial council to help women in need.[73] The committee helped women convert their *çarşaf* into overcoats, and if this was not possible because of the fabric of the *çarşaf*, the committee helped them obtain a new one. The head of the committee was the wife of the city's governor and she led the efforts every day at the party office where the committee worked. The committee also tried to collect money from charitable donors to help poor women and to cover sewing expenses. In Akşehir, a district of the province of Konya, tailors assiduously sewed overcoats when the party inspector visited the city at the peak of mobilization for the elimination of the *peçe* and the *çarşaf*.[74] Similarly, in Soma, a district in the province of Manisa, tailors sewed overcoats day and night after the city council banned the *çarşaf* and the *peştamal*.[75]

In the relatively wide space of action they enjoyed on the issue of anti-veiling campaigns, some local elites tended to follow a more gradual strategy, while trying to convince the centre that they had taken all the necessary measures to promote unveiling. For instance, in Çorum, the *peçe* was banned by a municipal decision. In order to do away with the *çarşaf*, however, a gradual approach was adopted. Like the governor of Maraş, the governor of Çorum had first tried to mobilize minor officials who were locals in the province and he gave them a certain period of time to adopt the new dress codes.[76] At the end of this period, on 15 September 1935 he organized a meeting at the People's House to which all minor officials were invited with their female family members who had now replaced their *çarşaf* with overcoats.[77] In the meantime, after having carefully observed public reactions to

70. See 'Kızılay fakirlere 50 manto dağıttı', *Halk*, 30 April 1936; 'Kızılay bugün 150 manto daha dağıtıyor', *Halk*, 4 May 1936; 'Kızılay mantoları dağıttı', *Halk*, 11 May 1936. See also BCA 490.01/17.88.1

71. See 'Halkeviçok fakir ailelere Manto yaptıracak', *Halk*, 27 February 1936. See also 'C.H. Partisi 100 Manto dağıtacak', *Halk*, 11 May 1936; 'Bugün 119 Manto daha dağıtılacak', *Halk*, 1 June 1936.

72. Letter from the RPP Maraş Administration to RPP Secretariat General, BCA 490.01/17.88.1, 10 January 1936.

73. 'Kentimizde kadın kılığı işi bütün hızıyla yürüyor', *Antalya*, 2 May 1935.

74. See 1935 Report of Adnan Menderes, deputy of Aydın, BCA 490.1/618.27.1, 2 December 1935.

75. 'Somada çarşaf ve peçe kalktı', *Cumhuriyet*, 10 September 1935.

76. From the Governor of Çorum to the Ministry of the Interior, EGM 13216-7/1, 20 August 1935.

77. From the Governor of Çorum to the Ministry of the Interior, EGM 13216-7/1, 16 September 1935.

mobilization against the *çarşaf*, he then invited the leading members of the local party branch and the municipality to a joint meeting. At the meeting, there were some who argued that people should be given six months to stop wearing the *çarşaf* because of economic reasons. However, others insisted that it needed to be handled sooner, and because of this pressure, the municipality banned the use of the *çarşaf* starting on 29 October 1935, the Republic Day. The governor also informed the ministry that they had not heard from the district capitals yet, but it should be considered as natural that they would follow the provincial capital on the issue of unveiling. Writing to the minister of the interior on 22 November 1935, a month after the ban on the *çarşaf* was put into practice, the governor reported that because women were under the influence of a long tradition of conservatism and a backward mentality, progress would be achieved gradually:

> Since the population of the city of Çorum is small, moral and traditional principles have taken on unique and personal importance. This has put women under the pressure of *şekilperestlik* [importance attached to outward appearance] and made it difficult for them to act according to their personal beliefs and initiatives. Official intervention and action have been considered necessary and appropriate to fight against this social pressure and to empower free thinking and personal initiative. And as a result of official control and implementations, the majority of women have stopped wearing the *çarşaf*. However, it is not possible to deny that one can encounter older or poor women wearing the *çarşaf*, thereby disobeying the ban, in some neighbourhoods. It is necessary to consider it just a matter of time that these women will also feel an obligation to comply and adopt the new styles. Village women who have been using the *çarşaf* in the remote parts of the city and at the markets are now coming to the city centre having abandoned the *çarşaf*. In the districts of the province, the *peçe* has been abandoned, but true success could not be attained in the complete elimination of the *çarşaf*. Without a doubt the initiative in the province centre has had an impact on the district capitals. The results of forcing a change, however, could result in the adoption of strange forms of clothing. The belief in and insistence on covering the head would play a major role in the emergence of such results. Without a doubt, gossip that comes about as the result of quick adaptation to new forms of clothing would slowly lose their impact, and a normal state of affairs would arise. This is because repeating something results in a change of manners, and stability would ensue in the emergence of tradition.[78]

Thus, the governor was in fact laying the groundwork for the acceptance of a slower pace of transformation in the province of Çorum, a sluggishness brought on by poverty and the strongly conservative character of the community. Likewise, the governor of Kırklareli also informed the minister of the interior and the inspector general of the Thrace Region that all state officials and their families had

---

78. From the Governor of Çorum to the Ministry of the Interior, EGM 13216-7/1, 22 November 1935.

stopped wearing *peçe* and *çarşaf* in the centre of the province, but in the district capitals and villages it was reported that only a small number of women could start wearing overcoats because of a lack of financial means.[79] Although they had stopped wearing the *peçe*, some of them continued to wear the *çarşaf* because it was expensive to get an overcoat. Therefore, the governor added, although the situation was being closely observed, it would be managed slowly. There was a similar situation in the province of Sivas. As the governor reported, the women of Sivas had easily and happily abandoned the *peçe* by themselves but the total elimination of the *çarşaf* was more difficult and necessitated further efforts.[80] It would be managed, the governor claimed, in a short period of time.

This tendency to lower the expectations of Ankara and to be content with gradual change might also be related to the fact that the circulars of Ankara were mainly concerned with and insisted on the modernization of the clothing of state officials and their families. Thus, in their reports to the centre, some local administrators emphasized the adoption of 'modern clothing' by state officials and the success they achieved on this matter, deliberately without mentioning the reactions of the general public and the possible impacts this change had on the clothing of ordinary citizens. The governor of Diyarbakır, a predominantly Kurdish province in the Southeast Turkey, reported, for instance, that the wives and close relatives of state officials were increasingly abandoning the *peçe* and *çarşaf* and starting to adopt 'civilized' clothing, and it was noted that they were happy to join public meetings wearing new styles of clothing.[81] The report of the governor, however, did not include any information regarding the attitudes of the rest of the population of Diyarbakır regarding this significant change.

Some local elite, on the other hand, presented a very positive picture. There was in fact a fairly common tendency among provincial administrators to represent the anti-veiling campaign in their cities as a total success and an effort that was embraced by the general public, especially the women of the city. This positive image regarding the results of the anti-veiling campaigns was reinforced by local newspapers as well. 'The women happily welcomed the decision of the city council' was a quite common expression attached to news reports about the bans on the *peçe* and the *çarşaf*. Some local newspapers were clearly taking this to extremes by making the claim that the total abandonment of veils was achieved overnight. On

---

79. From the Governor of Kırklareli to the Ministry of the Interior, EGM 13216-7/1, 27 September 1935.

80. From the Governor of Sivas to the Ministry of the Interior, EGM 13216-7/1, 3 September 1935.

81. From the Governor of Diyarbakır to the Ministry of the Interior, EGM 13216-7/1, 23 August 1935. The anti-veiling campaign in Diyarbakır had begun with an initiative of the members of the People's House in December 1934. News reports then was claiming that this initiative was celebrated by the women of the city. See 'D. Bekir Halkevi üyeleri kendi ailelerinin çarşaf ve peçelerini kaldırdılar', *Halk*, 24 December 1934. It should be noted that the governor was not mentioning such a compliance by ordinary women, and thus the news was probably exaggerating the situation.

1 July 1934, a local newspaper, *Yeni Mersin*, reported on the beginning of a *çarşaf* ban in Mersin, informing readers how easily and willingly the new ban had been accepted by the people of the city.[82] The *peçe* ban had begun twenty days earlier than the *çarşaf* ban, and so the newspaper claimed that not even a single woman had faced charges because of non-compliance. It was also noted that almost half of the women had already stopped wearing the *çarşaf* right after the council made its decision, without waiting for the ban to be put into practice. Claiming that the decision to ban the *peçe* and *çarşaf* had emerged from public demand in the city, the most significant sign of which was women's willingness to remove their veils, the newspaper announced 1 July as a 'day of liberty for the women of Mersin'. The next day, only one day after the *çarşaf* ban went into effect, *Yeni Mersin* announced the total disappearance of the *çarşaf* in Mersin.[83]

Likewise, on 2 May 1935, the local newspaper *Antalya* informed its readers that the campaign against the *peçe* and the *çarşaf* in the city of Antalya was continuing with great success, and that women's willingness to abide by the decision to abandon veils, despite the financial difficulties they faced, was worthy of appreciation.[84] The report of the party inspector, Adnan Menderes, on Antalya at the end of 1935 in fact confirmed the accounts provided by the newspaper. He indicated in his report that the *peçe* and the *çarşaf* had been abandoned in the city quite easily, without reactions or gossip, and that this could be interpreted as a lack of opposition to the revolution.[85] Türkân Baştuğ, one of the few female members of parliament and a deputy of Antalya, also reported on 27 November 1935 that the issue of veiling, 'which divides life into two spheres', had been settled, especially in the city centre of Antalya, as well as in some district capitals. She said that she had seen no veiled women in the city centre and reported that women were living a normal life together with men in the public sphere.[86]

Such reports by party inspectors and deputies indicate the state of the anti-veiling campaigns and the attitudes of local elites; and in this way, the regime had some means to monitor what was going on at the local level. However, inspectors were not specifically asked to report on the issue. In other words, we do not come across information about the anti-veiling campaigns in all reports. Rather, many of the governors reported to the minister of the interior after receiving his circular on 22 June 1935, and almost all of them reported a very positive picture. These reports by province governors shared a language that was strikingly similar,

---

82. 'Kadın Umacı Değildir', *Yeni Mersin*, 1 July 1934.

83. 'Çarşaflı kadına rastlanmıyor', *Yeni Mersin*, 2 July 1934.

84. 'Kentimizde kadın kılığı işi bütün hızıyla yürüyor', *Antalya*, 2 May 1935.

85. 1935 Report of Adnan Menderes, deputy of Aydın, BCA 490.1/618.27.1, 2 December 1935. For example, in the Korkuteli and Serik districts of the province of Antalya, where Menderes saw no trace of fanaticism or reactions to the revolution, the issue of the *peçe* and the *çarşaf* was reportedly easily settled. He characterized these districts as free of religious reactionaries because of the lack of a *medrese* tradition and the influence of religious hodjas.

86. Report of Türkân Baştuğ, deputy of Antalya, BCA 490.1/618.28.1, 27 November 1935.

usually repeating the same phrases used in the circulars coming from Ankara when referring to the *peçe* and the *çarşaf*. In other words, they were responding to Ankara by using Ankara's own language. Apart from these very similar introductions, the governors were assuring Ankara that the necessary measures had been taken, but they would very rarely explain in detail what those measures were, nor would they give detailed reports about how they were being put into practice. Moreover, as with some local newspapers, some governors also tended to exaggerate the success of the anti-veiling campaigns in their provinces. The governor of Afyon, for example, informed the ministry that a week after the ban on the *peçe* and the *çarşaf* was put into place, 90 per cent of women, who until then had always worn such veils, complied.[87] The governor of Giresun reported that the *çarşaf* was banned in the city and noted that women were very happy about the decision and were in full compliance.[88] The deputy governor of Balıkesir also reported how easily the abandonment of the *peçe* and the *çarşaf* had been accepted by the people of the province, and at liberation day celebrations held in the province capital on 7 September 1935, it was reported that there was not even a single woman wearing a veil among the thousands who gathered in the streets and squares.[89] In Çanakkale, the governor reported that propaganda efforts had been successful; he stated that in the province and district capitals, most of the women had begun wearing overcoats, following the example of the families of state officials, and in the villages, women had made their own overcoats.[90] In Kars, it was reported that 'a small signal' given by the governorship of the province was enough to achieve total success; the *çarşaf* was reportedly eliminated altogether without provoking gossip or discontent (*sızıltı*), meaning that it led to no discussions or opposition and appeared to be a natural transformation.[91]

Some governors tended to represent this success as a result of their own diligent efforts. The governor of Maraş, for example, regularly sent reports to the Ministry of the Interior from mid-1935 onwards explaining how his efforts resulted in a smooth transformation of women's clothing in a province which, in his words, had been held back by entrenched conservatism. On 13 August 1935, the governor informed the ministry that the women of Maraş were very bound to tradition and he noted that the first thing that caught his attention when he was appointed to the province was the *çarşaf* and the thick *peçe* women wore.[92] Five months later,

87. From the Governor of Afyon to the Ministry of the Interior, EGM 13216-7/1, 13 November 1935.

88. From the Governor of Giresun to the Ministry of the Interior, EGM 13216-7/1, 15 September 1936.

89. From the Deputy Governor of Balıkesir to the Ministry of the Interior, EGM 13216-7/1, 6 September 1935.

90. From the Governor of Çanakkale to the Ministry of the Interior, EGM 13216-7/1, 21 March 1936.

91. From the Governor of Kars to the Ministry of the Interior, EGM 13216-7/1, 27 April 1936.

92. Letter from the Governor of Maraş to the Ministry of the Interior, EGM 13216-7/1, 13 August 1935.

on 3 January 1936, he reported that all women in the capital of the province had stopped wearing the *peçe* and *çarşaf* thanks to the anti-veiling campaign.[93]

As mentioned in the previous chapter, the general secretary of the RPP had also asked local branches of the party to report on the situation regarding the anti-veiling campaigns. Like the governors, local party administrators rarely mentioned obstacles, problems or hesitation regarding the process. On 5 November 1935, the head of the party branch in Maraş, for example, informed the general secretary that together with the governor of the city he had explained the necessity of reforming women's clothing to the members of the city council and they all willingly agreed and signed a ruling that banned the *peçe* and the *çarşaf.* Such veils were to be abandoned in Maraş by 1 January. Writing on 10 January about the result of the ban, he reported, like the governor of Maraş, that it had been successfully implemented and that not a single woman went onto the streets or into the markets of Maraş wearing the *peçe* or *çarşaf* anymore, and he added that the *çarşaf* had been replaced by overcoats.[94]

The effect of the anti-veiling campaign in Maraş, however, was in fact very limited. In 1936, the party inspector reported that even the leading families of the city seemed to be unwilling to abide by the decision to ban the *peçe* and the *çarşaf,* linking this attitude to the same one that had arisen a decade earlier in response to the hat reform:

> No reactionary tendencies or counter-revolutionary activities are discernible. While there are people who curse their fellow townsmen for blackening the name of their hometown because they were formerly condemned for their opposition to the hat, there are also people who think that those who were condemned were ignorant and naïve, and that the opposition [to the hat] was overplayed. What is certain, however, is that the people are extremely religious (*koyu bir tassup içinde*) and even the wealthy people of today acquired their wealth by appearing religious (*mutassıp görünmekle*). As it was the rich, even the members of the administrative board of the party, who were the last people to start wearing the hat back then, today they are still the same rich families who continue to wear the *peçe* and the *çarşaf* because of the same concern [for appearing religious].[95]

According to another report written in 1940, in Maraş, aside from two or three exceptions, women from families that were supposedly liberal and young-minded were wearing long overcoats that hung to their heels and carried umbrellas to conceal themselves day and night. There were even women from upper-class families who did not go out at all, or visited the hamam and their neighbours only

---

93. Report of the Governor of Maraş to the Ministry of the Interior, EGM 13216-7/1, 3 January 1936.

94. From RPP Maraş Administration to RPP Secretariat General, BCA 490.01/17.88.1, 10 January 1936.

95. 1936 Report of Şevket Ödül, deputy of Kırklareli, BCA 490.01/686.328.1, 2 November 1936.

at night, regardless of how enlightened their families were.[96] In 1943, the party inspector reported that the only female member of the local party administration, Nuriye Bülbül, was seen in a negative light by the religious residents of the city because she was the first woman to abandon the *çarşaf* in Maraş, but he also mentioned that she played an important role in the anti-veiling campaign by doing so.[97]

As the documents discussed so far reveal, the Ministry of the Interior was the main actor in Ankara that tried to control and monitor the anti-veiling campaigns in the provinces. Accordingly, the governors, the primary addressees of the circulars sent out by the ministry, seem to have been quite influential in the process. This is also partly because of their high visibility in the archives. Governors were of course the representatives of the central authority and they were appointed administrators who were not natives of the provinces they governed. As such, it can be questioned to what extent they can be seen as 'local' actors. However, the examples analysed above indicate that even these appointed 'outsiders' were far from being a monolithic group that simply acted as transmitters of central policies. Some of them surpassed the limits drawn by orders from the government, while others merely acted as though they had fully implemented Ankara's decisions. Thus, even if they were at the heart of the state structure, governors were in possession of the capacity to act as local agents in the provinces. A more complex and diverse picture emerges regarding the role of the local elite when we peer deeper into the local context. Since the anti-veiling campaigns, or at least the bans on the *peçe* and the *çarşaf*, were initiated by city councils, municipalities appear to have been major institutions in the negotiation and domestication of reforms. Moreover, the members of local party administrations and the People's Houses could equally play a role, depending on the way the anti-veiling campaign was organized in a given locality. In particular, the city councils included quite diverse actors: locals and non-locals, professionals, merchants, hardline Kemalists, more hesitant moderates and even conservatives. It was generally at council meetings where firm opposition and the unwillingness of some local elites regarding the anti-veiling campaigns surfaced most.

One main conflict that emerged in a number of city councils concerned issuing an outright ban on veils, as some members openly resisted the idea. In Alanya, for example, a district of the province of Antalya, a debate arose among the members of the municipal council about whether the municipality should issue a ban on the *peçe* and the *çarşaf*. As party inspector Adnan Menderes reported, some members of the council rejected the idea by arguing that the municipality should not intervene in the matter and that they had no right to interfere with the desires of the people as regards their attire.[98] As a result, the municipal council of Alanya only mentioned

96. Copy of the Report of Mitat Aydın, deputy of Trabzon, BCA 490.01/612.125.2, 12 June 1940.

97. Copy of the Report of Mitat Aydın, deputy of Trabzon, BCA 490.01/273.1091.2, 7 May 1943.

98. 1935 Report of Party Inspector Adnan Menderes, BCA 490.1/618.27.1, 2 December 1935.

that 'the municipality would encourage the abandonment of the *peçe* and the *çarşaf*, which the inspector characterized as being vague and meaningless.[99] Kâmil Kemal, a member of the council and the party administration in Alanya, opposed this and attached an annotation. The district governor of Alanya had also intervened by revising the decision. Although there is no sufficient information concerning the result of this attempt, it seems that pro-regime members of city councils played an active role in trying to reach conclusive decisions on the issue at council meetings. In cases where they were ineffective or there was reluctance to reach a decision, governors and local party administrators became involved in convincing the council members accordingly. In Mersin as well, some people opposed the idea of banning the *peçe* and the *çarşaf*, arguing that it would be very difficult to apply such a ban and that the matter should be handled with a gradual approach.[100]

In some cases, the local elite also debated whether city councils actually had the right to ban the *peçe* and the *çarşaf*. The city council of Bergama, for example, decided to form a committee to investigate the municipal law. Having come to the conclusion that municipalities had the legal capacity to issue such bans, the city council of Bergama eventually banned the *peçe* and the *çarşaf*.[101] It seems that a similar debate had arisen in the Ereğli district of the province of Konya. In Ereğli, the *peçe* and the *çarşaf* were banned by the municipality in April 1935. In August, a Konya-based newspaper reported that all women in the distinct capital had replaced their *çarşaf* with overcoats.[102] The party inspector had visited Ereğli around the same time. In December 1935, while he reported that he did not see any visible opposition to the party in general, he said that he had heard that there was talk in the town about whether the municipality indeed had the right to ban the *peçe* and the *çarşaf*.[103]

In the Hadim district of the province of Konya, opposition came from within the RPP itself, revealing that even in the party structure opposing views existed. The party inspector's report mentioned that the local party president in Hadim had complained about the difficulties he faced while trying to ban the *peçe* and the *çarşaf* because of the opposition of the 'fanatically-minded' (*softa kafalı*) members of the local party administration.[104] While they appeared to be supportive of the decision, when it came to implementing the anti-veiling campaign, they were likely unwilling to encourage the women of Hadim to abandon their veils or promote regime ideals. This example confirms Lamprou's suggestion that as one moves downwards from the provincial to sub-provincial level, the composition of

---

99. Menderes also reported that there were regressive-minded (*geri kafalı*) people in Alanya and that the mayor was particularly so with his old agha mentality (*eski ve ağa kafalı*). See Ibid.

100. 'Mersin'in başardığı iki mühim iş', *Yeni Mersin*, 18 July 1934.

101. See 'Bergama'da Çarşaf, Peçe ve Kıvraklar Kaldırılıyor', *Anadolu*, 6 December 1934.

102. 'İlçe ve şehir haberleri', *Balıkık*, 10 August 1935.

103. 1935 Report of the Party Inspector Adnan Menderes, BCA 490.1/618.27.1, 2 December 1935.

104. Ibid.

the party cadres overlaps more with the social structure at large; hence even within the party structure there were people who opposed regime policies or were at least unwilling to actively promote them.[105]

Another striking example that shows how the anti-veiling campaigns were in fact shaped by power struggles among local elites who were part of different institutions is the case of Seyitgazi, a district of the province of Eskişehir. In Seyitgazi, the municipality had banned the *peçe* and the *çarşaf*, but this decision created discontent in the city. As the governor of Eskişehir reported to the Ministry of the Interior, negative sentiment about the municipal ban and the 'overcoat incident' was voiced not just by ordinary people, but also by elites participating in local politics.[106] Some neighbourhood delegates (*mahalle mümessilleri*) had wanted to prepare a report requesting that implementation of the ban be postponed. Moreover, some members of the city council had held a secret meeting to discuss the possibility of organizing a vote of no confidence for the mayor. Ahmet Akalın, a member of the council, wrote a notice to the district governorship stating that Mehmet Özdemir, with whom he was at odds, was carrying out such secret activities. Based on this notice and queries made by the police (*kaza zabıtası*), an investigation was launched. What is important here is that Mehmet Özdemir was not only a member of the city council, but also the president of the Seyitgazi branch of the RPP. In addition, the head of the local branch of the Turkish Aviation Society (*Tayyare Cemiyeti*), Mustafa Özdemir, who was probably from the same family, was also among the accused. Mehmet Özdemir's brother, a grocer named Veli, was also on the list. Thus, if the accusations were correct, some prominent members of the local elite, who were locals, including the head of the local party branch, were part of the 'movement' against the anti-veiling campaign. Even if they were not against it ideologically, they were at least taking advantage of the social discontent that emerged as an opportunity to challenge the mayor by a vote of no confidence. Although the governor informed the ministry that no movement was detected as a result of the secret investigation, a list of thirteen people, including the head of the RPP branch and his relatives, was turned over to the court for further investigation.[107]

Some members of the local elite informed Ankara when there was reluctance in the implementation of the anti-veiling campaign in their provinces, as they saw this as an opportunity to prove their loyalty to the regime. On 1 June 1936, an official from the 4th Bureau of the Directorate of the Police in Gaziantep, a certain Mr. Yazıcıoğlu, stated that, as a diligent official who took pride in his work, he wanted to forward to the General Director of the Police information he had received. He reported that there had been talk among the people of the province

---

105. Lamprou, *Nation Building*, 61–5.

106. Letter from the Governor of Eskişehir to the Ministry of the Interior, EGM 13216-7/1, 7 February 1936.

107. Unfortunately, there is no further correspondence in the file regarding the result of the trial.

of Gaziantep about the attitude of the governor regarding the issue of unveiling.[108] According to his letter, the governor had initially wanted to act firmly for the abandonment of the *çarşaf*, but stepped back from his initial position because of threatening letters he had received. The governor, according to this official, had left the people free to make up their own minds on the matter. Having received this letter, the minister of the interior wrote directly to the governor of Gaziantep asking whether this information was true and whether he had given the people the right to decide for themselves. The minister also demanded an urgent report from the governor about the measures and efforts that were being carried out on the matter in his province.[109] This shows that the attitude of the central elite in Ankara had changed considerably if they sensed a possibility of opposition or reluctance on the side of the local administrators. In such cases, Ankara preferred to act more assertively, favouring direct involvement mainly by putting pressure on governors or by having inspectors general intervene. The case of Gaziantep also shows that disagreements among the local elite and their rivalries for the approval of the centre had an impact on the course of the campaigns.

The case of Trabzon is perhaps one of the best examples illustrating the tensions that existed between local actors. It clearly shows the ways in which the anti-veiling campaigns were shaped at the local level through the struggles and negotiations of the local elite, and how Ankara intervened in these conflicts and competition if their outcomes were not in line with its expectations and if the tensions could result in a backlash. In Trabzon, the anti-veiling campaign first got underway with propaganda in local newspapers that started in October 1934, followed by a petition submitted by members of the youth and sports clubs, led by a youth club, the Trabzon Home for Adolescents (*Erginler Yurdu*), to the city council requesting a ban on the use of the *peçe* and the *çarşaf* in February 1935.[110] Although the petition of the youth club was welcomed by the mayor and presented to the council for discussion, the first decision of the council was to postpone the discussion until a report made by the administrative committee (*idare encümeni*) about the appropriateness of the proposal had been received.[111] At the next meeting of the council, however, the issue could not be discussed since there were not enough members present.[112] In fact, some members of the city council had

---

108. From Mr. Yazıcıoğlu to General Director of the Police Şükrü Sökmensüer, EGM 13216-7/1, 1 June 1936.

109. From the Minister of the Interior to the Governor of Gaziantep, EGM 13216-7/1, 9 June 1936.

110. 'Kadın Peçe Çarşaflarının kaldırılması hakkında erginler yurdu belediye meclizine muracaatediyor', *Halk*, 11 February 1935. A local newspaper in Izmir reported that it was *Trabzon İdman Yurdu* (a local youth and sports club in Trabzon) that had submitted the petition to the city council. 'Trabzon Kadınları da Çarşafları Atıyorlar', *Yeni Asır*, 16 February 1935.

111. Initially, it was expected that this would not take a long time. 'Belediye meclisi gençlerin teklifini kabul etti. Bugün mecliste kat'i karar verilecek', *Halk*, 14 February 1935.

112. 'Peçe ve çarşaf meselesinin konuşulması Nisan toplantısına kaldı', *Halk*, 18 February 1935.

opposed the idea by arguing that banning of the *peçe* and the *çarşaf* would be disgraceful for the city.[113] The sports clubs decided to submit the same petition to the provincial council in April 1935, most probably because of the reluctance of the city council and its desire to postpone the process.[114] It seems, however, that this move also did not yield the desired results, since at the April meeting of the provincial council the issue of the *peçe* and the *çarşaf* was not on the agenda.[115] Opposition in the city council continued for a year and opposing members were able to postpone the talks at the council meetings several times in order to prevent a decision from being made.[116] Meanwhile, in his reply to the circular sent by the secretary general of the party in October 1935, the head of the local party branch did not mention the council's opposition and merely indicated that the *peçe* had been eliminated in Trabzon. He noted that to eliminate the *çarşaf*, which only a few women still wore, he would consult the governor and they would put into place the necessary measures together.[117] In fact, the situation was quite different; the *peçe* had not disappeared and the *çarşaf* was still an issue. During this year, Trabzon-based newspapers published several articles, commentaries and news reports in an attempt to mobilize the people of the city, especially the women, to support the anti-veiling campaign by abandoning the *peçe* and the *çarşaf* and put pressure on the council to reach a decision. As mentioned earlier, some newspapers tried to use the discussion on the *peçe* and the *çarşaf* at the 4th Congress of the RPP in May in order to put pressure on members of the local party branch in Trabzon. A caption in the local newspaper *Halk* about the congress was emblematic of this strategy of forcing the Trabzon party elite to act: 'Members of the RPP promised to eliminate the *çarşaf* and the *peçe*.'[118]

The turning point in overcoming this resistance appears to have been the intervention of the local party administration. In October 1935, *Halk* reported that the administrative council of the Trabzon branch of the RPP and the party councils of the districts in the province had held a meeting at the local party office and discussed the measures that needed to be taken to eliminate the *peçe* and the *çarşaf* in Trabzon.[119] Local newspapers reported that the city council was expected to make a decision soon.[120] However, opposing delegates managed to get the issue postponed at the October and November meetings as well. In the end, under

113. 'Trabzon Gençliği', *İkbal*, 13 February 1935.

114. 'Çarşaf ve Peçeler', *Halk*, 18 April 1935.

115. 'Vilayet genel kurumu çalışmasını biterdi', *Halk*, 22 April 1935.

116. 'Belediye Meclisi', *Halk*, 4 April 1935; 'Belediye Meclisi Dağıldı', *Halk*, 16 May 1935; 'Belediye Meclisi', *Halk*, 23 September 1935. *Halk* claimed that it was the older members of the council who opposed the move.

117. From the head of the RPP Trabzon Administration to the RPP Secretariat General, BCA 490.01/17.88.1, 4 October 1935.

118. 'C.H.Parti üyeleri Çarşaf ve Peçelerin kaldırılmasına söz verdiler', *Halk*, 20 May 1935.

119. 'Peçe ve Çarşaf Meselesi', *Halk*, 17 October 1935.

120. 'Peçe ve Çarşaf Urayca Kaldırılıyor', *Halk*, 22 October 1935.

pressure from the local party administration and the governor, the city council of Trabzon banned the *peçe* and the *çarşaf* on 4 February 1936 with a majority decision (so some members still opposed the decision). 4 May was declared as the day the ban would go into effect.[121] As reported by a local newspaper, an official message about the banning of the *peçe* and the *çarşaf*, which was prepared by the local RPP administration (*CHP il yön. Kurul başkanlığı*) and co-signed by the provincial authority (*vilayet makamından tevdi edilen*) was approved to be put on the agenda by the city council.[122] In fact, the provincial council led by the governor was summoned for a general meeting on 1 February, two days before the regular meeting of the city council. Local newspapers had already reported a week earlier that the meetings would result in a ban on the *peçe* and the *çarşaf*.[123] It was thus clear that the local party branch and the governor had intervened in the process, and that was how a decision to ban the *peçe* and the *çarşaf* by the city council was secured in Trabzon. In fact, in the public declaration of the ban in local newspapers, mention was made of the fact that the decision of the city council had been approved by the governorship.[124] There are indications that the Trabzon RPP administration also followed up on the process after the declaration of the ban by the city council by issuing a notice for the entire party organization in the province of Trabzon and the People's House regarding the necessary measures that needed to be taken before the ban went into effect.[125] Based on this notice, the People's House administrative council decided to hold a general meeting which people were expected to attend with their family members.[126]

However, the tension regarding the anti-veiling campaign in the city probably had been felt in Ankara because the recently appointed inspector general of the region, Tahsin Uzer, took a firm stance and sought to make sure that the aims of the anti-veiling campaign were achieved. Towards the end of February, he mentioned the issue in a speech he delivered at the Trabzon People's House.[127] Having stressed that the *peçe* and the *çarşaf* could not have a place in a civilized Turkey, Uzer urged his audience to support the attempts of the Trabzon youth to 'civilize' the attire of Trabzon women so that they could become more active citizens. He argued that it was not a matter of women showing their faces but a means for women to use their social rights. In his speech he also asked members of the audience to convey this request to their sisters and daughters. Uzer's involvement in the process probably had an impact on other local actors and institutions. In fact, the announcement

---

121. 'Halkevinde Peçe ve Çarşaf mes'elesi görüşüldü', *Halk*, 26 March 1936.

122. 'Belediye Meclisi Peçe ve Çarşafın kaldırılmasına karar verdi', *Halk*, 6 February 1936.

123. 'Vilayet genel meclisi', *Halk*, 27 January 1936.

124. 'Peçe ve çarşafın yasağı hakkında sayın halkımıza ilan', *Halk*, 10 February 1936. This announcement was reprinted several times up through May.

125. 'C.H. Partısında', *Halk*, 26 March 1936.

126. 'Halkevinde peçe ve çarşaf meselesi görüşüldü', *Halk*, 26 March 1936; 'Halkevi aileli bir toplantı yapacak', *Halk*, 6 April 1936.

127. 'Halkevinde İnkılap konferansları', *Halk*, 24 February 1936.

of the local party administration mentioned above was probably a consequence of the pressure he was putting on the administration, or least a result of his influence. As the British Pro-Consul in Trabzon informed the British Embassy in Ankara in March 1936, Tahsin Uzer's main aim had in fact been to encourage 'modern' social life in Trabzon and especially to increase women's participation at the social activities organized and encouraged by the inspector general, and hence to fight against women's seclusion.[128] The inspector had criticized the failure of the Trabzon municipality to initiate a ban on the wearing of the *peçe* and the *çarşaf*, regretting that the ban had been delayed until 4 May. Inspector General Uzer also added that if he had been in Trabzon at the time he would not have permitted such a delay. The Pro-Consul also noted the plan of the inspector general to arrange an evening party to which only those renowned for their religious fanaticism would be invited along with their wives.

It seems, however, that the attitude of the inspector general increased tensions rather than alleviating them. A few weeks later, the British Pro-Consul reported to the embassy in Ankara that reactions against the anti-veiling campaign were on the rise in the city and that the mayor of Trabzon was receiving anonymous letters containing death threats. The wife of the mayor was attacked and other instances of violence also occurred because of the way the anti-veiling campaign was put into practice:

On April 13th the wife of the President of the Municipality was assaulted and injured in the street by a man who tore her dress and underclothes, calling them immoral. The police are now searching for the culprit who, if found, will, it is stated, be punished in an exemplary manner. It is reported that at Palatane [today's Akçaabat, a district of the province of Trabzon S.A.] a man killed a gendarme who according to the regulations obtaining there had forcibly removed his wife's veil. I understand that great animosity prevails locally against the municipality as a result of the decision regarding women's dress, and especially against the Third Inspector General and his staff who, owing to the conduct of most of them, are considered unfitted to the task of civilizing the region, being commonly referred as 'a band of debauchees'. I am informed that the recent visit of the Fleet to Trebizond and its surroundings was made with the object of cooling the reactionary feelings of the local population and of reminding them that force was behind the authorities.[129]

The case of Trabzon shows that local elites could be part of the opposition to the anti-veiling campaign and openly resist it by using their power, as exemplified by the efforts of some members of the Trabzon city council to block the council

---

128. Memorandum from British Pro-Consul in Trabzon to British Embassy in Ankara, FO 371/20087, 28 March 1936.

129. British consul in Trabzon to British Embassy in Ankara, FO371/20087, 16 April 1936.

meetings. It also shows, however, state reactions to such resistance and the ways it could put strong pressure on people with opposing views. In the case of opposition to the anti-veiling campaign, Ankara and all levels of the state administration were involved in the process.[130] However, despite this ideological determination and efforts to control and coordinate the campaigns, 'undesirable reactions' were not or could not be avoided, as was noted in the circulars of Ankara. The possibility of such tensions might have concerned many local administrators to the extent that even though a decision was made to eliminate the *peçe* and the *çarşaf* in some cities, its implementation was carried out rather reluctantly. For example, reporting from the Kadınhan district of the province of Konya in the fall of 1935, the party inspector indicated that no action had yet been taken on the issue of *peçe* and *çarşaf* despite the existence of a decision to abolish them.[131] Thus, both the efforts leading to an anti-veiling campaign and its implementation were complex processes, which were not and could not be determined by the orders coming from Ankara, nor they could be shaped solely by a particular group of elites such as state officials just because they were appointed, more powerful or educated. Their similarities and general characteristics notwithstanding, each anti-veiling campaign in 1930s Turkey was shaped by a complex matrix of dynamics on the ground.

It is also crucial to note that although the attitude of the local elite, which was a composite group in itself, was a very significant factor, it was not the only one. In other words, the local cannot be reduced to the attitude of the local elite and the ways in which they negotiated and domesticated the policies of Ankara either. Just like the central authority was one actor operating within the complexities of the local society, the local elites were also surrounded by the same complexities and had to act *in relation* to the attitudes and reactions of ordinary people. Hence, in addition to diversifying the concept of 'elite' by emphasizing the role of the local elite and the multiplicity of actors that compose the elite at the local level, the local also needs to be diversified. The role the non-elite actors and subordinated sectors of the society played should be analysed so that the diversity of the voices at the local level can be addressed.

Diversifying the local: Social opposition and resistance to anti-veiling campaigns

The general picture in terms of popular reactions to anti-veiling campaigns of the 1930s reveals that ordinary people followed relatively 'secure' strategies of resistance, confirming Hobsbawm's analysis that the subordinate classes are rather

---

130. The Inspectorship General of Trace was also active in controlling and coordinating the governors in his region. See Letter from the vice deputy inspector general of Thrace to the Ministry of the Interior, EGM 13216-7/1, 10 August 1935.

131. 1935 Report of Adnan Menderes, Deputy of Aydın, BCA 490.1/618.27.1, 2 December 1935.

more interested in 'working the system ... to their minimum disadvantage'.[132] The trouble these strategies of resistance created at the local level, particularly for the local authorities who had to deal with them on the ground, also reveals that such resistance was quite effective. The reactions, however, also reflect the diversity of possible responses to the policies of the state, which included engaging in negative propaganda and sending anonymous complaint letters. In fact, putting well-known rebellions and incidences aside, people largely refrained from organized, mass resistance to Kemalist reforms, and instead opted for comparatively safer and easier strategies, such as putting an anonymous letter on the door of a mosque or circulating gossip.[133] By doing so, they were at the same time involved in acts and expressed attitudes that went beyond passive resistance in their everyday experience; they could attempt to challenge, negotiate and influence the policies of the state.

Popular resistance to women's unveiling in fact predates the organized anti-veiling campaigns of the mid-1930s. Considering the increasing number of women, especially in big cities, who had 'modernized' their dress in some way since the late Ottoman times, combined with the earlier attempts of anti-veiling campaigns in the 1920s, it is predictable that reactions to this transformation would also follow. For example, in 1929, a preacher at the Büyük Mosque in Yozgat, Ethem Hoca, claimed during his sermon that unveiled women (*açık gezen kadınlar*) were prostitutes.[134] He was put on trial because of this provocative insult and other 'reactionary comments' he made. Apparently, he was also sent to court a year earlier for the same reason.[135] Such cases of religious-based opposition initiated by preachers or imams in the mosques continued in the 1930s, as well, and usually targeted the secularist policies of the regime, in general, categorized as opposition to regime in the official documents. However, in some reports, we see references to specific issues, such as women's unveiling. In May 1935, for example, at the

---

132. Eric Hobsbawm, 'Peasant and Politics', *Journal of Peasant Studies* 1, no. 1 (1973): 3–22. James Scott also suggests that 'such kinds of resistance are often the most significant and the most effective over the long run'. Scott, *Weapons*, xvi. For an analysis of the strategy of 'working the system' in the Ottoman/Turkish context, see Necmi Erdoğan, 'Devleti "İdare Etmek": Maduniyet ve Düzenbazlık', *Toplum ve Bilim* 83 (Winter 1999/2000): 8–31.

133. For examples of collective action to secular reforms, see Brockett, 'Collective Action'. For everyday forms of resistance, see Akın, 'Reconsidering State'; Alexandros Lamprou, '"CHP Genel Sekreterliği Makamına": 30'lu ve 40'lı Yıllarda Halkevleri'yle İlgili CHP'ye Gönderilen Şikayet ve Dilek Mektupları Hakkında Kısa Bir Söz', *Kebikeç* 23 (2007): 381–92; Cemil Koçak, *Tek-Parti Döneminde Muhalif Sesler* (Istanbul: İletişim, 2011).

134. Circular from the Minister of Interior to the Prime Ministry, BCA 030.10/102.668.8, 21 February 1929, quoted in Koçak, *Tek-Parti*, 232.

135. Koçak rightly indicates that such examples show the looseness of the regime rather than its rigidity; it was either considering it unnecessary to issue harsher punishments for these kinds of crimes, or was hesitant to do so. Koçak, *Tek-Parti*, 37–8.

peak of the anti-veiling campaigns all over the country, a certain Sheikh Musa was sent to court in Istanbul for criticizing the republican regime in his sermons. He was preaching against the regime's Westernizing policies, and particularly, its agenda to emancipate women and to remove the *çarşaf*.[136] Similarly, on 27 December 1935, in Mersin, a preacher by the name of Hadımlı Ahmet Hoca, told a crowd during his sermon at the Yeni Mosque that unveiled (*açık gezen*) women were shameless, and when they die, their funeral prayer should not be performed. Immediately, an investigation was launched into the case and Ahmet Hoca was arrested. Having heard of the incident, the Prime Ministry had felt the need to warn the Directorate of Religious Affairs. According to the Prime Ministry, the frequency of such examples demonstrated that the directorate was not careful enough when selecting preachers.[137]

In the absence of organized opposition, it seems that the most common way of resistance to anti-veiling campaigns was to engage in negative propaganda about women's unveiling. In addition to the preachers and imams, ordinary people were also involved in such propaganda activities. Rumour was the main way in which people tried to communicate their discontent and to decrease social support for, or at least compliance with, the anti-veiling campaigns. In the official communications between Ankara and various local actors in the provinces, as well, the fear of counter propaganda was in fact visible and such activities were usually mentioned as rumour or gossip. The phrases like 'there is no negative propaganda' or 'the *peçe* and the *çarşaf* have been removed without leaving any opportunity for discontent and gossip' or 'those with harmful ideas and aims were not allowed to act' were used by some governors in their reports, for example, probably to assure Ankara that they were successfully handling the threat of resistance.[138] In some cases, however, such propaganda activities against the anti-veiling campaigns were reported to Ankara by the local authorities. In the Seyitgazi district of the province of Eskişehir, for example, there were people who attempted to propagandize against the ban of the municipality on the *peçe* and the *çarşaf* by spreading the idea that unveiling was immoral and contrary to tradition. This was reported by the district governor of Seyitgazi to the governor of Eskişehir, who then forwarded the news to the Ministry of the Interior.[139] Having received the news, the ministry had asked the governor for the identities of those people and what measures had been taken

---

136. Caporal, *Kemalizmde*, 249.

137. For all correspondence between the Prime Ministry, the Directorate of Religious Affairs, the Ministry of Justice and the Office of the Public Prosecutor of Mersin, see BCA 030.10/26.151.7.

138. See Letter from the Governor of Sivas to the Ministry of the Interior, EGM 13216-7/1, 3 September 1935; Letter from the Governor of Yozgat to the Ministry of the Interior, EGM 13216-7/1, 12 November 1935; and from the Governor of Kars to the Ministry of the Interior, EGM 13216-7/1, 27 April 1936, respectively.

139. Letter from the Governor of Eskişehir to the Ministry of the Interior, EGM 13216-7/1, 22 January 1936.

regarding them.[140] Apparently, as mentioned in the previous section, the people of Seyitgazi had thought that the decision of the municipality to ban the *peçe* and the *çarşaf* would be implemented immediately and by force. Since the majority of them were poor farmer families, many women could not afford to buy an overcoat and thus had to wear men's overcoats. This created disquiet in the city and people begun publicly complaining about the situation. Consequently, the governor sent a letter to the ministry. In it he reported that, as further investigation revealed, people in fact were not engaged in negative propaganda against unveiling, but rather were complaining and gossiping about the immediate implementation of the ban.[141] The ban of Seyitgazi municipality advised that the *peçe* and the *çarşaf* be replaced by hats and overcoats; the complaints had grown out of the inability of people to obtain this 'modern' clothing.

What was interesting about the case of Seyitgazi was that in addition to ordinary people who were accused of making these complaints, there were people who were engaged in the local politics and part of this 'movement' (*cereyan*), as characterized in the report of the governor of Eskişehir and discussed in the previous section. Some neighbourhood delegates (*mahalle mümessilleri*) and members of the city council were accused of being involved in the opposition to the anti-veiling campaign. Thus, it seems, the public discontent over the implementation of the ban on the *peçe* and the *çarşaf* became part of a conflict between groups of local elites. If the accusations were correct, the head of the local party branch was indeed trying to challenge the mayor by a vote of no confidence, and interestingly, he was doing so by being part of, or at least by taking advantage of, the popular resistance that had emerged against the application process of the anti-veiling campaign. In fact, opposition or reluctance shown by some local elite in the course of the anti-veiling campaigns, especially against issuing of outright bans, often coincided with the social discontent already existing in the local community. In other words, while it was possible to encounter examples where some members of the city councils or even local party administrations in some cities opposed these bans and thus were accused of being 'fanatical' by the representatives of Ankara, there were also cases, such as Trabzon, where the resistance shown by some local elite in the city council and social resistance shown by ordinary people complemented, and probably, reinforced, each other. Therefore, it is also important to keep in mind that it is not always possible to differentiate resistance by the elite and popular resistance; a native owner of a grocery store could be a member of the city council and could be accused of being part of the same opposition 'movement' with an ordinary man complaining about the ban of the municipality, as in the case of Seyitgazi.[142]

---

140. Letter from the Ministry of the Interior to the Governor of Eskişehir, EGM 13216-7/1, 31 January 1936.

141. Letter from the Governor of Eskişehir to the Ministry of the Interior, EGM 13216-7/1, 7 February 1936.

142. See Letter from the Governor of Eskişehir to the Ministry of the Interior, EGM 13216-7/1, 7 February 1936.

Another form of resistance to anti-veiling campaigns was sending complaint letters to central authorities. These complaint letters could be written by lower-ranking officials who would accuse their superiors for their misconduct during implementation process of the campaigns, as in the case of Tosya district of Kastamonu, or by citizens themselves, as in the case of Ödemiş district of Izmir.[143] In fact, in the case of Ödemiş, we see a local notable, İsmail Efe, complaining to higher authorities after having already communicated with the local administrators himself. In his letter, İsmail Efe was saying that he had first told the district governor that the representatives in the parliament in Ankara did not have consent for the use of the police force in the issue of unveiling, but the district governor had paid no attention to this.[144] Thus, those local actors who were sending complaint letters were convinced that local administrators were acting without the consent of Ankara and thus exceeding their authority; or at least they had the hope that Ankara would not tolerate a forceful removal of women's veils. The complaint letters would also contain information about the social discontent such wrongdoings of local administrators created among ordinary people and thus warn Ankara about the possibility of a social reaction or harm in the image of the regime.

One sector of the society that constantly consulted the local authorities or tried to contact Ankara through letters against the anti-veiling campaigns was the weavers of the *çarşaf* or the *peştamal*. Since anti-veiling campaigns directly influenced their trade, the concern of the weavers of the *çarşaf* or *peştamal* was mainly economic. In fact, this group was not limited to the producers of these veils; in places where the bans included certain men's clothes, those who were employed in weaving the fabric for the manufacture of these clothes also reacted and sent petitions to the authorities. For example, an owner of a weaving loom that was producing the fabric for the local baggy trouser *karadon*, Biçuv İbrahim from the Kılıç Ali neighbourhood of Maraş, had sent petitions to the governorship, to the municipality, to the local party branch, as well as to the party headquarters in Ankara when *karadon* was banned together with the *peçe* and the *çarşaf* in the province.[145] In some cases, weavers tried to influence the authorities in Ankara and limit the impact of the anti-veiling campaign in their localities by reporting all

---

143. For the former, see Letter from Second Commissioner Tahsin to the General Directorate of Security, EGM 13216-7/1, 21 August 1935. For the latter, see İsmail Efe's letter dated 18 December 1937, quoted in Yılmaz, *Becoming Turkish*, 127–8.

144. İsmail Efe's letter is addressed to a certain Hamdi Bey, a high level state official, Yılmaz indicates. İsmail Efe urges Hamdi Bey to let Celal Bey, the prime minister, know about the situation. İsmail Efe had in fact known Celal Bayar personally, and had discussed this issue with him beforehand. This was how he knew that Ankara was against the use of force in the unveiling issue. Ibid., 130.

145. The local authorities tried to convince him that he could produce the fabric for the modern trousers that the men of Maraş were supposed to wear. They were also trying to help these weavers to establish a cooperative. Correspondence from RPP Maraş Administration to RPP Secretariat General, BCA 490.01/17.88.1, 24 January 1936.

the misconduct in which the local administrators engaged in the implementation process of the bans on the *peçe* and the *çarşaf*. A certain weaver from Aydın, Dokumacı Ahmet Şevki, for example, even sent a telegraph to president Atatürk, explaining that horrendous instructions (*dehşetli emirler*), which included stationing watchmen in the streets and tearing off the *peçe* and the *çarşaf* of women, had been given by the local administrators to remove the *peçe* and the *çarşaf* in the province.[146] He characterized these acts as a violation of basic individual freedoms and law (*hürriyet şahsiye kanun ayaklar altında çiğnenmektedir*). Dokumacı Ahmet Şevki also informed the president that he reported these acts to the governorship of Aydın. However, the governorship had considered it enough to reply to his complaints by referring to the decision that banned the use of the *peçe* and the *çarşaf*, and did not provide a further explanation. He asked the president to see to it that such actions be stopped if they were unlawful. As it is understood from his telegraph, Dokumacı Ahmet Şevki had also sent a telegraph to the president a year earlier, when there had been attempts made by the governorship to remove the *peçe* and the *çarşaf*. Apparently, this earlier telegraph Şevki sent had an impact, and although it is not clear what they were, certain orders were sent to the governor of Aydın. Thus, Şevki was following the same strategy and applying to the president in order to limit the attempts of the governorship of Aydın.

The governor of Aydın, on the other hand, informed the Ministry of the Interior on 17 August 1935, one day after the telegraph of Dokumacı Ahmet Şevki, that the decision of the city council dated 9 August to ban the *peçe*, the *çarşaf* and the *peştamal* had been received very well by the people of the province, and that no opposition or difficulty had been faced during the implementation.[147] The only opposition was that of a *peştamal* weaver, Şevki, who had informed the governorship that he would be left unemployed if the ban on the *peştamal* was implemented. Şevki was informed that he could continue weaving the *peştamal* cloth to be used at the public baths. The governor warned the ministry that the same weaver had send a telegraph to the president during the previous attempts at unveiling and managed to get some orders issued. According to the governor, it was also understood that Şevki would attempt to do the same this time as well. The governor finished his letter to the minister by characterizing Şevki as a person with a very low social status (*içtimai mevkii çok düşük*) and by indicating that they were also taking into consideration that 'this guy' could encourage some action on the matter, probably referring to the possibility that Şevki could engage in some propaganda activities against the anti-veiling campaign.

As indicated above, the governor was indeed right in expecting Dokumacı Şevki to send a new telegraph to the president. Apart from the resistance of a *peştamal* weaver and his insistence on directly complaining to the president about the local affairs, the case of Dokumacı Şevki is also interesting in that it reveals

146. Telegraph from Dokumacı Ahmet Şevki to President Atatürk, EGM 13216-7/1, 16 August 1935.

147. Letter from the Governor of Aydın to the Ministry of the Interior, EGM 13216-7/1, 17 August 1935.

how the Ministry of the Interior handled such cases. The ministry sent to the governor of Aydın a code (*şifre*) asking for the identity of Ahmet Şevki, whether the signature on the telegraph was true or factitious, and what this guy wanted.[148] In other words, the ministry asked that an inquiry be made about Ahmet Şevki by the governorship. The governor of Aydın, Salim Günday, responded to the code of the ministry with a detailed explanation of who Ahmet Şevki was and what he wanted.[149] According to the report of the governor, Ahmet Şevki was originally from Buldan, and he was mainly an artisan whose job was to weave and sell the *peştamal* garb. He was also known as the husband of a girl from Dinar, since he got married to a girl with 'loose morals' (*serbest kadın*) from Dinar when he was young. He had no reputable social position among the people and he was a half-wit (*yarım akıllı*). In previous years, when there had been attempts to remove the *peştamal* in Aydın, Şevki again sent 'exaggerated' telegraphs and petitions to Atatürk, to the Prime Ministry and to the ministries, and had managed to postpone the initiative. The governor again rejected Ahmet Şevki's accusations and assured the ministry that the implementation of the ban was uneventful and not a single woman was fined. Apparently, Ahmet Şevki had tried to encourage opposition against unveiling by showing people the response he received from Atatürk to his telegraph a year earlier. His actions, however, had been ineffectual, according to the governor. No opposition to or complaints about the ban on the on the *peçe*, the *çarşaf* or the *peştamal* in the province of Aydın had been received, and, having seen this, Ahmet Şevki had changed his attitude.

Unfortunately, there is no information in this correspondence regarding Atatürk's response to Ahmet Şevki's telegraph in 1934. It is interesting, however, to note that Atatürk indeed had replied to the complaint he received about anti-veiling campaigns, and apparently, due to his intervention, the campaign that year had been postponed, as it is indicated in the governor's letter. It is also not certain whether the president received Ahmet Şevki's telegraph in 1935. The ministry's reaction to Ahmet Şevki's constant complaints was quite sceptical, however, despite the fact that the governor explained the reason behind his opposition to the campaign as being mainly economic. In response to the governor's letter, the ministry reminded the governor in Aydın that Ahmet Şevki's intention could very well stem from his reactionary ideas, rather than from his economic concerns.[150] In other words, the ministry was not satisfied with governor's explanation and asked

---

148. Code from the Minister of the Interior to the Governorship of Aydın, EGM 13216-7/1, 26 August 1935. This code was sent as an urgent case and was a supplement to a previous code dated 23 August, which was less detailed. It seems that some additions were made probably by the minister or his undersecretary; the owner of the hand-writing in the document is not clear.

149. From the Governor of Aydın to the Ministry of the Interior, EGM 13216-7/1, 26 August 1935.

150. From the Minister of the Interior to the Governor of Aydın, EGM 13216-7/1, 7 September 1935.

him to follow Ahmet Şevki more closely, to send his photograph, and to investigate on whose behalf he was acting and whether he was a member a religious order (*tarikat*). The ministry also urged the governor that necessary measures should be taken to prevent Ahmet Şevki from disturbing high authorities. It is evident that the ministry was uncomfortable with Ahmet Şevki's telegraphs to the president. Having received the additional order, the governor sent another letter after a few weeks, summarizing the results of his investigation:

1. Dokumacı Ahmet Şevki's situation is being closely monitored.

2. Based on the investigations so far, although it is understood that he has a poor character and morals and is tainted by his addiction to gambling, no relationship had been detected between him and any religious order. In my opinion, he was provoked by a few backward-minded people on the issue of the *peştamal*, and encouraged by the reply he had received to his telegraph to Atatürk the previous year, he repeated the same initiative this year. He is a worthless person with no position in his own community, and with a tainted past. He has no relationship with the religious orders.

3. We are trying to find Ahmet Şevki's photograph. I respectfully submit that it will be sent as soon as it is obtained.[151]

The case of Dokumacı Ahmet Şevki of Aydın shows that any attempt at questioning or complaining about the anti-veiling campaigns was associated with a potentially more general ideological opposition to the regime and was thus approached with great suspicion by the Ministry of the Interior. A similar reaction of the ministry can be seen in another case as well. On 18 September 1935, the governor of the province of Konya sent a letter to the Ministry of the Interior indicating that a certain man named Taşçı Ahmet (Ahmet the stonecutter) from the sub-district of Sille had circulated a rumour that a gendarmerie soldier who had been assigned a task in one of the villages was killed because he tried to remove a woman's *çarşaf*.[152] Supposedly, he was killed by the brothers of the woman who was attacked. Ahmet had also told people of his hometown Sille that a policeman and a gendarmerie were also killed for the same reason in the centre of Konya. Having heard about such talk, the governorship had begun an investigation, and as a result, had found out that Ahmet was responsible for them. Upon being questioned, Ahmet said that he had heard about the killings while three men were talking at a coffeehouse in the province centre. However, he could not identify the people from whom he had heard the story. His case was sent to the court as the police was of the opinion that he himself had created false stories and helped spread them, even among the little children of Sille. The Ministry of

---

151. From the Governor of Aydın to the Ministry of the Interior, EGM 13216-7/1, 1 October 1935.

152. From the Governor of Konya to the Ministry of the Interior, EGM 13216-7/1, 18 September 1935.

the Interior again found the case suspicious and asked the governor of Konya to closely watch Ahmet's situation, to investigate his ethnic origin and whether he had any connections from outside and to send Ahmet's picture and fingerprints.[153] Twenty days later, the governor of Konya sent the picture and fingerprints, but assured the ministry that Ahmet was an ignorant man who had not engaged in any anti-regime activity in the past. There was also no information indicating that he had any connections from outside.

Based on the existing documents, it is impossible to tell for sure whether the stories told by Taşçı Ahmet about the killing of two gendarmerie soldiers and a policeman in the province of Konya were at all true. However, the killing of or attacks against the gendarmerie, the police officers or the municipal police forces because they intervened in women's clothing during the implementation of the anti-veiling campaigns were not pure construction. In the province of Trabzon, for example, the British Pro-Consul reported that a man had killed a gendarmerie soldier who had forcibly removed his wife's veil in the district capital of Akçaabat.[154] As discussed in the previous section, some local administrators had had a very hard time in handling cases of resistance to the implementation of the bans on the *peçe* and the *çarşaf* through the use of police force. The mayor of Trabzon had received anonymous letters threatening his life. His wife was physically attacked in the street and injured. Similarly, the governor of Gaziantep was accused of retreating from his initial firm position on the issue of unveiling because he had received threatening letters.[155] Thus, in addition to attacks against the police forces and soldiers, it seems that sending threatening letters to the local authorities who were seen as responsible for the anti-veiling campaigns, or even targeting their unveiled female family members, were ways some people used to stop the anti-veiling campaigns, or at least to prevent the authorities from using force while implementing the bans.

Overall, the examples discussed above reveal that although there was no mass protest or collective action against the anti-veiling campaigns, this hardly meant lack of resistance. Both the central authorities in Ankara and the local administrators had hard time dealing with the creative ways in which people responded to the campaigns and the various forms of selective adaptation they underwent. From circulating rumours to sending letters, people's 'repertoire of responses' was in fact quite rich.[156] Perhaps, the way the anti-veiling campaigns were put into practice determined the way people responded. Since the campaigns were mainly local in character and unveiling was not imposed by a central degree

---

153. From the Ministry of the Interior to the Governor of Konya, EGM 13216-7/1, 14 October 1935.

154. Letter from the British Pro-Consul in Trabzon to British Embassy in Ankara, FO 371/20087, 16 April 1936.

155. From Mr. Yazıcıoğlu to General Director of the Police Şükrü Sökmensüer, EGM 13216-7/1, 1 June 1936.

156. Brockett, 'Collective Action', 61.

or law, the reactions were mostly organized against the local authorities. In some cases, reactions involved both members of local elite and ordinary people, blurring the distinction between elite and popular resistance. In fact, if we look at cases where local administrators acted more hesitantly in the anti-veiling campaigns, it becomes clear that they were dealing with the opposition of local forces on the ground and acting accordingly. This was why, for example, some local elites tried to avoid issuing an outright ban on the *peçe* and the *çarşaf*, while at the same time justifying this 'choice' by claiming that their city was already very 'modern' or that the people were in fact conscious regarding revolutionary ideals and the necessities of modern life.[157] In effect, the creative ways ordinary people tried to react to the anti-veiling campaigns affected not only the attitudes and choices of the local elites, but also the outcomes of the campaigns. Resistance by male societal actors also made women's attitudes all the more important, since it was them at the end of the day who would make the 'choice' to keep wearing their *peçe* and *çarşaf* or not. As the main target of the anti-veiling campaigns, women were indeed in a central position to influence the process at the local level. Hence, any attempt to recover the voices of the local also needs to restore women's story as the 'agents of the narrative'.[158] It is to these questions of women's responses and contribution in the shaping of the anti-veiling campaigns we now turn.

---

157. Such claims were usually expressed in local newspapers. For example, in Akseki, a district of the province of Antalya, no measure was taken on the issue of *peçe* and *çarşaf* because the guidance was considered sufficient given that the level of awareness concerning this issue among the people of Akseki was quite high. 'Akseki Mektubu', *Antalya*, 15 August 1935. For another example from Konya, which explains the lack of local activity on the issue of unveiling by referring to the social maturity of the women of the city and their will for progress, see A. Evren, 'Konya Kadınlığı Uyanıktır', *Yeni Asır*, 19 December 1934. See also 'Peçe ve Çarşaf', *Babalık*, 20 December 1934.

158. Joan Wallach Scott, 'Women in History: The Modern Period', *Past & Present* 101 (November 1983): 141–57.

Chapter 4

WOMEN, THE KEMALIST 'PROJECT' AND THE ANTI-VEILING CAMPAIGNS

Rethinking women's agency in the Ottoman/Turkish context

A great deal has been achieved by feminist historians in making women a subject of historical enquiry.[1] From major historical developments to the histories of ordinary people, 'her-story' has begun to be told and thus the conventional historiography, in which women were mainly invisible, has been challenged. Feminist historians, aiming to go beyond simply incorporating women into old schools of social history or writing women's history as supplementary to the existing grand narratives, have increasingly begun to use gender as an analytic category.[2] The objective in doing this has been to emphasize that gender is not a separate or complementary topic of analysis but rather a fundamental and essential part of any historical narrative. Studying gender, in other words, is a method for rewriting history; it consists of not only analysing men and women in relation to one another, but also studying how gender shapes social, economic and political structures. In such an approach, as Joan W. Scott suggests, the study of female agency exposes 'the often silent and hidden operations of gender which are nonetheless present and defining forces of politics and political life'.[3]

The debate in the field of gender studies on how to approach women's agency and especially how to analyse it in relation to power and male domination has been an ongoing one, having transformed, in particular, how patriarchy has been understood. The idea that women's choices, behaviours and reactions are not entirely determined by the structure (i.e. patriarchy) and that they have a capacity to act upon their world, to bargain with or contest given gender norms, has dramatically altered the way we approach any historical question regarding

---

1. For a general discussion on the achievements of feminist historians, see Joan Wallach Scott, 'Feminism's History', *Journal of Women's History* 16, no. 2 (Summer 2004): 10–29. See also commentaries to Scott's article in the same issue.

2. Joan W. Scott, 'Gender: A Useful Category of Historical Analysis', *The American Historical Review* 91, no. 5 (December 1986): 1053–75.

3. Joan W. Scott, 'Women in History: The Modern Period', *Past & Present* 101 (November 1983): 156.

women's roles in and reactions to socio-economic and political processes.[4] The impact of such debates has been geographically uneven, however.[5] While greater distance has been covered in European and American history, in Middle Eastern history, the progress has been relatively slower in integrating women into social history and gendering historiography. Studies about women in modern Middle Eastern history have mainly focused on outlining women's roles in the nationalist movements of the late nineteenth century and in the modernizing reforms that were put into practice once nation-states were established in the region. In other words, the most popular topic has been the centrality of the 'woman question' to nationalism and modernization. Consequently, relatively fewer studies have attempted to deal with the issue of how gender fundamentally altered the way modernity was imagined and constructed, and how central women's agency was in this construction.[6] Because portraying Muslim women as submissive and passive receivers of patriarchal policies has been historically very salient, especially in the West, feminist scholars of the region have paid particular attention to the question of Middle Eastern women's agency. Although an important contribution has been made in this vein, the focus has largely been on women's movements, which were mainly composed of upper-middle-class educated women. In other words, understandably, vanguards of feminism and women's rights in major countries of the region were the topic of early works and the emphasis, thus, has remained largely on feminist agency.

Nevertheless, a wider discussion on women's agency has also emerged in the field of Middle Eastern women's studies and the question of how to approach and analyse this agency has received more attention over the last decades. This can be traced mainly in anthropological works dealing with the questions of new forms of veiling since the 1980s, women's participation in Islamic movements, the emergence of new female religiosities and Muslim feminist activism. While they adopt different definitions of women's agency, these studies have collectively been instrumental in shifting the scholarly attention away from feminist to ordinary women's agency.[7] In this regard, Saba Mahmood's work, which conceptualizes agency 'not simply as a synonym for resistance to relations of domination,

---

4. For example, see Deniz Kandiyoti, 'Bargaining with Patriarchy', *Gender and Society* 2, no. 3 (September 1988): 274–90.

5. Afsaneh Najmabadi, 'From Supplementarity to Parasitism', *Journal of Women's History* 16, no. 2 (Summer 2004): 30–5.

6. For example, see Lila Abu-Lughod, ed. *Remaking Women: Feminism and Modernism in the Middle East* (New Jersey: Princeton University Press, 1998).

7. For example, see Arlene E. MacLeod, 'Hegemonic Relations and Gender Resistance: The New Veiling as Accommodating Protest', *Signs* 17, no. 3 (1992): 533–57; Azam Torab, 'Piety as Gendered Agency: A Study of Jalaseh Ritual Discourse in an Urban Neighborhood in Iran', *The Journal of the Royal Anthropological Institute* 2, no. 2 (June 1996): 235–52; Rachel Rinaldo, 'Pious and Critical: Muslim Women Activists and the Question of Agency', *Gender and Society* 28, no. 6 (December 2014): 824–46.

but as a capacity for action that specific relations of *subordination* enable and create,[8] has been particularly influential and her take on the question of women's agency has had an impact in the field going far beyond the analysis of women in contemporary piety movements. Her proposal to enlarge the existing feminist analyses by taking into consideration the instances where women do not engage in an explicit feminist agency or resistance to relations of male domination, played a significant role in putting an inquiry into women's agency at the centre of gender scholarship on Muslim contexts, including historical scholarship on women in the Middle East.

In the field of Ottoman women's studies, too, there has been an increasing effort to rethink the state policies and modernizing reforms around a more nuanced understanding of women's agency. The body of literature that focuses on Ottoman women in the late nineteenth and early twentieth centuries has especially been pioneering an approach that locates Ottoman women within the wider history of Ottoman integration to global capitalism and as subjects 'in co-temporal history with Western geographies, responding to similar developments'.[9] Documenting the responses of late Ottoman women unearthed the various ways they were engaged with larger social, economic and political processes and structures while they shaped their own lives as workers, peasants, middle-class housewives or educators. Such studies also implied an alternative approach to questions of modernization or state building not as fixed, solely top-down processes with entirely foreseeable and consistent outcomes, but as dynamic transformations that are subject to contestations and negotiations, prone to take unexpected twists and likely to bring inconsistent outcomes in practice. In her study of the politicization of reproduction in the nineteenth-century Ottoman Empire, Gülhan Balsoy, for example, shows how policies that mainly aimed at establishing a legal and medical control over women's lives, enabled women to situate themselves as agents.[10] The Ottoman government's laws and regulations banning abortion, she argues, were not just signs of absolute state domination over women's bodies; they became means through which Ottoman women gained legal subjectivity.[11] Reminding us about the limits of state 'projects' as well as their unexpected consequences, such

---

8. Saba Mahmood, 'Feminist Theory, Embodiment and the Docile Agent: Some Reflections on the Egyptian Islamic Revival', *Cultural Anthropology* 16, no. 2 (2001): 210. Emphasis in the original.

9. Duygu Köksal and Anastasia Falierou, 'Introduction: Historiography of Late Ottoman Women', in *A Social History of Late Ottoman Women: New Perspectives*, eds. Duygu Köksal and Anastasia Falierou (Leiden: Brill, 2013), 3.

10. Gülhan Balsoy, *The Politics of Reproduction in Ottoman Society, 1838–1900* (London: Pickering & Chatto, 2013).

11. For a similar analysis, see also Tuba Demirci and Selçuk Akşin Somel, 'Women's Bodies, Demography, and Public Health: Abortion Policy and Perspectives in the Ottoman Empire of the Nineteenth Century', *Journal of the History of Sexuality* 17, no. 3 (2008): 377–420.

analyses demonstrate that discourses and policies of modernization could be both empowering and oppressive, entailing opportunities for women.[12]

When it comes to the early republican period, however, the impact of the 'agency turn' has been far more limited compared to the historiography of late Ottoman women. While there is a flourishing literature on the social history of interwar Turkey, the conventional feminist analyses of the 'Kemalist project' and its implications for women remain largely intact. As briefly discussed in the Introduction, these analyses, as transformative and informative as they have been, have predominantly focused on the Kemalist discourse on women's emancipation and confined women's agency mainly with the feminist movement that was represented, institutionally, by the Women's Union. The idea that the Kemalist policies did not touch the majority of women's lives and thus opened up an 'opportunity space' essentially for women of elite and educated background in the major urban centres has prevailed.

This chapter aims to provide a different analysis of women's experiences under the 'Kemalist project' by focusing on how that 'project' touched the lives of women in the provinces and was negotiated, domesticated and thus transformed by women's reactions and 'ordinary' agencies. By documenting the diverse ways in which women responded to the anti-veiling campaigns of the 1930s, my aim is to demonstrate that, first, the anti-veiling campaigns in early republican Turkey and the ways in which women reacted to them reflect a multilayered notion of agency that cannot be confined to the dichotomy of resistance and subordination. The analysis of the various ways in which women in the provinces engaged with the anti-veiling campaigns reveal that there was a range of possibilities and options that women could utilize in reacting to such social and political changes that impact their lives, including but not limited to open resistance and full compliance. It should also be noted that what seems to be resistance or compliance in the first instance may very well not be intended as such by women themselves. Or, even if women's first reaction was compliance, it might not mean submission to what was imposed. On the contrary, it might be one way of, and possibly the most rational/effective tactic for, handling the situation. I take inspiration from Torab's point here that compliance provides security and social recognition for women in certain contexts, and can be turned into an advantage, a source of empowerment. Thus 'compliance is often the result of rational assessment of the situation and its viable alternatives. It is not always a matter of simple choice, nor does it automatically entail agreement.'[13] Likewise, there may be instances of 'resistance' that are 'momentary, fragile and often not even conscious.'[14] Similarly, women may behave such that simultaneous processes of compliance and resistance can be seen. It is imperative to explore, therefore, women's reactions and attitudes through a multifaceted conception

---

12. See Balsoy, *The Politics*, 51–80. For similar analyses, see also the contributions in Çiğdem Oğuz, ed. 'Women's Agency in the Late Ottoman Empire', special issue, *Journal of Ottoman and Turkish Studies Association* 6, no. 2 (2019): 9–130.

13. Torab, 'Piety as Gendered', 245.

14. Ibid., 238.

of agency, which allows us to take into consideration that women do not act in isolation, but in relationship to one another and within the constraints as well as opportunities generated by male-dominated structures and processes.

Second, by focusing on the forms the Kemalist 'reforms' like anti-veiling campaigns took in practice, the ways they were implemented at the local level and experienced by women, the chapter aims to demonstrate the complex dynamics Kemalist modernization entailed for women. My argument is that although the anti-veiling campaigns were ultimately interventions in women's lives and thus can be seen as mechanisms of control and regulation, they, at the same time, were shaped by women's agency and provided them a potential space, a milieu to negotiate gender norms. In other words, ordinary women's encounters with the Kemalist ideal of modern Turkish woman had the potential to lead to various changes and transformations in practice that cannot be captured with conventional narratives of 'top-down' modernization. The change in women's dress in the early republic was not a straightforward consequence of an imposed ideal or solely determined by a reform assumed to be implemented consistently. Rather, it was a social process equally shaped by women's reactions and choices, the involvement of various actors and local dynamics that were hard to entirely control. This dynamic and complex process reveals that the Kemalist imagination and discourse of 'modern woman', albeit quite visible and powerful in visual representations and elite-level articulations, were much more cautious and open to negotiations in practice than they have been thought to be. In fact, the Kemalist 'modern (unveiled) woman' remained very much an ideal that would be realized, the Kemalist political elite hoped, by women's embracing it gradually and with their own efforts.

Finally, the case of the anti-veiling campaigns shows that when we focus on the implementation and actual effects of state policies, it becomes clearer that the Kemalist modernization process potentially opened up 'opportunity spaces' for women. These opportunity spaces were indeed highlighted by feminist scholars of Turkey by pointing at the legitimacy the Kemalist reforms enabled for educated, middle-class women of the major urban centres, providing them the avenues through which they could, in the long run, participate in public life.[15] I suggest to expand this argument to include wider segments of women, to reflect the legitimacy and opportunity that became available to women in the provinces as well. As Bozdoğan emphasizes, the feminist critique of Kemalism as an essentially patriarchal project 'does not alter the progressiveness of the reforms as viewed in their own time, especially by women themselves, who felt empowered by their new rights and new visibility in public life'.[16] In other words, patriarchal and

---

15. Yeşim Arat, 'Women's Movement of the 1980s in Turkey: Radical Outcome of Liberal Kemalism?', in *Reconstructing Gender in the Middle East: Power, Identity and Tradition*, eds. Fatma Müge Göçek ve Shiva Balaghi (New York: Columbia University Press, 1994), 100–12; Deniz Kandiyoti, 'End of Empire: Islam, Nationalism and Women in Turkey', in *Women, Islam and the State*, ed. Deniz Kandiyoti (Philadelphia: Temple University Press, 1991), 22–47; Kandiyoti, 'Gendering the Modern'.

16. Bozdoğan, *Modernism*, 82.

limited as they were, the legal and social reforms introduced by the Kemalist regime significantly *increased* the space and capacity for women's visibility and participation in the public life, as well as for their potential empowerment in their personal lives. Similar to Najmabadi's analysis of Iranian modernization, one can argue, then, that the Kemalist project of modernity can also be seen as simultaneously regulatory/controlling and empowering for women.[17] Moreover, some women, at least, were active supporters and even initiators of the Kemalist reforms. Especially the policies such as the anti-veiling campaigns, which were mainly local in character and put into practice based on the discussions and negotiations at the local level, allowed even larger space for women's agency. If all the complexities of the campaigns that were discussed in the previous two chapters are taken into consideration, one can understand better that there was in fact a wide range of possibilities for the new dress codes to be manipulated in the public sphere and women had the capacity to adapt, modify and/or resist them in various ways. Thus, the feminist critique of early republic needs to be revisited and enlarged in order to reflect this complexity of women's reactions and roles in the shaping of the Kemalist experience.

Women and the anti-veiling campaigns: Non-compliance, resistance, selective adaptation

As discussed in detail previously, anti-veiling campaigns in the 1930s were much more effective than the earlier attempts to remove the *peçe* and the *çarşaf* in the 1920s. They were more organized, widespread and determined; they more consistently targeted the use of the *peçe*, the *çarşaf* and other local veils and replaced them with 'modern' clothing through the power of local institutions and actors, including municipalities, members of the local sports clubs, governors and members of teachers' associations. They had a strong impact on the shaping of new gender roles and codes not only in the political sphere, state offices and educational institutions, and the urban space, but also in the daily life of ordinary people, at the heart of gender relations in the private sphere. In this sense, however inconsistent and ambiguous in practice and diverse in discourse they were, it should be underlined that these campaigns nevertheless touched the lives of many women.

Public discourse on anti-veiling campaigns in the 1930s, as it was reflected in the local newspapers, overwhelmingly emphasized women's compliance. News reports and articles about the anti-veiling campaigns tended to mention women's approval of the changes and their willingness to adopt the new clothes. This was partly a result of the propaganda the local newspapers had initiated; they shared a similar language to imply how the bans on the *peçe* and the *çarşaf* were well-received and

---

17. Afsaneh Najmabadi, 'Crafting an Educated Housewife in Iran', in *Remaking Women: Feminism and Modernism in the Middle East*, ed. Lila Abu-Lughod (New Jersey: Princeton University Press, 1998), 91–125.

enthusiastically supported, particularly by women, by using titles like 'women remove their *peçe*' or 'women throw off their *çarşaf*'. In fact, such reports highlighted women's agency on purpose; it was a strategy, a part of the attempt to present these campaigns as local initiatives, as changes stemming from women's genuine desire to alter their clothing. However, below the surface of this propaganda, there were many ways in which women tried to resist anti-veiling campaigns or at least to limit the influence the campaigns had on their own choices.

One common way women used to resist unveiling was disobedience. There were women who continued to wear the *peçe* or the *çarşaf* in the public sphere despite the existence of open bans in their cities.[18] In Bursa, for example, a local newspaper reported on 10 October 1935 that because of women's disobedience, the municipal police had to apply legal sanctions, and, as a result, over a hundred women were fined for wearing the *peçe* or the *çarşaf* in a few months' time.[19] It seems, however, that such actions of the municipal police were insufficient to overcome women's disobedience in the city. In the following months, the existence of women who insisted on wearing the *peçe* or the *çarşaf* continued to draw the attention of a handful of local newspapers and a number of members of the city council in Bursa.[20] There were discussions on the implementation process of the ban, and some argued for an even more vigorous enforcement of the council decisions.[21] Another place where women insisted on wearing the *çarşaf* despite the ban and the threat of fine was Sivas. Two sisters who were fined for entering a government office with their black *çarşafs* did not hesitate to write a letter to Ankara, complaining about the fines issued by the local authorities, arguing that there was no law banning these veils.[22] In Denizli, there were also women who continued to wear the *peştamal* veil in certain neighbourhoods in the provincial

---

18. In addition to women's incompliance, there were also worries about men who would use the *peçe* and the *çarşaf* to hide themselves. As mentioned in Chapters 1 and 2, this had been a major concern of the authorities since the Ottoman times. It seems that this continued to be a source of fear during the anti-veiling campaigns in the 1930s as well. For example, the governor of the province of Elâziz was reporting that although women abided by the ban on the *peçe* and the *çarşaf*, there could still be harmful people who would wear women's veils and would enter the province for bad purposes. The security forces were watchful for such cases. See the letter from the Governor of Elâziz to the Ministry of the Interior, EGM 13216-7/1, 5 November 1935.

19. 'Çarşaflar Kalkıyor', *Hakkın Sesi*, 10 October 1935. The same newspaper was reporting at the beginning of November that the municipal police had drew up a total of 700 records (*zabıt varakası*) on various matters in the last four months, and some of these records were on the cases of disobedience to the *çarşaf* ban. See 'Uray zabıtası dört ay içinde neler yaptı?', *Hakkın Sesi*, 7 November 1935.

20. See 'Kendi kendilerini cezalandıranlar...', *Hakkın Sesi*, 30 November 1935 and 'Peçeli Kadınlar', *Hakkın Sesi*, 24 December 1935.

21. 'Dünkü Uray Kurulunda', *Hakkın Sesi*, 15 February 1936.

22. See Metinsoy, 'Everyday Resistance', 101.

centre, and in some district centres and villages.[23] Local newspapers of the city reported some of those women who were fined by publicly listing their names.[24] Similar news about women who tried to avoid authorities by hiding from them or reports mentioning women's insistence on using the *peçe* or the *çarşaf,* especially in the remote neighbourhoods away from city centres, can also be seen in other provinces.[25] Sometimes, the continued use of the *peçe* and the *çarşaf* in some cities could create reactions in other cities where the bans were implemented. The situation in the big cities, such as Istanbul, Ankara and Izmir, had a particularly great impact on people living in the provinces. The head of the local party branch in Yozgat, Yusuf Duygu, for example, complained that people from Yozgat who travelled to these big cities and saw women there wearing the *peçe* and the *çarşaf* were surprised about Yozgat's insistence on unveiling when they returned.[26] Thus, he indicated to the General Secretary of the RPP that it was critical that these veils be removed very rapidly, altogether everywhere, especially in big cities. This consistency was significant in order to prevent rumour and discontent in the periphery.

If women did not or could not challenge the bans by open disobedience, they tried to find other ways to handle them. One way was to minimize, as much as possible, the frequency at which they left their houses. In other words, some women tried to avoid adopting the newly imposed outdoor clothes such as overcoats by

---

23. Uyar, 'Tek Parti', 573.

24. Uyar cites two news reports from the newspapers *Denizli* and *Babadağ* that mention the names of ten women in total from various neighbourhoods and towns of Denizli who were fined in November and December 1935: in the province centre, a certain Hatice from Kaplanlar neighbourhood, Ganime from Eskimüftü neighbourhood and Fatma (the wife of Kalak O. Ömer) from Gerzile village; in the district of Sarayköy, Ayşe from the Hatipoğlu neighbourhood, Zeliha from Yeniköy village and Şerife from Bereketler village; in the district of Honaz, Hatice from the Beylerce village, Ayşe from the Irlıganlı village and Hatice (the wife of İbrahim) from Haydar neighbourhood; and Rabia from Şahanlar neighbourhood of the district of Acıpayam. See ibid., 573, fnt. 82.

25. For example, for Konya, see 'Zaman ilerler ilerlemezden sürükler', *Babalık*, 18 January 1936; for Çorum, see, Letter from the Governor of Çorum to the Ministry of the Interior, EGM 13216-7/1, 22 November 1935. As reported by the police, in Adana as well, many women continued to wear the *çarşaf* even after the decision of the city council to ban the *peçe* and the *çarşaf*. The date of the report is not stated. Metinsoy, 'Everyday Resistance', 92. In 1939, the governors of the provinces of Tokat and Urfa were also reporting to Ankara that women continued to wear the *çarşaf*. These reports are quoted in Ibid. However, it is not clear in Metinsoy's account whether there were organized anti-veiling campaigns in these two provinces in the 1930s.

26. Letter from the Head of Yozgat RPP branch to the Secretariat General of RPP in Ankara, BCA 490.01/17.88.1, 13 November 1935. Yusuf Duygu was one of those delegates who supported a general law banning the use of the *peçe* and the *çarşaf* at the party congress in May 1935. See Chapter 2.

remaining in their private spheres. A complaint letter sent from Tosya, a district of the province of Kastamonu, to the General Directorate of Security indicates that the decision of the city council to ban the *peçe* and the *çarşaf* was implemented in the district centre by using the gendarmerie.[27] As claimed in the letter, the soldiers forcefully removed some women's *çarşaf* in the middle of the street, leaving them in a very difficult situation.[28] Having seen or heard of these instances, women in the district centre and in the villages refrained from leaving their houses. Village women who were accustomed to regularly visiting the district centre on the day of the city market stopped going to Tosya.[29] Similarly, in Maraş, there were women who did not step outside their houses for years, as reported by the governor in 1939. Some of them preferred to travel in carriages at night to visit their relatives.[30]

Another way in which women dealt with the ban on the *peçe* and the *çarşaf* was using alternative means to cover themselves. The most noteworthy of these alternative means was to use umbrellas to replace the *peçe*. Women would hide their face with the umbrellas they carried so they could follow the norms of veiling without violating the ban. As mentioned in the previous chapter, the governor of Ordu complained that some women began to carry umbrellas unnecessarily.[31] Similarly, in Maraş and Kilis, women were using umbrellas day and night to hide themselves.[32] In Rize, the use of umbrella for veiling purposes reached such a level that the decision of the city council to ban the *peçe* also asked women to not carry umbrellas.[33] In addition to the use of umbrellas, some different combinations of outdoor attire that would provide women with a middle ground, which would not violate either the bans on the *çarşaf* or the traditional customs, also prevailed. Hence, using long and wide (usually black) headscarves, and preferring overcoats that reached the heels, thus providing a veiling closer to full-body covering, could also be seen as means employed by women to overcome the difficulty the banning of the *çarşaf* had created for them.[34]

---

27. From Second Commissioner Tahsin to the General Directorate of Security, EGM 13216-7/1, 21 August 1935.

28. The author was claiming that women were left with their 'pants' in the middle of the street: ... *kadınları 'donları ile' sokak ortasında bırakmaktadırlar.* Quotation marks in the original letter.

29. Similarly, a complaint letter from the Ödemiş district of the province of Izmir was also stating that women could not go out to the market in the city because of the anti-veiling campaign. Yılmaz, *Becoming Turkish*, 78.

30. The report of the governor of Maraş dated 23 March 1939 is quoted in ibid., 73.

31. Copy of the Declaration on the *Peçe*, the *Çarşaf* and the *Peştamal* ban by the Governor of Ordu, EGM 13216-7/1, 5 March 1937.

32. For Maraş, see the copy of the Report of Mitat Aydın, deputy of Trabzon, BCA 490.01/273.1091.2, 7 May 1943. See also Yılmaz, *Becoming Turkish*, 73. For Kilis, see 'Kiliste Şemsiye Modası', *Son Posta*, 17 December 1935.

33. See 'Rizede Peçeler ve Çarşaflar Kalkıyor', *Yeni Asır*, 1 March 1935.

34. Such preferences by women were also stigmatized as resistance to the anti-veiling campaigns by some local authorities. See Chapter 3.

One indication of women's reluctance to adopt the new clothes was the frequency of notices published in the newspapers calling on women to abide by the decisions. In Trabzon, for example, where there was also resistance by some male members in the city council against issuing a ban, a lot of women were hesitant to remove their *peçe* and *çarşaf*.[35] Therefore, several articles and notices were published in the local newspapers to convince women that the *peçe* and the *çarşaf* were inappropriate customs, not Islamic, and were the major obstacles to women's progress and participation in the social life. The emphasis on the 'non-Islamic' character of the *peçe* and *çarşaf* was particularly visible, showing that there was a widespread perception that those women who insisted on wearing these veils were doing so because of religious reasons.

There was also a perception that women were reluctant to comply with the necessities of a 'modern' social life because of the conservative attitude of the Turkish society in general, or because traditional norms (not necessarily religious) were very dominant. Those who stressed this dominance of the traditional norms as the major obstacle before the modernization of women's clothing also referred to the social resistance to women's public visibility in general. The same local newspapers in Trabzon that complained about women who insisted on wearing the *peçe* and the *çarşaf* also complained that women were not active in the public life of the city in general. For example, women were not willing to participate in the activities of the People's House. The inability of the theatre section of the Trabzon People's House to stage plays, for example, was directly related to the disinclination of women to appear on stage.[36] Even the women teachers in the city were reluctant to participate in such activities.[37] Having seemed to understand that women were trapped between traditional norms and the necessities of the 'new' life, these male authors would nevertheless not abstain from blaming women for their inability to overcome this difficulty – for not being brave enough to challenge this social pressure. Cemal Rıza, a columnist in *Halk*, addressed the women of Trabzon by saying that it was unacceptable for them to still be reluctant to join modern social life, and not to be able to get rid of the *peçe* and the *çarşaf* after all the progress they had accomplished in other fields:

> The revolution has given you the rights you have been denied for centuries. You
> have gained all the seats you deserve. Is there any point in looking at your rights
> from behind the *kafes*? You too know, see and enumerate the meaninglessness of
> bad customs, of useless habits. Why do you not get rid of the *peçe* and the *çarşaf*?

---

35. There were also complaints that women's insistence on wearing the *çarşaf* would harm the image of Trabzon as a 'modern', 'progressive' city. For example, see 'Eni konu konuşmalar ... ', *Halk*, 11 April 1935.

36. 'Gösterit işleri neden çalışamıyor?' *Halk*, 3 October 1935.

37. There were similar complaints in other places as well. The reluctance of women teachers to participate in the plays staged by the People's Houses was an issue even in places like Izmir, a relatively more advanced and less conservative province. Alexandros Lamprou, 'Negotiating Gender Identities during Mixed-Gender Activities: Amateur Theatre in the 1930s and 1940s in Turkey', *British Journal of Middle East Studies* 42, no. 4 (2015): 618–37.

There is a sun, a life, a light awaiting your new existence that got rid of the *peçe* and the *çarşaf?* What difficulty do you see in front of reaching this life, this light as soon as possible?[38]

Another common theme in explaining resistance or hesitance of women to removing the *peçe* and the *çarşaf* was that they were forced by men to continue to wear these veils.[39] Male authors of the newspapers were especially alert to men's attitudes regarding unveiling, and did not hesitate to address them directly in their articles: Turkish men would not represent their sisters to the world in a bad way, as backward women[40]; and their reluctance (rather than women's) could be the real reason for the slow pace of progress in unveiling.[41] There was also propaganda calling on women to be strong vis-à-vis the men who force them to veil. In Trabzon, for example, where women's compliance with the bans on the *peçe* and the *çarşaf* was low, local newspapers were trying to convince women not to obey their husbands or other closely related men. In an anonymous article, the local newspaper *Halk* was particularly addressing those women who wait until the deadline imposed by the city council to remove their *peçe* and *çarşaf*, warning them to not listen to the men who preach to them to do so.[42] Women were advised by the newspaper to reply those men in following words:

I am the one who creates the society. The society awaits me. We will get out of this backward veil that slaps our social existence for once and all; we will throw off the *çarşaf* just like you have removed and mangled the fez. Like you, we will adopt civilized clothing. ... Even if it came late, the decision of the municipality has emerged out of our deep desire to be part of the civilized life, out of our long lasting interest in joining society.

Such news reports and comments on them usually did not use incriminating language against women who continued to wear the *peçe* and the *çarşaf*. However, there were some examples of a more radical tone that tended to represent especially those women who continued to dress in the black *çarşaf* as reactionaries who opposed the revolutionary ideas of the new regime. Their continuing to participate in the public sphere dressed like this was viewed by some as a direct attack on the creation of a civilized, modern public life, which was seen as the first condition for entering the world of civilized nations. In one of his articles emblematic of such a tone, Aka Gündüz, a prominent columnist and play writer of the time, claimed

---

38. 'Peçe ve Çarşaf, Şehrimizin Sayın Bayanlarına', *Halk*, 19 December 1935. See also 'Peçe ve Çarşaf, Şehrimizin Sayın Bayanlarına', *Halk*, 23 December 1935.

39. In fact, the idea that women were wearing the *peçe* and the *çarşaf* because of men was very influential in the official circles as well. This was visible both in the discussions held at the General Congress of the RPP in 1935 and some circulars sent from Ankara. See Chapter 2.

40. 'Peçe ve Çaşaf', *Halk*, 17 October 1935.

41. 'Trabzon gençliği ve müsbet hamlesi', *Halk*, 19 March 1936.

42. 'Çarşafı Atalım', *Halk*, 13 April 1936.

that there were three groups of women who continued to wear the *çarşaf* in 1930s Turkey: elderly women, young women who are forced to wear this veil and young women who willingly insist on wearing it.[43] Elderly women who continued to use the *çarşaf* could be excused, according to Gündüz, because it was understandable that they would remain loyal to old traditions. It was, however, unacceptable for young women to follow the example of these older women. If they did, Gündüz suggested, this meant that they either deliberately opposed the new regime's ideals, or that they were forced to wear the *çarşaf*. The latter could be excused; but conscious disobedience to the dictates of the civilized life by younger generations, who insisted on participating in the public sphere in 'uniform-like' *çarşaf*, was unacceptable. That is why he argued that one should be very sceptical about those groups of women who wore black *çarşaf*s in similar styles and wandered in the most crowded areas in cities together. For him, this could not be seen as normal and should be approached as a kind of demonstration; what he called a '*çarşaf* demonstration' (*çarşaf nümayişi*). He characterized women who dressed in black *çarşaf* as 'demonstrators' of a different kind; those who did not protest in usual gatherings or by organizing uprisings, but by simply wandering around in the public sphere with their 'silk, chic and black' *çarşaf*. '*Çarşaf* demonstrations' were a clear sign of reaction to the new – to what was civilized and modern. This 'black unity', in his own words, must have been organized and planned by the 'backward mind' that was still alive and awaiting to be crashed by the forces of the revolution. Aka Gündüz here warned his readers about the possibility of unconventional political demonstrations: demonstrators against the regime should not always need to carry Derviş Mehmet's flag and shout; they could also use a fashionable, silk, black *çarşaf*.[44]

It is important to note that although Gündüz's article was originally published in a well-known pro-regime national newspaper, *Hakimiyeti Milliye*, it was then reprinted in some local newspapers. Thus, such concerns about women who continued wearing the *peçe* and the *çarşaf* also had local resonance, and this was because of still high visibility of women wearing these veils. In other words, there was awareness that anti-veiling campaigns could remain limited in impact, at least in the short run. In fact, Gündüz's article was motivated by the same awareness; because these veils were so durable and because many women were reluctant to remove them, he claimed that decisions by local authorities to ban these veils were important, but it would take a long time for these decisions to be publicly accepted as a norm. His aim was to warn the public that some women's resistance should be taken seriously, and this struggle should continue if Turkey wants to be part of the civilized world. One fear was that Turkey's image would be harmed because of the visibility of women wearing the *peçe* and the *çarşaf*. As explained in Chapter 2, this question of 'what the Europeans would think about us' was in fact a major motivation behind the anti-veiling campaigns in general. However, it seems that

---

43. Aka Gündüz, 'Çarşaf Nümayişleri', *Yeni Asır*, 17 July 1934.

44. Gündüz refers here to the Menemen incident happened four years ago, an attempt by a small group of Islamists to organize a counter-revolutionary movement. For more, see the discussion and references cited in Chapter 2.

there was a more particular concern about women's non-compliance with the anti-veiling campaigns; there was a fear that this non-compliance would be seen as resistance to the regime in the West as well. In fact, an article published in an American newspaper, *Daily Eagle*, had alerted both the Ministry of the Interior and the Ministry of Foreign Affairs.[45] As the Turkish Embassy in Washington, DC, reported, the article claimed that in Kastamonu and in some other Anatolian cities, groups composed of six to eight women would prefer to go out to the streets wearing thick *peçes* and *çarşafs*. This was interpreted as a protest against the 'modern' clothing that had been introduced by the regime. The article was based on a telegraph the newspaper had received from Ankara. The Ministry of the Interior sent a circular to the Ministry of Foreign Affairs asserting that such news were fabrications of those who wished to generate or strengthen the idea in the West that Turks were backward-thinking (*geri düşünceli*).[46] The Ministry of Foreign Affairs was asked to refute the article.

Women between patriarchal pressure and economic hardship

Although it is hard to find detailed information, there are indications that women's compliance with the ban on the *peçe* was higher than their compliance with the ban on the *çarşaf*. Some provincial governors indicated in their reports to Ankara a similar tendency; while women had 'easily and happily' removed their *peçes*, the *çarşaf* was only 'partially' removed in the course of the anti-veiling campaigns.[47] It was probably easier, or more acceptable, or desirable for women to expose their face than to replace their *çarşaf*. The fact that the struggle against the *peçe* had a longer history, and that it was much strongly stigmatized as the 'veil' to be removed because of the symbolic meanings attributed to the opening of the face, it can be argued that the removal of the *peçe* began earlier than the removal of head covering or full body covering as provided by the *çarşaf*. It was also probably perceived as more 'doable' by the general public compared to the removal of the *çarşaf*. An article in a Trabzon newspaper, for example, complained that while women easily got rid of their *peçe*, the *çarşaf* proved more durable despite all the propaganda against it.[48] Specifically targeting the *çarşaf*, the author claimed that the removal of

---

45. Circular from the Deputy Minister of Foreign Affairs to the Ministry of the Interior, EGM 13216-7/1, 28 October 1935.

46. Circular from the Ministry of the Interior to the Ministry of Foreign Affairs, EGM 13216-7/1, 19 November 1935. There is another circular sent from the General Directorate of Security to the General Directorate of Press (*Matbuat Umum Müdürlüğü*) informing the later about the circular sent to the Ministry of Foreign Affairs asking the ministry to refute the article. See the circular from the General Directorate of Security to the General Directorate of Press, EGM 13216-7/1, 27 November 1935.

47. See, for example, the letter from the Governor of Sivas to the Ministry of the Interior, EGM 13216-7/1, 3 September 1935.

48. 'Çarşaf', *Halk*, 12 November 1935.

the *peçe* was in fact more important and symbolic to reflect the civilized character of the nation, and the will of Turkish women had succeeded in achieving this task. Yet, although the *çarşaf* was a foreign tradition and thus should be easier to remove according to the author, women of Trabzon were very reluctant to do so.

This reluctance of women cannot, of course, be understood without taking into account the patriarchal and conservative social dynamics by which they were surrounded. In fact, references to social pressures in explaining the unwillingness of women to remove their veils were common in the reports of the local authorities to Ankara, and these cannot be read only as attempts of these actors to create excuses for their inability to enforce a successful anti-veiling campaign in their localities. Especially in socio-economically less developed or smaller provinces or in places where there was a more homogeneous local culture, ethnically or religiously, the conservativeness of the society regarding women's public appearance was a major concern for women in the issue of veiling/unveiling as well. Thus, the strictness of patriarchal social control of women played a key role in their decision to veil or unveil. The governor of Sinop, for example, reported in March 1935 that many of those local women who had removed the *çarşaf* and came to the municipality building with an overcoat during the national elections a month earlier, in February 1935, again switched back to wearing the *çarşaf* due to the influence of old customs.[49] It seems that the local propaganda regarding the modernization of women's clothing in Sinop had some effect on the women of the city, at least in the beginning, and many women had chosen to unveil only during the elections, perhaps because there was more public attention on them during this first voting process after women gained their political rights in December 1934. Once the elections were over, however, many of them continued to use the *çarşaf* instead of the overcoat. Similarly, in Çorum, the governor attributed women's insistence on wearing the *çarşaf* despite an open ban on the entrenched moral and traditional norms in the province.[50] Under such circumstances, he maintained, it was very difficult for women to make up their own minds and adopt new forms of attire at the expense of having to face social pressure and exclusion.

The poor and older women proved particularly determined to wear the *çarşaf*. Even in the circulars sent from Ankara to the provinces, this idea that the *peçe* and the *çarşaf* were surviving in the provinces due to social pressures was salient. As quoted in Chapter 2, the circular of the minister of the interior on 22 June 1935 claimed that these veils had been totally removed in big cities like Istanbul, Ankara

---

49. From the Governor of Sinop to the Ministry of the Interior, EGM 13216-7/1, 4 March 1935.

50. From the Governor of Çorum to the Ministry of the Interior, EGM 13216-7/1, 22 November 1935. A similar argument was employed by the governor of Maraş. See, the Governor of Maraş to the Ministry of the Interior, EGM 13216-7/1, 13 August 1935. The governor of Çankırı was also complaining in 1939 about communal pressure on women and religious fanaticism, which made it very difficult for most of the women of the city to adapt to the new clothing norms. Metinsoy, 'Everyday Resistance', 100.

and Izmir, but were in use in other provinces because of the power of traditions and because women were afraid of gossip.[51] In fact, the minister indicated that women living in places where the *peçe* and the *çarşaf* were surviving would adopt the overcoat when they visited big towns, but then would go back to wearing the veils when they returned to their hometowns. A contemporary observer also points at how local community pressure influenced women's ability to unveil. In her tour through Eastern Anatolia, Lilo Linke notes the reaction of a woman she met on a train from Malatya to Adana in mid-1935 to the banning of the *peçe* and the *çarşaf* in the city. Having learned the news of the ban, the woman stated that women of Adana were lucky since they did not need to worry about what people would say about them if they removed their *çarşaf*.[52] The bans, it seems, were making it easier to unveil for those women who would like to unveil but were not able to do so because of the social pressure they were surrounded by.

The extent of pressure the patriarchal and conservative character of the society put on women can also be seen in the harassment and attacks some women faced because they removed their veils. In other words, in addition to labelling, gossiping and exclusion, which would already make women's daily life very difficult and thus hard to bear, women also had to cope with the threat of physical harassment in case of unveiling. In the province of Afyon, for example, women who had removed their *çarşaf* were harassed and assaulted by some men in the streets. As the governor reports, these 'malicious men' would make a pass at women, saying 'what nice domestic goods we have' (*ne iyi yerli mallarımız varmış*),[53] or use ruder language words, and even physically attack them.[54] A certain Emine, for example, a twenty-year-old woman who was the daughter of Mevlüt and wife of İsmail from the neighbourhood of Nurcu in the centre of Afyon, was physically harassed by Abdurrahman, son of Ahmet from the Kırkalioğulları family in the Mecidiye neighbourhood. Abdurrahman had harassed Emine because she was unveiled when she was passing by the İstasyon Avenue of Afyon with her child

---

51. From the Minister of Interior to General Inspectorships and Provinces, EGM 13216-7/1, 22 July 1935.

52. Linke, *Allah Dethroned*, 231.

53. Here, the verbal assault cited in the report of the governor, 'what nice domestic goods we have', probably had a double connotation and was also referring to another contemporary campaign to promote the use of domestic, locally produced goods. In the aftermath of the Great Depression, the 1930s in Turkey witnessed a national campaign to encourage saving and promote the use and consumption of domestic products. For this task, a special association, the National Economy and Savings Society (*Milli İktisat ve Tasarruf Cemiyeti*), was established in December 1929. The association was very organized in the provinces and established various committees for propaganda purposes. It also organized events during the Savings and Domestic Products Week (*Tasarruf ve Yerli Malı Haftası*), celebrated each year between 12 and 19 December. See Doğan Duman, *Ulusal Ekonominin Yapılanmasında Yerli Malı Haftaları* (Izmir: Dokuz Eylül Yayınları, 2001).

54. From the Governor of Afyon to the Ministry of the Interior, EGM 13216-7/1, 13 November 1935.

on 12 November. He had grabbed Emine's arm and began dragging her down the street. Emine was rescued only by the assistance she received from people around them. Abdurrahman was captured and handed over to the police. As indicated in a subsequent report from the governor, however, he was acquitted of this crime.[55] Similarly, the decision of the city council of Bergama, a district of the province of Izmir, to ban the *peçe*, the *çarşaf* and the *peştamal* also included an article indicating that those who would hurt and harm women wearing 'national' (meaning 'modern') attire would also be fined.[56] This shows that such acts either happened in Bergama or at least there was a strong concern that they could happen once women unveiled. In order to apply it more effectively, the committee that prepared the ban also proposed to the city council that the chairs placed in front of the coffeehouses should also be removed. These chairs, according to the committee, were occupied by unemployed men (*işi gücü olmayan*), who could harm those women who would pass by in national attire. Having heard of these cases of harassment and attacks against women, Ankara had urged the local authorities to strengthen their measures against such actions, to apprehend immediately those who were involved, and to report on the results of the legal procedures.[57] It seems that Ankara was concerned that such kinds of events could be used as excuse for open or secret opposition and provocation.

Women also had to confront the pressures coming from the state authorities and various local actors pushing for unveiling. Considering especially the cases where fines were imposed and the municipal police, the police or the gendarmerie were involved in the implementation process of the bans, it would not be an exaggeration to argue that some women were coerced, and probably had to remove their veils even if they did not want to.[58] In other words, women were caught between two patriarchal forces. On the one hand, religious concerns, traditional habits, social and family pressures surrounding women certainly played an indispensable role in their attitudes towards unveiling; on the other hand, the pressures coming from the state authorities created yet another obstacle to women trying to realize their own preferences and choices as individuals.

---

55. From the Governor of Afyon to the Ministry of the Interior, EGM 13216-7/1, 25 May 1936.

56. 'Bergama'da Çarşaf, Peçe ve Kıvraklar Kaldırılıyor', *Anadolu*, 6 December 1934. Metinsoy claims that in the 1930s, 'numerous men who verbally attacked women in the streets were sentenced to imprisonment or a heavy fine' after the Ministry of Justice issued a circular in 1929 ordering the judicial authorities to take legal action against those men who harassed women. Metinsoy, however, does not explain in detail whether these cases of imprisonment or fines were related to women's unveiling. Metinsoy, 'Everyday Resistance', 102.

57. For example, see the letter from the Minister of Interior to the Governorship of Afyon, EGM 13216-7/1, 28 November 1935.

58. In addition to the case of Tosya mentioned above, there were other instances where women were physically attacked. As mentioned in the previous chapter, a complaint letter from Aydın claims that women's *çarşaf*s were forcefully removed. Telegraph from Dokumacı Ahmet Şevki to President Atatürk, EGM 13216-7/1, 16 August 1935.

In addition to these factors, economic reasons also had a great impact on women's ability to comply with the new dress codes. Because anti-veiling campaigns promoted the replacement of the *çarşaf* with an overcoat and presented it as the 'modern' outdoor clothing of women, the removal of the *çarşaf* was equated with the adoption of an overcoat, which was unfamiliar to many people in the provinces, in short supply and more expensive than the *çarşaf* or other local body veils, such as the *peştamal*. The *çarşaf* or the *peştamal* had become customary, were locally produced and thus easily available for people. Considering that the majority of the population lived in the rural areas and in poor conditions, acquiring an overcoat was not easy. Some women openly complained about this by writing letters to newspapers and explaining their inability to afford overcoats.[59] In fact, the inability of the poor people to abide by the decisions of the local institutions banning the *çarşaf* was also observed by the authorities.[60] Thus, the widespread tendency of the local administrators to allow more time for the removal of the *çarşaf* in the decisions was not a coincidence. Poverty also explains why local institutions such as the People's Houses, the Red Crescent, the party branches and chambers of commerce were mobilized to provide poor women with overcoats. In some cities, the wives of the governors or mayors were personally in charge of these organizations to help poor women to replace their *çarşaf*. As mentioned earlier, in Antalya, for example, a special committee was formed by the provincial council to help poor women and the head of this committee was the wife of the governor.[61] In Trabzon, the wife of the mayor, Emine Kadri Evren, was in charge of the efforts of the Red Crescent to provide poor women with overcoats.[62] In fact, even for these initiatives, it was hard to provide enough overcoats for women in need.[63] They tried to mobilize donors to collect money for the initiative and help women convert their *çarşafs* into overcoats

---

59. A woman from Çorum and groups of women from Milas had written to the newspaper, *Köroğlu*. They were not against unveiling but they were complaining that overcoats were very expensive. A group of men from Akseki had also written a letter to the same newspaper indicating that they were unable to afford an overcoat since they were poor people living on bread. This letter was reported in the newspaper with the title 'Overcoat or Bread?'. Metinsoy, 'Everyday Resistance', 96.

60. For example, see the letter from the Governor of Çorum to the Ministry of the Interior, EGM 13216-7/1, 20 August 1935 and the letter from the Governor of Kırklareli to the Ministry of the Interior, EGM 13216-7/1, 27 September 1935.

61. 'Kentimizde kadın kılığı işi bütün hızıyla yürüyor', *Antalya*, 2 May 1935.

62. 'Kızılay fakirlere 50 manto dağıttı', *Halk*, 30 April 1936.

63. In some news reports, this difficulty was implicit in the language. It was emphasized that these institutions would 'search for ways' to provide the overcoats. See, for example, 'Halkevi çok fakir ailelere manto yaptıracak', *Halk*, 27 February 1936. As it can be followed by local newspapers, all initiatives combined, they could provide 319 women with overcoats in Trabzon: 200 by the Red Crescent, 119 by the local party administration. See 'Kızılay fakirlere 50 manto dağıttı', *Halk*, 30 April 1936; 'Kızılay bugün 150 manto daha dağıtıyor', *Halk*, 4 May 1936; 'Bugün 119 Manto daha dağıtılacak', *Halk*, 1 June 1936.

in cases where the cloth of the *çarşaf* was suitable for such a change.[64] In Çanakkale, for example, village women tried to produce overcoats out of the local cloth they had woven themselves.[65] In places where such initiatives did not exist or could not provide the number of overcoats needed, women had to find other ways to handle the difficult situation in which they found themselves. In Seyitgazi, for example, a district of the province of Eskişehir, the ban on the *çarşaf* was put into practice immediately, thus those women, who could not afford to buy an overcoat but had to go out to work, had to wear men's overcoats and jackets.[66] This 'awkward scene' created a reaction in the district. The people of Seyitgazi, the majority of whom were poor farmers, complained that the municipality should have postponed the implementation of the ban on the *çarşaf* until the end of harvest season so that people could at least save some money to comply with the new dress codes.

Such examples also point to the various ways in which women in different cities reacted to the clothing change. In other words, the effectiveness and the influence of the anti-veiling campaigns were uneven; depending on the social, cultural and economic factors in different cities, and differences across social classes in a particular city, there were significant variations regarding how women dressed.[67] Age would also matter.[68] Even within the same family, generational differences would play a role; a mother would continue to use some kind of a headscarf, while her daughters could be totally unveiled. Also, a woman who used to veil by wearing the *çarşaf*, might adopt a turban or a hat for some time, but then prefer to use a headscarf as she gets older. Thus, just as in the case of the 1920s, it is rather more appropriate to talk about a coexistence of many forms of veiling and unveiling in the 1930s.[69] The *peçe* and the *çarşaf* never totally disappeared, but decreased at

---

64. This was the case in Antalya, for example.

65. Letter from the Governor of Çanakkale to the Ministry of the Interior, EGM 13216-7/1, 21 March 1936.

66. Letter from the Governor of Eskişehir to the Ministry of the Interior, EGM 13216-7/1, 7 February 1936.

67. In fact, even before the anti-veiling campaigns of the 1930s, these factors had already caused a change in women's clothing. Graham-Brown suggests, for example, that the change in women's clothing was partly a result of the shift in the meanings attributed to certain dress forms: 'In Turkey, in 1890, the wearer of a *yashmak* and a *charchaf* would have been assumed to come from a well-to-do elite family. In 1930, a woman from that class would have been recognizable by the fashionable cut of her dress and coat or suit ... ' Graham-Brown, *Images of Women*, 132. Yashmak (*yaşmak*) is a veil that was used together with the *ferace*, which consisted of two pieces, a head-veil and a face-veil. It was replaced by the *peçe* with the spread of the *çarşaf*.

68. For a similar observation by a contemporary author who underlined the difference between the old generation of women and the new in terms of adopting modern clothing in Istanbul in 1934, see A.E., 'Yüzü kapalı gezen kadın', *Son Posta*, 6 August 1934.

69. For various examples of women's adaptation to new clothing and their new ways of covering their hair, see Oya Baydar and Feride Çiçekoğlu, eds. *Cumhuriyet'in Aile Albümleri* (Istanbul: Tarih Vakfı Yurt Yayınları, 1998).

least during the campaigns, though perhaps more in some places than others.[70] More 'modernized' forms of veiling, ranging from larger headscarves to turbans, became common. In fact, women's insistence on veiling, more particularly, on covering their hair, whether in a more traditional form or in more modernized, modified forms, clearly influenced the outcome of the anti-veiling campaigns. In other words, the insistence on the covering of the hair had an impact on the general public discourse on women's clothing, and also, on the expectations of the Kemalist elite. As mentioned above, even a Kemalist as radical as Gündüz was willing to accept the fact that it would take a long time for the ideals to be internalized by the masses. As a matter of fact, however dominant the image of 'modern' Turkish woman was in the popular press, there was not a total disappearance of women with some forms of head covering, for example.[71] In other words, since the co-existence of many forms of women's clothing in practice was undeniable, the tendency of the Kemalists to opt for a more gradual transformation in the matter of modernization of women's dress grew; the 'symbolic "revealing" of the face and body operated within constraints recognized and accepted by authorities prompting dress reform'.[72] Thus, in addition to the patriarchal concerns of the Kemalist male elite and their fear of 'over-Westernization' of Turkish women,[73] it was women's insistence on having a say on what they wear that drew the boundaries and limits of the anti-veiling campaigns.

Women's role in the transformation of the female dress

It would be misleading to think that women's compliance can be seen as purely a matter of propaganda. Although it is impossible to know the exact percentages, there were in fact many women who removed their *peçe* and *çarşaf*. Likewise,

---

70. Yılmaz argues that the regional differences can in part be explained by the limits of the RPP penetration in the periphery. Yılmaz, *Becoming Turkish*, 103. Yılmaz also refers to a report by the governor of the province of Hakkari, where he indicated that the notable native families continued to wear the *peçe* and the *çarşaf* despite the anti-veiling campaign. The governor was pointing at a difference between the civil servants who were natives of the region and those who were not; native ones also continued to wear the *peçe* and the *çarşaf*. Ibid., 104.

71. See Libal, 'From Face Veil'.

72. Ibid., 49.

73. Even during the heyday of the anti-veiling campaigns in the mid-1930s, the control over women's sexuality and the obsession with preventing women from being 'too much Westernized' were very visible. Various commentaries in local newspapers were warning women to remain loyal to moral codes in the public life. The length of women's skirts, their hair styles or how much make-up they should put were all constant issues of concern. For example, see 'Kadın ve Erkek', *Babalık*, 2 December 1934; Orhan Selim, 'Çok Boyanıyorsun Kadınım … ', *Babalık*, 18 December 1934; 'Çok Açılıyorsun Kadınım', *Babalık*, 19 December 1934; 'Kız talebeler hakkında verilen güzel kararlar … ', *Hakkın Sesi*, 28 February 1936.

it would also not be correct to attribute this compliance of women solely to the repressiveness of the campaigns and women's fear of the regime or local authorities. Some women willingly removed their *peçe* and *çarşaf*, having seen anti-veiling campaigns as an opportunity to adopt the new clothing, to relax the rules of seclusion, to follow fashion, or simply because they thought it was more convenient to do so.[74] Since anti-veiling campaigns addressed all women and aimed at achieving a mass movement of change in women's clothing, they also created a chance for individual women, who had the intention or desire to remove these veils, to do so in groups. In other words, it can be argued that those women who were prepared to remove these veils but were afraid or reluctant to do so on their own might have found it easier and more preferable to change their outdoor clothing together with other women and as part of a politically supported and socially propagated local campaign. In fact, although less obviously, such opportunities were available even before the main wave of anti-veiling campaigns had begun in 1934. Women participating in public education or joining the workforce were among the factors that significantly increased their capacity to socialize with unveiling as a norm, or at least to familiarize with the idea that their clothing can change just like their social status. In Tarsus, for example, a local factory distributed over 300 overcoats to women workers in November 1933 so that they could remove their *peçe* and *çarşaf*.[75] Some other working women in the town also followed this example and begun wearing an overcoat instead of the *çarşaf*. The public cotton factory in Adana went one step further in 1934 and introduced a uniform for its 1,200 workers, composed of both men and women. As reported in a national newspaper, especially the new elegant dress for women workers, 'a black dress with a white belt', had emancipated them from the baggy trousers, the *peçe* and the *çarşaf*.[76]

As briefly discussed in Chapter 2, the beginning of the 1930s witnessed an increasing stigmatization of the *peçe* and the *çarşaf* as uncivilized attire and the promotion of European dresses as the norm in a number of media, ranging from propaganda posters of the RPP to the various milieus of popular culture. As Shissler argued in the context of beauty contests, the new practices and norms introduced or legitimatized under the new regime in the 1930s 'shifted the parameters of where women could go and what they could do'; they entailed a 'redefinition of

---

74. Yılmaz indicates, based on her sources, that 'local elites found many of the state-promoted reforms and lifestyles acceptable and desirable'. However, it should be underlined that it is hard to generalize this to all local elites since not all of them were 'already modernized, urban and educated' to easily adopt the new dress norms. Yılmaz, *Becoming Turkish*, 105. She quotes one of her informants, Meliha Tanyeli, who recalled that women of her family in Trabzon very easily adopted the new dress norms: 'Everyone put on a *manto* [overcoat] right away. First they put headscarf (*eşarp*) above it. Later hats become fashionable'. Ibid., 107.

75. 'Tarsus kadınları', *Cumhuriyet*, 29 November 1933.

76. 'Adana Amele Kıyafeti', *Son Posta*, 3 August 1934. It was also stated in the news that male workers were seen quite elegant in public with their new dresses, a blue trouser and a worker's shirt (*işçi gömleği*).

the concept of respectability or honour, *namus*, and an expansion for women of the limits of the social contract'.[77] Similarly, the anti-veiling campaigns also enhanced women's capacity to make choices and expanded the space in which women could realize them. This does not mean that this happened to the same degree everywhere, or that all women enjoyed the advantages of this redefinition equally. However, it should not be overlooked that anti-veiling campaigns and the discourse and propaganda regarding women's clothing in the press and popular culture significantly contributed to the relaxation of certain social norms, by marking the removal of the veil as 'normal', acceptable and even desirable, by redefining 'socially acceptable standards of women's dress'.[78]

This redefinition was reinforced by the encouragement of the adoption of 'new' clothing to replace the *çarşaf* in various ways, the most important of which was the flourishing of the sewing courses for women in the provinces. In other words, women were not only persuaded to remove their 'old' clothes, but they were also trained to create their new clothes by learning modern sewing techniques and the latest fashion patterns. Usually called the *Biçki Dikiş Yurdu*, these tailoring schools that provided sewing courses for women were opened by both private initiative and public institutions like the People's Houses.[79] The opening of such a place in a certain city was usually announced in the local newspapers and included detailed information such as its address or the school from which the head of the course graduated.[80] It was also common for such schools to provide courses on hat making, which would make women's access to 'modern' headwear easier and cheaper. This would be especially emphasized in the ads about sewing courses. These sewing schools also frequently organized fairs, exhibitions, and fashion shows to display the clothes, hats, flowers and other home decoration items they produced for the general public. Always reported on in the local newspapers, such organizations were sometimes hosted by the People's Houses or the party buildings, and attended by the highest local administrators and other leading

---

77. Shissler, 'Beauty', 107.

78. Libal, 'From Face Veil', 54.

79. The idea of training women in sewing goes back to the late Ottoman era. They emerged as part of the debate on the 'national dress' as briefly mentioned in Chapter 1. *Teali-i Nisvan Cemiyeti* (Association for the Advancement of Women) had established first a course centre and then a sewing house, which was called *Beyaz Dikiş Yurdu* (White Sewing Home), in Istanbul in 1913. Later, *Malumat-ı Dahiliye İstihlaki Kadınlar Cemiyet-i Hayriyesi* (Women's Organization for the Consumption of Local Products) opened workshops in a few neighbourhoods in Istanbul where women were educated as dress makers by using locally produced materials. There were also other organizations, like the *Türk Kadınları Biçki Yurdu* (Turkish Women's Tailoring Home) that organized sewing courses for women. See van Os, 'Feminism, Philanthropy', 230–40.

80. See, for example, 'Elçin Biçki ve Dikiş Yurdu', *Halk*, 6 February 1935; 'Münevver bir kızın muvaffakiyeti', *Hakkın Sesi*, 25 January 1936. One of the sewing courses was called 'Modern Family Sewing Course' (*Asri Aile Dikiş Yurdu*) in Trabzon. See 'Trabzon Halkevinde Biçki ve Dikiş Sergisi', *Son Posta*, 1 August 1934.

members of the local society in the provinces.[81] In some cities, the contribution of the sewing schools to replacing the *çarşaf* with the overcoat during the anti-veiling campaigns was particularly emphasized. In Trabzon, for example, only a few weeks before the enforcement of the ban on the *peçe* and the *çarşaf*, the sewing schools were working at higher capacity, day and night, by bringing more women into their workforce.[82]

In addition to the sewing courses offering short-term training for women, seemingly organized predominantly for women in the provinces, a more limited number of women had the chance to acquire a longer education and thus more complex skills in sewing at the Girls' Institutes (*Kız Enstitüleri*). As vocational schools established in 1929 specifically for training girls, these institutes aimed at creating educated, modern and rational housewives.[83] One of the main components of this project was equipping women with the knowledge necessary to make their own clothes, and preferably, to help spread 'modern' clothing as the norm. Graduates of the institutes would be the role models for all other Turkish women, and through the clothes they created, for sale, for exhibition or for themselves and women around them, they would symbolize the transformation of ordinary Turkish women under the republic.

Women's positive attitude towards the removal of the *peçe* and *çarşaf* was not limited to their simple compliance with the bans or campaigns initiated by men. There were, in fact, many women, mostly from the local elite families or among state officials, who organized meetings, gave speeches and supported unveiling by being part the campaigns. Especially local women's associations, women members of other associations and sports clubs or of the local branches of the Red Crescent and the Aviation Society were actively involved. The Diyarbakır Women's Association, for example, organized a meeting where the head of the association, Behiye Baturay, declared their wish for the removal of the *peçe* and the *çarşaf*, which, she argued, had no connection with women's honour or Turkish women's dignity.[84] Equally, women could act as facilitators and initiators of these campaigns. In fact, one of the earliest examples of an anti-veiling campaign was the decision of a group of women in Bursa on 29 October, Republic Day, in 1933 to remove their *çarşaf* and to declare this publicly in order to inform and encourage other women in the city.[85] A similar decision was made by a group of women in Kütahya in May 1934.[86]

---

81. For example, see 'Malatyada Biçki ve Dikiş Sergisi', *Son Posta*, 14 June 1934; 'Trabzon Halkevinde Biçki ve Dikiş Sergisi', *Son Posta*, 1 August 1934; 'Samsunda Biçki ve Dikiş Sergisi', *Son Posta*, 4 August 1934; 'Halkevinde açılan sergi', *Halk*, 11 July 1935; 'Elçin Dikiş Yurdu sergisi açıldı', *Halk*, 25 June 1936; 'Halkevinde Sümer Biçki, Dikiş, Nakış yurdu açıldı', *Halk*, 27 July 1936.

82. 'Peçe ve Çarşaf tarihe karıştı', *Halk*, 23 April 1936.

83. Like the sewing courses, the origins of the Girls' Institutes also go back to the late Ottoman Era. For more the Girls' Institutes, see Elif Ekin Akşit, *Kızların Sessizliği: Kız Enstitülerinin Uzun Tarihi* (Istanbul: İletişim, 2005).

84. 'Diyarbekir kadınlar derneği ... ', *İkbal*, 27 January 1935.

85. 'Bursada artık çarşaf giymeyecekler', *Cumhuriyet*, 29 October 1933.

86. 'Kütahya hanımları ve çarşaf', *Cumhuriyet*, 6 May 1934.

Women's role as facilitators or initiators of the anti-veiling campaigns was particularly valid for women who were politically active. As it was briefly discussed in Chapter 2, Turkey in the 1930s witnessed an increase in women's political mobilization. Women's acquisition of the right to participate in the local elections in 1930 was a turning point and their membership in the party began to be promoted by the regime leadership in Ankara. Women's attainment of political rights, along with their right to participate in the national elections beginning in December 1934, created an even stronger momentum for women's greater involvement in political life, in the party, in provincial and municipal councils, and also in other institutions, like the People's Houses. Although it was promoted by the regime leadership, women's increasing involvement in political life clearly widened the space for their participation in the public life in general. In other words, as can be followed from the provincial newspapers, not only did women's membership in the party begin to increase by the beginning of 1935, but their membership in other institutions and associations also grew along with their political mobilization.[87] Many women willingly became politically and socially active, and they usually participated very enthusiastically and vocally in the institutions they joined. This was especially so in issues related to women, including unveiling. As it was mentioned in Chapter 2, in the General Congress of the RPP in May 1935, among those who supported the idea to enact national legislation banning the *peçe* was a women delegate from Niğde, Naciye Osman Kozbek. In fact, in its report on the congress, one local newspaper claimed that it was a women delegate who first submitted a proposal to the congress for such legislation.[88] The newspaper argued that this women delegate had promised her fellow women in her constituency that the *peçe* and the *çarşaf* would be removed. Some local decisions to ban the use of the *peçe* and the *çarşaf* were in fact made on the basis of the proposals of women members of the local councils. In Mersin, for example, the capital of the province of İçel, Zekiye Hanım, a women member of the city council, submitted a proposal to ban the *çarşaf*.[89] In Tarsus, a district of the province of İçel, the proposal to ban the *peçe* and the *çarşaf* was submitted to the city council, again by a women member, Meliha Dağseven.[90] In Bursa, the suggestion to have the *kafes* removed from windows was made to the city council by the deputy mayor, Zehra Hanım, the first women deputy mayor of Turkey.[91] In Maraş, it was Nuriye Bülbül, the only women member of the local party administration, who was the first woman in the city to remove her *çarşaf*.[92] In Antalya, a women's committee of the People's House was the forerunner of the anti-veiling campaign.[93]

---

87. See, for example, 'Samsunda Kadınların Toplantısı', *Kars*, 24 January 1935; 'Parti Kongrelerinde Kadın Üyeler', *Hakkın Sesi*, 20 October 1935.

88. 'Kurultay ne yaptı', *Ak Günler*, 3 June 1935.

89. 'Mersin'de çarşafların Men'i İstendi', *Cumhuriyet*, 7 April 1934.

90. 'Tarsus Belediye M. Toplantısı', *Yeni Mersin*, 4 February 1935.

91. 'Belediye Meclisinde', *Hakkın Sesi*, 3 February 1935.

92. Mentioned in the Report of Mitat Aydın, deputy of Trabzon, on the province of Maraş, BCA 490.01/273.1091.2, 7 May 1943.

93. 'Antalyada Çarşaf ve Peçelerle Mücadele Başladı', *Yeni Asır*, 23 December 1934.

Women's roles as facilitators and initiators of the anti-veiling campaigns were not limited to a small number of women who were members of the local councils or the People's Houses. Women became the vanguards of the campaigns in relatively higher numbers especially in the context of their acquiring the right to vote and to be elected. In gatherings women organized in various cities to celebrate this right, the removal of the *peçe* and the *çarşaf* was advocated as part of women's efforts to be worthy of this reform. A news report states that in Ordu, for example, women who gathered to celebrate and to send telegram messages to Atatürk and Prime Minister İnönü indicating their appreciation for having gained this right, decided to no longer wear the *çarşaf*, which they saw as the legacy of the sultanate.[94] Likewise, in Kilis, about a hundred and fifty women gathered to celebrate their political rights and decided to remove the *peçe*.[95] In Muğla, a group of women also led the call to organize a campaign to remove the *çarşaf* as part of their decision to be politically more active.[96] They had gathered to discuss the issue of becoming members of the party, the People's House and other institutions, and to remove their *çarşaf*. In Bor, a district of the province of Niğde, about forty women organized a meeting at the library of the People's House, where they all removed their *peçes* and requested that these veils be kept in the museum as the remnants of the past. They also asked the municipality to issue a ban on the use of the *peçe* in their city.[97] At similar meetings in Izmir and Konya, women's speeches drew a direct link between the opening of the doors of public life in the republican regime and their liberation from the social seclusion symbolized by the *peçe* and the *çarşaf*: 'The Turkish woman, who, until yesterday, was supposedly incapable of doing anything else than napping behind her *kafes* and stumbling in her *çarşaf*, has progressed as fast as an eagle in flight in her short life of 11 years.'[98]

This equating of the removal of the *peçe* and the *çarşaf* with the gaining of women's political rights continued in subsequent years. It was in fact reinforced by women themselves and used to mobilize other women in the struggle against segregation and veiling. It became for women a milestone that differentiated between a period characterized by women's segregation and their degraded status in the society, and a new era marked by women's increasing public visibility and roles.[99] At a meeting

---

94. 'Türk Kadınlığının Kıvancı', *Yeni Asır*, 9 Aralık 1934.

95. 'Atatürk Kadınlarımıza Değerli İşler Dileyor, Her Tarafta Kadınlar Kıvanç İçinde', *Yeni Asır*, 11 December 1934; 'Kiliste kadınların tezahüratı', *Kars*, 13 December 1934; 'Kilis bayanları', *Yeni Adana*, 12 December 1934.

96. 'Muğla Kadınları Çarşafları Kaldırıyor', *Halk*, 31 December 1934; 'Muğla Bayanları', *Yeni Adana*, 30 Aralık 1934.

97. 'Kadınlar peçelerini müzeye koydular', *Yeni Adana*, 11 January 1935.

98. 'Kadınların söylevleri', *Babalık*, 16 December 1934. For women's speeches in Izmir, see 'İffeti Kara Peçede ve Kafesin Arkasında Arıyan Zihniyet Yıkılmıştır, Bayanlarımızın Heyecanlı Söylevleri', *Yeni Asır*, 16 December 1934.

99. For an article by a women author in a local newspaper emphasizing this historical break, see Melahat Saim, 'Türk Kadınının Saylav Seçimi', *Kars*, 14 January 1935. See also 'Türk Kadının Cemiyetteki mevkii', *Halk*, 26 March 1936.

at the Antalya People's House held to celebrate the first anniversary of the political rights of women, Nihal Güzey pointed to this difference in her speech addressing the Turkish woman:

> In days when the women of the advanced nations were living in total freedom, the sultanate had reserved you a space behind the *kafes* and covered your face with a thick and black piece of cloth. It had seen no harm in insulting you by believing that this *kafes* and piece of cloth would be the guardians of your chastity. The Atatürk revolution, on the other hand, could not tolerate this insult that was deemed worthy of you. It has showed that you are not a slave but a human being that deserves respect worthy of civilized people. It has given you freedom. You have come into existence. You have also lifted and taken away that black cloth on your face that was of use for nothing.[100]

Women also wrote in the local newspapers to promote unveiling, directly addressing the women of their city. The idea frequently emphasized by women was that they could modernize the way they dressed themselves, without any need for men's guidance, in conformity with modernization and with the aim of reaching a better position in society. In her poem entitled 'Let's Throw off the *Çarşafs*', which was published in a local newspaper, Hayriye Ural, a woman from Trabzon, emphasized how Turkish women easily adjusted to the major changes the Kemalist revolution had introduced, and called on them to do the same on the issue of unveiling as well.[101] In her opinion, it was meaningless for the women of Trabzon to adhere to the meaningless and outdated veil called the *çarşaf* at a time when all archaic beliefs were in fact being eliminated. Having emphasized that the *çarşaf* had nothing to do with religion and had been removed in other cities, she invited the women of Trabzon not to fall behind in bringing about this change.

The discrepancy in terms of veiling (and in fact, in terms of women's social status in general) between Istanbul and Ankara, on the one hand, and Anatolia, on the other, had often been mentioned as a sign of the disadvantaged position of the women living in the periphery of the country, and, thus, the anti-veiling campaign was promoted as an opportunity to fill the gap by women themselves in the provinces. In her article entitled 'Let's Do away with Veiling', Nihal Güzey drew the attention of the women of Antalya to this opportunity:

> Why do we [as women of Anatolia] not benefit from the right that our revolution has given to women? Are we still going to continue to wear this dress, which does not belong to us, at a time when we passionately struggle against foreign culture and get rid of the Arab alphabet?[102]

---

100. 'Aydın Antalya kadınları siyasi haklarını kutluladılar', *Antalya*, 12 December 1935.

101. Hayriye Ural, 'Çarşafları atalım', *Halk*, 30 March 1936. For a similar call written again by a women author, Mürşide Akyol, in the province of Adana, see 'Adana'da Türk Kadını', *Ak Günler*, 29 October 1936.

102. Nihal Güzey, 'Örtünmeden Vazgeçelim', *Antalya*, 10 January 1935.

For her, women of Anatolia should also adopt civilized clothing in order to be part of the social life, and 'enlightened' women should be the vanguards for them, especially in removing the *peçe* before all else. She also warned these enlightened women against wearing fancy overcoats and hats, since ordinary women were possibly not removing their *çarşaf* because it would be too expensive to replace them with modern clothes. That is why she stressed the necessity of creating options to adopting modern clothes in an affordable manner, one solution of which would be training women to make their own overcoats and hats at free courses. She suggested that these free courses could be organized by People's Houses.

This acceptance of new ways of dressing by a significant number of women was represented as 'women's struggle against the *peçe* and the *çarşaf*. These examples, indeed, reflect some women's support for the anti-veiling campaigns. Equally, these examples are also an indication of the regime's satisfaction with the gradual change that this support was supposed to bring in the future. In the eyes of the Kemalist elite at the centre, women's approval and adoption of modern clothing was the most significant precondition of the success, and unlike in other reforms, they were more patient to wait for the ultimate success, trusting in women's agency to spread the reform. Moreover, particularly educated women did not think of these campaigns and the propaganda concerning them as instrumentalization of women. In fact, as presented above, they participated in the campaigns to 'modernize' women's clothing, primarily because the clothing change was so thoroughly related to the ideas opposing women's seclusion and supporting their participation in the public life. In other words, for those women, it was not about a few veils; it was about the struggle against the mentality that limited women's visibility in and access to public life and confined them to the private sphere. This sure meant being in alliance with the regime, for particular groups of women at least – an alliance through which they gained the political support for their decades-old struggle against traditional norms and achieved the right to participate in the public sphere as the agents of modernization. However, this alliance should be seen as a negotiation rather than instumentalization of women. Women were not victims to be liberated or passive instruments to be deployed; the roles attributed to women were indeed far more complex. It can be argued that one of the goals of the anti-veiling campaigns was to create modern female subjects that would not passively follow the Kemalist male elite, but would actively participate in and further the modernizing reforms, especially at the local level. Thus, like in other state policies, the anti-veiling campaigns entailed regulation and control of women's bodies and choices while at the same time providing opportunities for them to position themselves as agents. This potentially empowering aspect of the Kemalist policies on women should be taken into account alongside their patriarchal and interventionist character.

Chapter 5

THE TURKISH CASE IN THE WIDER MUSLIM CONTEXT

Modernist discourses that emerged in the so-called 'Muslim world' in the nineteenth and early twentieth centuries, especially around issues of gender and women's social roles, were strikingly similar. Given the great extent of intellectual and cultural exchange within the wider global Muslim context, the main producers of these discourses, the modernist Muslim elites, were influenced by each other.[1] As Cronin has maintained, '[A]cross the Arab, Ottoman and Iranian worlds, across the Caucasus and Central Asia, and among the Muslim communities of the Balkans, reformers, operating within a newly integrated transnational Muslim intellectual environment, identified the same problem of "backwardness" resulting from the same general and specific causes, and proposed the same remedies.'[2] With these strong historical ties and political parallel in the background, the Kemalist modernization, however Western-oriented, was nevertheless also deeply embedded in this transnational Muslim environment. The developments under the new regime in Turkey were in fact, as it is often emphasized, closely followed by its Muslim contemporaries. Mustafa Kemal's role as the 'saviour of Turkey' had contributed immensely to his popularity among the Muslim-majority countries in the 1920s and the reforms introduced in interwar Turkey inspired a number of other Muslim leaders.[3] In certain cases, the relations would exceed inspiration,

---

1. See Cemil Aydın, *The Idea of the Muslim World: A Global Intellectual History* (Cambridge: Harvard University Press, 2017).

2. Stephanie Cronin, 'Introduction: Coercion or Empowerment? Anti-veiling Campaigns: A Comparative Perspective', in *Anti-Veiling Campaigns in the Muslim World: Gender, Modernism and the Politics of Dress*, ed. Stephanie Cronin (London: Routledge, 2014), 7.

3. François Georgeon, 'Kemalizm ve İslam Dünyası (1919–1938): Bazı İşaret Taşları', in *Kemalizm ve İslam Dünyası*, eds. İskender Gökalp and François Georgeon (Istanbul: Arba, 1990), 11–53.

going as far as to include actual collaboration in modernization efforts.[4] Although the admiration for Kemalism in Muslim societies suffered a serious backlash with the abolition of the caliphate in Turkey in 1924, and the subsequent reforms involving secularization, the Kemalist experience continued to be a constant reference point, negative or positive, in major political discussions and disputes in the Middle East and beyond.[5]

The political elite and intellectual circles in Turkey were of course aware of these influences. Particularly crucial for them was the image of Kemalist Turkey in Iran and in Arab countries that were formerly under Ottoman control. Not only was news about reforms in Turkey translated from Syrian, Egyptian and Iranian newspapers into Turkish and published in national and local newspapers, similar developments in these countries were equally followed and reported in the Turkish press.[6] The underlying idea behind the Kemalist interest in modernizing reforms in other Muslim countries was that Turkey was the 'model country' in the 'Muslim world'; the country was depicted as a mirror, reflecting light towards its 'less developed' Eastern neighbours.[7] Such depictions were not only concerned with promoting Kemalism outside Turkey; they would also reinforce the proud national identity constructed under the new regime inside the country and help legitimize the Kemalist reforms by invoking comparable initiatives in countries that were closest in terms of culture and history. In other words, the aim was also to send the message that Turkey was not alone among the Muslim-majority countries in pursuing radical modernization efforts.

---

4. Turkey sent advisors and experts to Afghanistan, for example, and hosted Afghan students, including women, for education. Afghan students' travelling to Turkey, having removed their veils, became an issue of opposition against the Afghan king. Yaiha Baiza, *Education in Afghanistan: Developments, Influences and Legacies since 1901* (London: Routledge, 2013), 79–80. See also Amin Saikal, *Modern Afghanistan: A History of Struggle and Survival* (London: I.B. Tauris, 2012) and Amin Saikal, 'Kemalism: Its Influence on Iran and Afghanistan', *International Journal of Turkish Studies* 2, no. 2 (1982): 25–32. For more on the transnational impact of Kemalism, see *Kemalism: Transnational Politics in the Post Ottoman World*, eds. Nathalie Clayer, Fabio Giomi and Emmanuel Szurek (London: I.B. Tauris, 2018).

5. See Gain Minault, *The Khilafat Movement: Religious Symbolism and Political Mobilization in India* (New York: Columbia University Press, 1982). Some Uzbek historians, for instance, argue that in Uzbekistan 'the idea of women's emancipation was carried forward by the example of Turkey'. Quoted in Marianne Kamp, *The New Woman in Uzbekistan: Islam, Modernity, and Unveiling Under Communism* (Seattle: University of Washington Press, 2006), 178.

6. For example, see 'İran'da teceddüt hareketleri', *Yeni Adana*, 19 October 1934; 'Meşhedte yeni elbise aleyhine gösteri', *Kars*, 27 July 1935; 'Mısır'da Peçe aleyhinde Nazire Zeyneddinin Faaliyetleri', *Hakkın Sesi*, 6 February 1936; 'Mısır kadınlarının tebriği', *Kars*, 14 February 1935; 'Suriyede bey, paşa kalmadı', *Hakkın Sesi*, 5 February 1936.

7. Georgeon, 'Kemalizm', 40. For example, see Musa Ateş, 'Çarşaf ve Peçeden Sonra Kafes!', *Hakkın Sesi*, 28 January 1935.

This was particularly crucial for those reforms that had a greater risk of fuelling social opposition. Changes regarding women were among the most salient ones. This was why any development related to them, particularly women's clothing and veiling, in other Muslim-majority countries would be closely followed by Turkish public opinion and receive great attention in the press. Moreover, in reporting these developments, the Turkish press would highlight Turkish women's vanguard position among the Muslim women. The idea that Turkish women's removal of the *peçe* and the *çarşaf* was celebrated by women in countries like Egypt and Syria, and this encouraged them to initiate a similar rebellion against 'backwardness' is visible in some of these articles translated from Arab newspapers.[8] In fact, some opponents of unveiling in Arab countries directly referred to unveiled Turkish women, since they were seen as setting a negative example.[9] So the public interest in what was going on in Turkey was there; but it was exaggerated by the Kemalist elites to the point that they would link all reforms regarding women in other Muslim-majority countries to the developments in Turkey. This idea that Turkey was the 'model country' in women's emancipation was strong even at the local level. For example, during a discussion at the city council of Bursa, council member Rıza Yücer would support a firmer implementation of the ban on the *peçe* and the *çarşaf* by claiming that the removal of these veils could no longer be seen only as a national concern. For him, it was unacceptable that there were still women in Bursa wearing the *peçe* and the *çarşaf* while 'even' the women of those countries that were following Turkey in their modernization efforts had already begun to remove them:

> In one of our meetings, we decided to ban the *peçe* and the *çarşaf*. There is no doubt that this decision is being carried out. However, the issue has reached such a point that the *peçe* and the *çarşaf* are no longer only the concerns of Turkey. Even those countries like Egypt, Iran and Syria, which consider us as their guide on the road to revolution and civilization and have begun to walk on the revolutionary road that we indeed have paved, are prohibiting the *peçe* and the *çarşaf*. Under these circumstances, we definitely do not want to come across women still wearing the *peçe* and the *çarşaf* in our streets. We should speed up the implementation of our decision.[10]

The word 'even' that Yücer uses reflects the degree to which Turkish elites, even those at the local level, had internalized the idea that Turkey was (or had to be) more 'advanced' compared to her other Muslim counterparts. This was of course subjective at many levels, yet politically useful for Kemalist purposes. In

---

8. For example, see 'Mısır'da Peçe aleyhinde Nazire Zeyneddinin Faaliyetleri', *Hakkın Sesi*, 6 February 1936. See also 'Mısır Kadınlar Briliği ve Türk Kadını', *Yeni Adana*, 10 January 1935; 'Mısır kadınlar birliği başkanının ajans muhabirine beyanatı', *Halk*, 31 January 1935.

9. William L. Cleveland, 'Atatürk Viewed by His Arab Contemporaries: The Opinions of Sati'al-Husri and Shakib Arslan', *International Journal of Turkish Studies* 2, no. 2 (1982): 19.

10. 'Dünkü Uray Kurulunda', *Hakkın Sesi*, 15 February 1936.

reality, the exchange among the Muslim-majority countries and their influences on each other were never one-sided.[11] While it was correct that Turkey was among the forerunners in terms of achieving national sovereignty and introducing modernization reforms, this hardly meant that it was the model for others. Rather, it was one among many references and sources of inspiration, which itself was inspired and influenced by other examples. Muslim-majority countries were partly in solidarity and partly in competition with one another in the struggle for modernization, and influenced each other not so much on the stance to take on the question of veiling, but on how to deal with it. In other words, the veil had to be removed; this was perceived as a given if one wanted to be modern. The question, however, was how to go about removing it.

Un/veiling in Muslim contexts during the interwar period: A brief overview

While analysing women's unveiling in different contexts, it is crucial to take into consideration the scope of these experiences. In other words, the issue of whether unveiling remained as a debate among the intellectuals and thus affected only a limited number of elite women, or blossomed into a general call for all women is an important dimension to take into account. Can we talk about a campaign against veiling if there was no banning of the veil, local or general, for example? How are we to analyse the case of Egypt, where it is debatable whether there was a movement or mobilization for unveiling, in relation to the case of Turkey, where there were local yet widespread bans on certain types of veiling? Equally important is to clarify what the concepts of veiling and unveiling referred to in each particular context. In other words, just as veiling, unveiling has meant multifarious things depending on the context, and could acquire different meanings over time in a particular context. The most remarkable difference between the unveiling debate in the Arab world and the one in Iran or Turkey, for example, seems to be that the former was mainly about the removal of the face veil. As Baron underlines, the widespread dispute in early-twentieth-century Egypt was about *al-sufur*, unveiling, which referred to taking off women's face cover, since *al-hijab*, veiling, was a generic term signifying the covering of the face.[12] In Syria and Lebanon under the French mandate as well, the debate on unveiling was mainly concerned with the removal of the face cover.[13]

---

11. For more details on this subject, see Aydın, *The Idea of Muslim.*

12. Baron, 'Unveiling', 370. This would change, however, with the 'return to the veil' movement of the 1970s. The term 'hijab' would come to mean the covering of the head. Margot Badran, *Feminists, Islam, and Nation: Gender and the Making of Modern Egypt* (Princeton: Princeton University Press, 1995), 22.

13. Elizabeth Thompson, *Colonial Citizens: Republican Rights, Paternal Privilege, and Gender in French Syria and Lebanon* (New York: Columbia University Press, 2000), 127–40.

In Egypt, the country that perhaps influenced the Arab world the most, while the debate on veiling had begun earlier, some of the urban elite women began to remove their face cover in the early twentieth century. This was a process during which unveiling became a metaphor for Egypt's independence from British rule. Studying the visual representations of the Egyptian nation in the press, Baron indicates that when Egypt began to be depicted as a woman, from the early 1900s onwards, she had no face covering but she was always modest in dress.[14] The real momentum for the removal of the face veil in Egypt, however, was created by feminists. The leading Egyptian feminist Huda Sharawi's removal of her face veil in 1923, the year when the Egyptian Feminist Union was established with Sharawi as its president, is referred to by scholars as a turning point leading to the unveiling of many Egyptian women.[15] Saharawi's was an individual but symbolic act, and perhaps a political statement that had helped with the unveiling of many others. Egyptian feminists would also try to inform the public about unveiling in other countries, such as Turkey and Lebanon, through their publication, *L'Egyptienne*. Towards the end of 1930s, the face veil had largely been removed by urban women. The fact that the face veil had not become a national symbol in Egypt and thus the new unveiled Egyptian woman could be deployed as a symbol of a modern and independent Egypt against British colonialism helped women to legitimize and advance their claims against the face veil.[16] In 1937, Al-Azhar declared that the Hanafi School of Islamic jurisprudence did not oppose the removal of the face veil, and the Maliki School did not require the covering of the face. This was an indication for the extent of legitimacy enjoyed by Egyptian feminists in their struggle against the face veil.[17]

In the debate on unveiling in other Arab countries, early advocates were largely male intellectuals, like the Iraqi poet Jamil Sidqi al-Zahari.[18] Women's organizations were concerned primarily with women's education and health, refraining from open mobilization for unveiling. The first women's organization established in Iraq in 1923, the Women's Awakening Club, for example, was disbanded because of the reactions that came from conservative circles; the word 'awakening' was perceived by the ulema as a call to discard the veil.[19] Thus, women in Arab countries who were advocates of the uncovering of the face mostly opted

---

14. Beth Baron, 'Nationalist Iconography: Egypt as a Woman', in *Rethinking Nationalism in the Arab Middle East*, eds. James Jankowski and Israel Gershoni (New York: Columbia University Press, 1997), 105–24.

15. Baron, 'Unveiling', 371. Sharawi initially kept her headscarf, but later preferred to cover her hair occasionally.

16. Beth Baron, *Egypt as a Woman: Nationalism, Gender and Politics* (Berkeley: University of California Press, 2005), 47–8.

17. Badran, *Feminists*, 93–4.

18. Noga Efrati, *Women in Iraq: Past Meets Present* (New York: Columbia University Press, 2012), 115–17.

19. Ibid., 122.

for individual removal of the face veil. Sometimes such symbolic public acts of unveiling were performed by women in groups on different occasions. A group of Syrian women first removed their face veil in nationalist demonstrations in Damascus in 1922; Muslim and Christian women of Jerusalem also unveiled during similar nationalist demonstrations in 1929; some intellectual Arab women removed their face veil for their public lectures on women's issues, like Habibah Manshari in Tunis in 1929 and Anbara Salam in Beirut in 1927.[20] The publishing of *Unveiling and Veiling* (al-Sufur wa al-Hijab) by Nazira Zayn al-Din, in Beirut in 1928, accelerated the debate and had reverberations not only in Greater Syria but across the Middle East. Speaking from within an Islamic framework, Zayn al-Din's book argued that covering the face was against the spirit of Islam. Moreover, addressing the French state, it 'made an explicit appeal for the precedence of civil law over religious law in issues of the veil and personal status'.[21] The book was translated into several languages in a year and received positive reactions especially from modernist circles. News about Zayn al-Din and her activities in Beirut even reached the pages of provincial newspapers in Turkey. A Bursa newspaper, for example, published an article from a Beirut newspaper, celebrating Zayn al-Din as a 'heroine Arab woman'.[22]

It seems that unveiling remained limited to elite circles in most Arab countries of the interwar period. In Greater Syria, for example, in the 1930s, upper-class women's adoption of French-style dress and their participation in the public life gradually increased, but this also triggered increasing reactions and even physical attacks against them by men.[23] Even in Beirut, where elites adopted European customs more rapidly compared to the elite of Damascus, Muslim women would continue to wear veils until the early 1940s; they would remove them when they visited the Europeanized parts of the city but would put them on when they returned to their own neighbourhoods.[24] In the 1930s, the agenda of the women's movement in Syria and Lebanon also became more moderate, emphasizing patriotic motherhood rather than the issues of unveiling or suffrage. This was a move that should be understood within the context of colonialism. They believed that the support of a unified women's movement could help nationalists win their struggle against the French, much as women had done in Egypt's 1919 Revolution. It was expected that an independent nationalist state would be secular and reform-minded, and would wield greater power over religious law than the French mandatory regime could.[25] Thus the colonial context significantly altered the dynamics of the demand for

---

20. Badran, *Feminists*; Thompson, *Colonial Citizens*; Farzaneh Milani, *Veils and Words: The Emerging Voices of Iranian Women Writers* (London: I.B. Tauris, 1992), 3.

21. Ibid., 131.

22. 'Mısır'da Peçe aleyhinde Nazire Zeyneddinin Faaliyetleri', *Hakkın Sesi*, 6 February 1936.

23. Thompson, *Colonial Citizens*, 171–224.

24. Ibid., 180.

25. Ibid., 146.

and the debate on unveiling. In other words, just like the discussions on women's suffrage, the issue of women's un/veiling was overshadowed by the dynamics of the colonial rule.[26] It was easier in a colonial context to denounce unveiling as an imitation of the West; it could easily be a matter of controversy between men and women as a result of gender anxiety and men's fear of emasculation under colonial rule. It could, thus, easily be postponed until the nationalist victory. This points to an important difference in non-colonial contexts, such as Turkey and Iran, despite the fact that the anxieties stemming from the fear of 'becoming too Western' were also part of the debate in these societies.[27]

A sort of in-between case was Afghanistan. A buffer zone under the impact of imperialist rivalries in the nineteenth century, Afghanistan was under the heavy influence of the British until it became independent in 1919. To achieve this, however, King Amanullah Khan had given up an important income of the state, the annual subsidy the British government had been paying to control Afghanistan's foreign affairs, which significantly limited the capacity of the state mechanism available to him.[28] Wide suggests that the extremely weak economic situation of the country in the 1920s and thus low capacity of the state should be taken into account in discussing both the reform agendas of King Amanullah, including reforms regarding women, and reasons behind their very limited impact, and even, in some cases, failure.[29] The initiative to promote unveiling in the country, again implying only the removal of the face veil, was quite symbolic. It started with the removal of the face veil by Queen Soraya during a speech given by King Amanullah in October 1928. The moment he uttered in his speech that Islam does not dictate that women cover their faces, the queen stands up and removes her transparent face veil, and several other women attending the lecture follow her.[30] Apart from this performance, however, there was neither a law nor a decree that enforced unveiling. The use of the face veil and *chadari* (usually known as *burqa*) were discouraged through presenting royal women as examples; but this had limited effect on society other than the upper classes of Kabul.[31] The attempt

---

26. Thompson, *Colonial Citizens*, 117–26.

27. Thompson, while referring to the difference the colonial context brings to the picture, contrasts the case of Syria and Lebanon not only from Turkey but also from Egypt. Ibid., 139–40. This, I think, risks blurring the difference between Turkey and Egypt.

28. Saikal, *Modern Afghanistan*, 66.

29. Thomas Wide, 'Astrakhan, Borqa', Chadari, Dreshi: The Economy of Dress in Early-Twentieth-Century Afghanistan', in *Anti-Veiling Campaigns in the Muslim World: Gender, Modernism and the Politics of Dress*, ed. Stephanie Cronin (London: Routledge, 2014), 179.

30. According to Moghadam, 'some one hundred Afghan women had reportedly discarded the veil by October 1928'. Valentine M. Moghadam, 'Nationalist Agendas and Women's Rights: Conflicts in Afghanistan in the Twentieth Century', in *Feminist Nationalism*, ed. Lois A. West (New York: Routledge, 1997), 82.

31. L.B. Poullada, 'Political Modernization in Afghanistan', in *Afghanistan: Some New Approaches*, eds. George Grassmuck, Ludwing W. Adamec and Frances H. Irwin (Ann Arbor: University of Michigan Press, 1969), 99–148.

to prohibit the use of the veil on certain streets of Kabul also proved short-lived; the state was simply incapable of imposing any systematic change on clothing.[32]

Compared to the Arab countries and Afghanistan, where unveiling mainly meant the uncovering of the face and was largely limited to symbolic efforts or elite segments of the population, Soviet Central Asia and the Caucasus followed quite a different trajectory on the issue of unveiling in the 1920s. Although arguably motivated by the reforms regarding women in Turkey in order not to fall behind this bourgeois counterpart,[33] anti-veiling campaigns in Soviet Muslim republics ended up being atypical examples in many ways. Particularly the case of Soviet Uzbekistan stands apart as the most violent experience. Launched publicly on International Women's Day in 1927 at a large demonstration, the *Hujum* (literally, attack), the Communist party-led anti-veiling campaign aimed at the removal of the full-body covering robe (*paranji*) and face veil (*chachvon*).[34] The vanguards would be the party members and their immediate families, and they would perform this role through collective unveilings at party meetings and conferences.[35] The burning of the veils at these gatherings became the symbol of the *Hujum*. There was no outlawing of the veil, but the state increasingly used force to create consent.[36] While there were different individual and collective reactions to the campaigns, resistance was strong in general. The Muslim clergy called upon Uzbek men to attack women who were unveiled. An estimated 2,500 Uzbek women were murdered by the male opponents of unveiling.[37]

This unparalleled level of violence came to characterize the Soviet anti-veiling campaigns in the literature. Northrop argues that although the *Hujum* was initiated by Soviet women activists in the Uzbek Communist Party, Uzbek women were almost completely absent in the party ranks and thus the campaign was mainly guided by the Zhenotdel, the women's section of the Communist Party of the Soviet Union. According to him, not only in Uzbekistan but also in other Muslim countries of Soviet Union, unveiling was experienced as an imposition from outside, a reflection of the 'civilizing mission' of the Bolsheviks, and hence, should be analysed as 'part of a wider narrative of European interactions with the colonial subject'. This colonial nature, Northrop suggests, also transformed the

---

32. Baiza, *Education*, 91. Wide mentions an announcement in the official newspaper prohibiting the use of the burqa, but he states that there is no source showing that this was ever implemented. Wide, 'Astrakhan', 189.

33. Douglas Northrop, *Veiled Empire: Gender and Power in Stalinist Central Asia* (Ithaca: Cornell University Press, 2004), 81–2.

34. The *Hujum* was the general term for the campaign of the Communist Party to 'liberate' Muslim women. Kamp, *The New Woman*, 150.

35. Northrop, *Veiled Empire*, 84.

36. Kamp, *The New Woman*, 3.

37. Marianne Kamp, 'Feminicide as Terrorism: The Case of Uzbekistan's Unveiling Murders', in *Sexual Violence in Conflict Zones: From the Ancient World to the Era of Human Rights*, ed. Elizabeth Heineman (Philadelphia: University of Philadelphia Press, 2011), 56–70.

meaning of the veil for the Central Asian Muslims: '[W]earing a veil became more than a narrowly religious or moral matter; for many people it also became an act of political and national resistance to an outside colonial power.'[38] In this sense, he finds the closest example to the Soviet anti-veiling campaigns of the 1920s in colonial Algeria in the 1950s, where the veil became the ultimate symbol of the struggle against the French.[39]

Kamp's analysis of the *Hujum* differs from that of Northrop in essentially two ways. First, she emphasizes the pre-Soviet roots of the discussion of women's emancipation and unveiling among the modernists of Central Asia. In other words, there was an indigenous drive for women's modernization already under way in Muslim Central Asia and Caucasus before the Bolshevik Revolution.[40] Second, Kamp underlines women's agency in the anti-veiling campaigns, particularly the vanguard role Muslim women activists played in the early 1920s.[41] She suggests that instead of approaching the *Hujum* against the backdrop of a struggle between the colonizer (Soviet Russia) and the colonized (Uzbeks), it should be analysed as a multisided struggle in which the Uzbek women and men were the primary actors.[42]

Similar to the Uzbek case is Soviet Azerbaijan, where the party-led anti-veiling campaign launched in 1928 in fact originated in the debate among the Azeri women themselves. Already in 1917, at the Congress of Muslim Clergy of Transcaucasia, Azeri women had appeared without the face veil and the *chador* (full-body cover, equivalent of Turkish *çarşaf*) and these initiatives continued through the activities of the Muslim women's clubs after the Bolsheviks seized power in 1920.[43] In 1926, inspired by reforms in Turkey and news about unveiling in Uzbekistan, the debate on the *chador* accelerated in Azerbaijan and soon turned into a party-led initiative. Although there was never a law or a decree, there were directives issued by party and state organizations.[44] Like in Uzbekistan, the unveiling momentum of the women's activists in Azerbaijan became a project at the hands of the party; a shift that Kamp characterizes as significant. This shift not only changed the parameters of women's activism and the symbolic meaning of the veil, but transformed

---

38. Northrop, *Veiled Empire*, 13.
39. He suggests that the French authorities were directly inspired by *Hujum*. Ibid., 29.
40. Kamp, *The New Woman*, 32–52.
41. Women from all over Central Asian were part of the debates in the modernist press even before the 1917 Revolution. Marianne Kamp, 'Women-initiated unveiling: state-led campaigns in Uzbekistan and Azerbaijan', in *Anti-Veiling Campaigns in the Muslim World: Gender, Modernism and the Politics of Dress*, ed. Stephanie Cronin (London: Routledge, 2014), 209.
42. Kamp, *The New Woman*, 6.
43. Kamp, 'Women-initiated', 214–15; Farideh Heyat, *Azeri Women in Transition: Women in Soviet and Post-Soviet Azerbaijan* (London: Routledge, 2002), 89–94.
44. The activists of the Women's Division of the party in Kazakhstan, Turkistan and Tajikistan also organized meetings for unveiling. Kamp, 'Women-initiated', 219–21.

unveiling into a violent conflict.[45] The murder of a housewife, Sareyye Khalilova, by her father because she was unveiled in Baku in January 1930 became a turning point in Azerbaijan. Meetings were organized across the country to denounce the veil and to declare commitment to 'the path of Khaliova'.[46] By the end of 1930s, the majority of the younger generation Azeri women were unveiled.

Similarities have been drawn between the Muslim Soviet republics, on the one hand, and the anti-veiling campaigns in Turkey and Iran, on the other, in broad terms, with regard to the role of the state in diminishing the power of the clergy and decreasing the public visibility of religion. They were also certainly similar in terms of the scale of the campaigns, their systematic nature and comprehensive understanding of unveiling, going beyond the removal of the face veil. However, as Kamp suggests, the Soviet republics differ in that the state had greater coercive power at its disposal than did the state in Turkey and Iran.[47] In addition, although Kamp rightly argues that colonialism should not overshadow the analyses of the anti-veiling campaigns that were put into practice in Muslim societies under Soviet Union and should not blur the role played especially by Muslim women activists, the Soviet domination was nevertheless a significant factor changing the dynamics of the unveiling debate in fundamental ways, ones similar to the Arab context. The fact that Turkey and Iran were independent states and that they were never directly colonized certainly sets them aside as the two closest examples of modernization in the wider Muslim context, in general, and of change in women's clothing, in particular.

Iran, Albania and Turkey: Some comparative remarks

The similarity between the anti-veiling campaigns Iran, Albania and Turkey is actually part of a more general parallelism that existed between these countries during the interwar era: not only in the changes regarding women's clothing, but also in many other fields; reforms initiated in these countries were guided by very similar modernization projects. This parallelism has received greater attention in the case of Iran and Turkey. Interwar Turkey and Iran have been viewed as distinct from other Muslim-majority countries because they were formally independent nation-states that were never directly colonized. Moreover, they had adopted very similar laws and reforms under comparable authoritarian regimes, which were closely informed by each other. Thus, it has been argued that they show sufficient similarity for a historically grounded comparison.[48] In fact, the

---

45. The level of violence in Azerbaijan remained limited compared to Uzbekistan. But unveiled women faced assault in streets, were stoned by children and beaten by men. There were even cases of murder. Heyat, *Azeri Women*, 92–8.

46. Ibid., 99.

47. Kamp, *The New Woman*, 178–81; 'Women-initiated', 206.

48. Touraj Atabaki and Erik J. Zürcher, 'Introduction', in *Men of Order: Authoritarian Modernization under Atatürk and Reza Shah*, eds. Touraj Atabaki and Erik J. Zürcher (London: I.B. Tauris, 2004), 1–12. See also Roger Owen, *State, Power and Politics in the Making of the Modern Middle East* (New York: Routledge, 1992), 26–30.

analogies with interwar Albania are not any less significant. Albania was also an independent nation-state, where modernization reforms were put into practice by an authoritarian regime led by strong and Western-oriented political elites. Just as Atatürk and Reza Shah had emerged as 'men of order' in response to the intellectual, political and economic questions originated in the nineteenth century, the Albanian nation-state under the leadership of King Zog I was shaped by very similar concerns that fashioned the authoritarian regimes of Southeast Europe, including Turkey.[49] In all three countries, the nationalist agenda emphasizing the national identity, history and language emerged and developed side by side an equally strong desire to attain recognition as a modern, equal nation among the 'civilized' states of the West. The 'woman question' and change in the way people dressed were central to this process.

However, while there have been some attempts at comparing the policies of the Kemalist and Pahlavi regimes regarding women's clothing, they have not gone beyond outlining the issue in very general terms, and Albania has never been included in the picture as an analogous example. Among the three, the Iranian case has received more attention, partly because most of the official documents related to the anti-veiling campaign of the first Pahlavi era were published by the Islamic regime in the 1990s and thus the issue was more accessible and perhaps politically more 'urgent' for scholars to explore because of the compulsory veiling imposed on Iranian women after the 1979 Revolution. More importantly, the anti-veiling campaign in Iran in the 1930s has been singled out in the literature as the most decisive, authoritarian and harshly implemented example. As one of the pioneers of Iranian Studies has indicated, *kashf-e hijab* (unveiling) was the most radical component of the Women's Awakening project of the Pahlavi regime, reflecting a 'unique absolutist approach' to the issue of women's dress.[50] This 'uniqueness' stemmed from the argument that Iran under Reza Pahlavi was the only country to make unveiling compulsory countrywide. While most scholars claim that veiling was banned by the shah, without detailing how, some specify the means through which it was banned. Kashani Sabet, for example, claims that the prohibition of *chador* (Iranian equivalent of *çarşaf*) was decreed and legislated,[51] while Paidar suggests that the removal of the veil was ordered by a decree of the shah in January 1936.[52] Moreover, even when scholars agree on the means through which the veil was banned in Iran, ambiguity remains as to what exactly was banned as the veil. Both Ettehaideh and Paidar, for instance, argue that a decree was issued by the

---

49. See Berd J. Fischer, ed. *Balkan Strongmen: Dictators and Authoritarian Rulers of Southeast Europe* (London: C. Hurst & Co. Publishers, 2006).

50. Nikki Keddie, *Modern Iran: Roots and Results of Revolution* (New Haven: Yale University Press, 2006), 100.

51. Firoozeh Kashani-Sabet, *Conceiving Citizens: Women and the Politics of Motherhood in Iran* (Oxford: Oxford University Press, 2011), 155–6.

52. Parvin Paidar, *Women and the Political Process in Twentieth-Century Iran* (Cambridge: Cambridge University Press, 1995), 106–7.

shah; but while the former claims that the decree prohibited the *chador*, the latter says it prohibited both the *chador* and the headscarf.[53]

The Iranian case became such an important benchmark that while little was known about women's unveiling in Kemalist Turkey except for some general remarks, many scholars have come to the conclusion that it was far less radical compared to Iran. The lack of a comparable law banning veiling in Turkey has been interpreted as the absence of intervention in women's clothing by the Kemalist regime. As a result, there emerged in the literature a consensus that in Turkey, 'it was wisely considered that an outright ban on the veil would provoke a catastrophic storm'[54] and thus 'there was never any forced unveiling'.[55] Despite the fact that scholarly attention on comparative aspects of the Kemalist and Pahlavi modernizations has been on the rise, the comparison of the anti-veiling campaigns in Turkey and Iran has remained limited to such general conclusions, lacking detailed and solid information regarding the precise content, implementation and consequences of these campaigns.

Recent research on both Iran and Turkey has attempted to fill this gap and has produced a different picture. As Rostam-Kolayi and Matin-asgari maintain, recent studies have actually revealed that anti-veiling campaigns in Turkey and Iran had more in common than previously acknowledged.[56] Rostam-Kolayi and Matin-asgari changed the parameters of the comparison, since they suggested that 'Iran's *kashf-e hijab* was neither legislated nor "decreed" by Reza Shah';[57] there was in fact no banning of the veil countrywide in Iran. And again, contrary to what has been argued, there was in fact systematic anti-veiling campaigns in Turkey, albeit at the local level, as this study has demonstrated in detail throughout previous chapters. Moreover, if there was one country that indeed legislated against the veil, it was Albania; yet, very little has been said about this 'uniqueness'. Equally little explored is the degree to which Albania can be discussed as part of the most sensible comparison; the one between Turkey and Iran. This section is an attempt to discuss these three cases together, with the aim of revealing the distinguishing characteristics of the Turkish case more clearly. One significant handicap is that

---

53. Ibid., 107; Mansoureh Ettehaideh, 'The Origins and Development of the Women's Movement in Iran, 1906-41', in *Women in Iran from 1800 to the Islamic Republic*, eds. Lois Beck and Guity Nashat (Chicago: University of Illinois Press, 2004), 85–106.

54. John Norton, 'Faith and Fashion in Turkey', in *Languages of Dress in the Middle East*, eds. Nancy Lindisfarne-Tapper and Bruce Ingham (London: Curzon Press, 1997), 162.

55. Houshang Chehabi, 'Banning of the Veil and Its Consequences', in *The Making of Modern Iran: State and Society under Riza Shah, 1921–1941*, ed. Stephanie Cronin (London: Routledge, 2003), 193.

56. Jasamin Rostam-Kolayi and Afshin Matin-asgari, 'Unveiling Ambiguities: Revisiting 1930s Iran's *Kashf-e Hijab* Campaign', in *Anti-Veiling Campaigns in the Muslim World: Gender, Modernism and the Politics of Dress*, ed. Stephanie Cronin (London: Routledge, 2014), pp. 121–39.

57. Ibid., 121.

we do not know as much about the Albanian case as we do about Turkey and Iran. Nathalie Clayer's article seems to be the most detailed account available in English, in addition to sources on general parameters of modernization in Albania.[58] Thus, comparative remarks about Albania are mainly derived from her account.

As a European Muslim-majority country, Albania was established as a secular state. The idea of reforming Islam was on the agenda of the political elites even before the gaining of independence in 1920, and remained so, along with the idea of attaining state control over religious institutions once the state was established.[59] King Zog I, formerly known as Ahmet Zogolli, received his high school education in Istanbul, at Lycée Impérial de Galatasaray, where he was exposed to the ideas of the Young Turks.[60] Directly involved in the Albanian national struggle against the Ottomans and then in the state-building process, he was determined not only to break Albania away from its Ottoman past, but also to refashion the nation as a truly modern European one.

Although this was also the goal of the Kemalist regime in Turkey, the Ottoman legacy continued to influence both countries in many ways. In fact, Albania was late among the Balkan states in achieving independence from the Ottoman Empire, and when it 'emerged from the First World War it was still in many respects Ottoman, from its architecture to its religious make-up as well as many aspects of its economic, social and political structure'.[61] On top of this Ottoman legacy shared by the two countries came similar authoritarian regimes. In particular, policies regarding religion in interwar Albania show striking similarities to those followed in Turkey under the Kemalist regime. Both countries opted for reforms like abolishing the religious courts, the change of the weekly holiday from Friday to Sunday, and the adoption of a secular Civil Code. Particularly the last one differentiates Turkey and Albania from Iran and other Muslim-majority countries of the interwar period where family laws were never fully secularized.[62]

---

58. Nathalie Clayer, 'Behind the Veil: The Reform of Islam in Interwar Albania or the Search for a "Modern" and "European" Islam', in *Anti-Veiling Campaigns in the Muslim World: Gender, Modernism and the Politics of Dress*, ed. Stephanie Cronin (London: Routledge, 2014), 231–51.

59. Nathalie Clayer, 'Adapting Islam to Europe: The Albanian Example', in *Islam und Muslime in (Südost) Europa im Kontext von Transformation und EU-Erweiterung*, eds. Christian Voss and Jordanka Telbizova-Sack (München: Verlag Otto Sagner, 2010), 53–69.

60. For more, see Jason Hunter Tomes, *King Zog of Albania: Europe's Self-Made Muslim Monarch* (New York: New York University Press, 2004).

61. Bernd J. Fischer, 'Introduction', in *Balkan Strongmen: Dictators and Authoritarian Rulers of Southeast Europe*, ed. Bernd J. Fischer (London: C. Hurst & Co. Publishers, 2006), 2.

62. The Albanian Civil Code, which was adopted in 1929, three years after the adoption of the Swiss Civil Code in Turkey, was mainly based on the French Code Napoléon. Owen Pearson, *Albania in the Twentieth Century: A History, Vol. I, Albania and King Zog: Independence, Republic and Monarch, 1908–1939* (London: I.B. Tauris, 2004), 307.

As in all other countries, the use of the face veil in Albania was predominantly an urban issue. However, the *perçe* (face veil) did not necessarily refer to religious differences. As Isa Blumi indicates, while rural women, both Muslims and Catholics, would work in the fields unveiled, women living in the cities, again both Muslims and Catholics, would be veiled in late-Ottoman northern Albania.[63] Nevertheless, in the 1920s when un/veiling became a political debate in newly independent Albania, the measures and propaganda mainly targeted the Muslim community. Women's unveiling became an issue as part of the discussions on improving women's social position, during which Turkey was one of the reference points.[64] Abolishing women's veiling was discussed as a necessary reform at the congress of the Albanian Muslims in Tirana in 1923.[65]

The first open official action was taken in 1929. The Ministerial Council banned the *perçe* and the *ferace*, with the Ministry of Justice giving the necessary orders to the police stations not to offend people during the application of the ban and to work together with the district councils to convince women to remove these veils. Although it is not clear who was behind the initiative, it seems that some religious leaders among the Islamic community were also supporting unveiling.[66] Associated not only with backwardness and fanaticism but also with the Ottoman past, the characterization of the *perçe* and the *ferace* in the discourse of the Albanian secularist elite was very similar to the perception of the *peçe* and the *çarşaf* in the Turkish context. It is also telling that although there had been a central decision, it nevertheless envisaged the involvement of the local administrative units to 'convince' women, adding a strong local dimension to the process, as in Turkey. Similarly, this decision shows that the caution taken to avoid reactions was also present in the Albanian case. In fact, the punitive measures remained unclear. Clayer indicates that in the years following the ban, the anti-veiling campaign was implemented mainly through propaganda. Women who were government employees, such as teachers and midwives, were closely checked, however; as in other countries, these groups of women were the easiest target for the Albanian state to control and pressure.[67] One important way in which the Albanian anti-veiling campaign was different was that unlike in Turkey and Iran, where the *çarşaf* and the *chador* were equally part of the unveiling debate, in Albania, the campaign in the 1920s was concerned with the *ferace*, which was a lighter outdoor dress compared to the *çarşaf* and the *chador*. The support of some religious intellectuals should also be noted; it seems that the anti-veiling campaign in Albania was a result of a wider consensus.

---

63. Isa Blumi, *Rethinking The Late Ottoman Empire: A Comparative Social and Political History of Albania and Yemen 1878–1918* (Istanbul: The Isis Press, 2003), 147.

64. Clayer, 'Behind the Veil', 237.

65. Miranda Vickers, *The Albanians: A Modern History* (London: I.B. Tauris, 2001), 108–9.

66. Clayer, 'Behind the Veil', 233.

67. Clayer also indicates that in the year 1935, punitive measures were taken against some women for not obeying the ban. Ibid., 234.

Although the Turkish example was a reference point in the early unveiling debates in Albania, the country undeniably went further than Turkey. There was no equivalent in Turkey of the Albanian ministerial decision to ban veiling in the 1920s. Compared to Albania, in both Turkey and Iran, systematic efforts at changing women's clothing came later and were first preceded by attempts at reforming men's clothing.[68] Unlike unveiling, in both countries, the changes in men's headgear were issued through legislation. While Turkey's Hat Law came in 1925, in Iran, the Pahlavi hat was made compulsory in 1928 as part of the Uniform Dress Law, which included all aspects of men's clothing.[69] The European hat would be later made compulsory in Iran in 1935, following Reza Shah's visit to Turkey in 1934. In both countries, the regulations to modernize men's clothing in the 1920s did not concern women, but echoed a similar change in women's clothing in the public debates, as well as in the social protests that emerged against them.

In Iran, as in Turkey, while the discussion of women's veiling goes back to the nineteenth century and had remained an issue for a long time mainly among the elite, no attempt was made by the state to remove it until the mid-1930s.[70] There were no equivalents in Iran of the local attempts at unveiling initiated in the 1920s in Turkey. Although there was some relaxation in gender segregation and veiling beginning with the constitutional period after the 1906 Revolution, in the early decades of the twentieth century, there was no consensus among the modernist intelligentsia about unveiling, and women's rights activists had different opinions even on the use of the face veil (*picheh*).[71] However, there was a small but active group of feminists who had unveiling on their agenda in the early 1920s. As one of the pioneers, the president of the Patriotic Women's League (*Jam'iyyat-e Nesvan-e Vatankhah*) Mohtaram Eskandari had removed her veil in Tehran in 1925, but was stoned and harassed in

---

68. Pearson indicates that in Albania 'a stricter code of dress for men was also introduced which stipulated that the wearing of national costume was to be confined to national holidays'. But he does not provide further details. Pearson, *Albania*, 385. Vickers mentions that this banning of the national costume for men came a few months after the unveiling law in 1937. Vickers, *The Albanians*, 135.

69. Houchang Chehabi, 'Staging the Emperor's New Clothes: Dress Codes and Nation-Building under Reza Shah', *Iranian Studies* 26, no. 3–4 (Summer/Fall 1993): 209–29; Kashani-Sabet, *Conceiving Citizens*, 153.

70. See Camron Amin, *The Making of the Modern Iranian Woman: Gender, State Policy, and Popular Culture, 1865–1946* (Florida: University Press of Florida, 2002), 16–79; Afsaneh Najmabadi, 'Authority and Agency: Revisiting Women's Activism during Reza Shah's Period', in *The State and the Subaltern: Modernization, Society, and the State in Turkey and Iran*, ed. Touraj Atabaki (London, I. B. Tauris, 2007), 159–77.

71. Najmabadi, 'Authority and Agency'; Firoozeh Kashani-Sabet, 'Dressing up (or down): Veils, hats and consumer fashions in interwar Iran', in *Anti-Veiling Campaigns in the Muslim World: Gender, Modernism and the Politics of Dress*, ed. Stephanie Cronin (London: Routledge, 2014), 149–62.

the street for her actions supporting unveiling.[72] Similarly, Sadigheh Dowlatabadi, the editor of another women's journal, Women's Voice (*Zaban-e Zanan*), had also discarded the *chador*.[73] In the late 1920s and early 1930s, while an increasing number of urban elite women had indeed removed their face veil, the removal of the *chador* still remained controversial. Najmabadi claims that the regime seemed to be against the removal of the *chador* as late as 1932, and there were disagreements on the issue within and outside government circles.[74]

In the mid-1930s, a more resolute agenda for the modernization of women's clothing emerged in all three countries. The change in women's attire was already underway, but as the regimes became more authoritarian, they became more resolute about shaping it. In Iran, the move for unveiling took off with the founding in May 1935 of the *Kanun-e Banuvan* (The Women's Centre), which was a direct regime initiative. It should be also underlined, however, that some prominent members of the 1920s' generation of feminists, such as Fakhr Afaq Parsa and Sadigheh Dowlatabadi, were also members of the board of the centre; they 'began to cooperate with the state in the hope of fulfilling their long overdue dreams'.[75] One of the aims of the centre was the removal of the veil. It initiated an open campaign for it by getting its own members to convince their relatives and others in their social milieu and by encouraging the participants of its meetings to unveil.[76] As Sadeghi indicates, 'the centre provided the organizational apparatus for propagating the idea of unveiling and its implementation.'[77] Reza Shah's oldest daughter was the president of the centre, thus the female members of the royal family were very visible in the campaign for unveiling. This was in fact one important similarity between Iran and Albania: the role the royal women played in the unveiling process. In the Albanian case, as well, King Zog's three sisters were the role models in their 'European dress', making public appearances, tours and visits throughout the country to push for unveiling.[78]

Albania, however, is distinct from both Iran and Turkey in that it is the only country to pass a law banning the veil. The Albanian parliament approved the Law on the Ban on Face Covering, which prohibited women from covering their face, wholly or partially, on 8 March 1937.[79] Women who did not abide by the law would be punished with a fine not exceeding 500 gold francs.[80] As mentioned earlier, the

---

72. Hamideh Sadeghi, *Women and Politics in Iran: Veiling, Unveiling, and Reveiling* (Cambridge: Cambridge University Press, 2007), 81. For more on the Patriotic Women's League, see Eliz Sanasarian, *The Women's Rights Movement in Iran: Mutiny, Appeasement, and Repression from 1900 to Khomeini* (New York: Praeger, 1982).

73. Some argue that Dowlatabadi was the first woman to remove the *chador* in public. Rostam-Kolayi and Matin-asgari, 'Unveiling Ambiguities', 138, fnt. 25.

74. Najmabadi, 'Authority and Agency', 162–3.

75. Sadeghi, *Women and Politics*, 82.

76. Kashani-Sabet, *Conceiving Citizens*, 154.

77. Sadeghi, *Women and Politics*, p. 83.

78. Vickers, *The Albanians*, 135.

79. Clayer, 'Behind the Veil', 234.

80. Pearson, *Albania*, 385.

face veil was in fact banned in Albania in 1929. It seems, however, that this earlier attempt was ineffective and the regime felt the need to ban it again, this time by enacting a law. The implementation of the law was supported by propaganda and with additional activities that were organized especially in the provinces.[81] In addition, it is important to note that when unveiling became an issue of legislation in Albania, its scope was narrowed and kept limited to the face veil; the earlier ban in 1929 also included the *ferece*, which was not touched by the law issued in 1937. As in the earlier attempt, this time, a degree of support from the religious leaders was seen as necessary. The head of the Islamic Community had issued a fatwa eight days before the enactment of the law, declaring that it was not forbidden in Islam for women to show their face.[82] According to the law, men who attempted to prevent women from obeying the law, who engaged in propaganda in favour of the veil, and who did not exert their authority to implement the law would also be fined.[83] These were measures taken against social opposition to unveiling. In contrast to the official account, which claimed that the reform was a success, there was in fact significant unrest. While the police tried to control in the streets women's compliance with the law, some women refused to do so or adopted new forms of veils, which they could use to cover their faces occasionally, when encountering a police officer.[84] Conservative Muslims' discontent with the unveiling law seemed to be one of the driving forces behind the unsuccessful revolt that broke out in May 1937 in the south of the country.[85]

Turkey and Iran opted for a different strategy: avoiding direct legislation, handling the issue mainly at the local level, and guiding and monitoring the local administrators through certain ministries. As was the case for Ankara, the initial position of Tehran on unveiling was cautious. The first directive on unveiling sent to certain provinces by the Ministry of the Interior of Iran on 9 December 1935 was very similar to the tone and language used by the Turkish Ministry of the Interior in its initial directives to the provinces:

[To local] governments of Arak, Hamedan, Garrus, Malayer, Kermanshah, Sanandaj and Golpaygan: The subject of *kashf-e hijab* must be encouraged by [local] governments and the police without forcing *kashf-e hijab* on anyone. Preachers and others who might oppose or talk against it must be immediately

---

81. A Turkish newspaper reported ten days after the enactment of the law in Albania that the king had ordered the opening of literacy courses for women in the provinces, as well as courses on social manners. 'Arnavudlukta peçe menedildi', *Cumhuriyet*, 18 March 1937.

82. Clayer, 'Behind the Veil', 234. Clayer thinks that the exclusion of the *ferece* from the law was a result of the compromise between the political and religious authorities.

83. Ibid. Pearson indicates that 'anyone attempting to prevent women from complying with this law was to suffer even more stringent a penalty' compared to the penalty introduced for women. Pearson, *Albania*, 385.

84. Clayer, 'Behind the Veil', 235.

85. Vickers, *The Albanians*, 135.

arrested and punished by the police. Act in a very prudent and dignified manner. Report the progress of this matter routinely via secret code.[86]

The subsequent directives were primarily issued by the minister of education, to be implemented by the minister of the interior by monitoring the governors. In fact, Rostam-Kolayi and Matin-asgari suggest that the key actor in Iran's anti-veiling campaigns was the Ministry of Education, since the directives sent by the Ministry of the Interior also referred to its directives, emphasizing the importance of girls' enrolment in school, the role of women teachers and finally, other state officials. The Minister of Education Ali-Asghar Hikmat was responsible for the campaign's initial conception and implementation.[87] As in Turkey, the state officials, especially female teachers, would be the vanguards, and the process would be managed by organizing conferences, meetings and social gatherings.[88] Different from Turkey, however, in Iran, the instrument emphasized in the directives on unveiling to get women to adopt European dress was the national education system. One of the most detailed directives on unveiling was one sent by the Ministry of Education to all local officials in charge of education in the provinces.[89] This directive called for all public elementary schools to be co-educational and for all elementary and secondary schools to adopt a uniform dress for all students, which they had to wear in school as well as on the street. Although mentioned implicitly, it was obvious in the directive that the dress codes for students excluded the *chador*. The transformation of the clothing of ordinary adult women, on the other hand, would be achieved through the conferences, meetings and gatherings to be organized in the provinces by Ministry of Education officials. Local administrators and heads of police were required to attend such organizations with their wives having removed the *chador*, and thus, to foster the development of mixed-gender environment.[90]

Hence, as far as the content of the directives issued by the state are concerned, it seems that unveiling in Iran was compulsory only for school girls, female government employees and wives of male government employees. And for many of these women, it meant not only the removal of the face veil and the *chador*, but also the headscarf, even if it was not explicitly dictated in the official documents.[91] In other words, the norm set by the families of the Shah, the high-level bureaucrats and the urban elite in general was the full adoption of European dress, including the replacement of headscarf with a hat. This seems to correspond to the Turkish case, where most urban and provincial elite, as well as female government employees had largely removed their headscarf as well. However, what is different

---

86. Quoted in Rostam-Kolayi and Matin-asgari, 'Unveiling Ambiguities', 127.

87. Rostam-Kolayi and Matin-asgari, 'Unveiling Ambiguities', 132.

88. Chehabi, 'Staging', 219.

89. Rostam-Kolayi and Matin-asgari, 'Unveiling Ambiguities', 129.

90. Ibid., 130.

91. On some occasions, however, wives of government employees in the provinces appeared in compulsory gatherings wearing headscarves rather than hats. Chehabi, 'Staging', 218–19.

in the Turkish case is that the anti-veiling campaigns in Turkey deliberately targeted changing ordinary women's dress; the bans issued by municipal councils were concerned with the removal of the face veil and the *çarşaf* by all women. The unveiling of school girls and female teachers in Turkey was achieved much earlier, through the regulations of the Ministry of Education, as mentioned in Chapter 1. Thus, to the extent that the content of the state directives and local decisions were concerned, the anti-veiling campaigns of the 1930s in Turkey can be seen as more comprehensive compared to the ones during the same period in Iran.

However, in practice, this difference tended to lose its significance, since, in the Iranian case as well, the anti-veiling campaigns surpassed the limits of the ministerial directives. In both countries, the local character of the anti-veiling campaigns and the ambiguity of the attitude of the centre gave the provincial authorities greater latitude for action. As it was discussed in previous chapters, in some provinces in Turkey, local authorities tried to limit veiled women's access to public places, such as parks, movie theatres or state offices, contrary to the circulars sent by the Ministry of the Interior. A similar tendency can be seen in the conduct of Iranian local administrators. A British consular report from Tabriz in February 1936, for example, mentioned that veiled women were excluded from public baths, public carriages and movie theatres. Moreover, doctors were ordered not to admit veiled women to hospitals.[92] As in Turkey, in Iran as well, unveiling was imposed on some women by force, although it was discouraged officially. Like Ankara, Tehran knew about this misconduct. In fact, there are oral historical accounts of police violence even in Tehran; Sadeghi tells the story of a woman who was stopped by a policeman for wearing a scarf, which he pulled off forcefully.[93] Reports of occasional use of violence led the Iranian minister of the interior to warn the local authorities, once again, against such offenses in 1938. The minister had emphasized the need to be prudent and to act with good intentions in order to avoid reactions, misunderstandings and problems, especially in conservative provinces such as Qom and Mashad.[94] Thus, it seems there was room to act differently in more 'appropriate' provinces; such unclear points were perhaps one source of difficulty (and opportunity, by the same token) for local administrators in interpreting the directives coming from Tehran.[95] The caution taken by the Pahlavi regime to not disturb traditional segments of the society and to not contradict the Islamic norms had in fact proved partly effective. There was no fatwa issued against unveiling by a major cleric in Iran[96]; some clerics even supported it.[97] Iranian

92. Kashani-Sabet, *Conceiving Citizens*, 113–14.

93. Sadeghi, *Women and Politics*, p. 87.

94. Rostam-Kolayi and Matin-asgari, 'Unveiling Ambiguities', 134.

95. Chehabi, for example, mentions that some local authorities requested more policemen from Tehran be employed in the anti-veiling campaign. It is not clear, however, if this was a reflection of implicit approval of the use of force by the regime centre, or if the policemen were being asked to fight against the opposition being waged rather than to enforce unveiling per se. Chehabi, 'Staging', 219.

96. Rostam-Kolayi and Matin-asgari, 'Unveiling Ambiguities', 135.

97. Chehabi, 'Staging', 220.

women used various strategies to find their way. Hiding or adopting the use of long overcoats and scarves were common; in some instances, the authorities interpreted this as resistance to the policy of unveiling. When unveiled, some women faced harassment and violence by members of the local populace for abiding by the new dress codes. Confronted by these various reactions on the ground, but at the same time, ordered by Tehran to fight against veiling and encourage unveiling, the authorities struggled to follow a consistent policy at the local level.[98]

Where does this brief comparative survey of the anti-veiling campaigns in Albania, Iran and Turkey leave us? First of all, it reveals the similarities particularly between the campaigns in 1930s Turkey and Iran. Both Ankara and Tehran tried to adopt a gradual strategy, took pains not to create reaction and sought to foster unveiling mainly through the help of the state officials and local elite. Although a complete Europeanization of women's dress was the ideal, for the most part, state intervention was directed mainly against face veil, *çarşaf* and *chador*, otherwise allowing a range of possibilities to adapt to the new codes. In fact, just as what unveiling entailed in mid-1930s Iran – primarily, the removal of the face veil and discarding of the *chador* – happened to be seen 'acceptable' under the Islamic Republic, the target of the anti-veiling campaigns in mid-1930s Turkey – again, removal of the face veil and discarding of the *çarşaf* – was essentially achieved, since when the 'Islamic dress' re-emerged and became a political issue in the 1980s, women's new veiling style – a long overcoat and a headscarf – was very much in line with the Kemalist standards of unveiling. As Rostam-Kolayi and Matin-asgari claim for the Iranian case, this is an ironic conclusion for the Turkish case as well.[99] Nevertheless, it reflects the extent to which the authoritarian regimes of Iran and Turkey in the 1930s were careful not to contradict existing patriarchal and even Islamic norms. It also shows that these regimes tended to adapt to local circumstances to a certain degree, no matter how keen they were to transform them. This was probably an issue of state capacity and penetration into society, rather than a question of ideological flexibility.

The question of state capacity is also a major factor in explaining the differences among the three countries. In comparisons between Turkey and Iran, it has also been emphasized that Turkey's early experience with modernization, and consequently, its relatively more centralized state and better organized bureaucracy was an advantage.[100] The fact that 'state initiated and privately backed reforms had a much longer history, scope, and cumulative effect in the nineteenth century Ottoman Empire compared with the few, short-lived, and limited measures at reform in Qajar Iran'[101] contributed immensely to the

---

98. Chehabi notes that this increased the frequency of violence against unveiled women. Chehabi, 'Staging', 220.

99. Rostam-Kolayi and Matin-asgari, 'Unveiling Ambiguities', 121.

100. Jean-François Bayart, 'Republican Trajectories in Iran and Turkey: A Tocquevillian Reading', in *Democracy without Democrats? The Renewal of Politics in the Muslim World*, ed. Ghassan Salamé (London: I.B. Tauris, 1994), 282–300.

101. Najmabadi, 'Hazards of Modernity', 55.

republican regime's efforts at modernization after the collapse of the Ottoman state. As Atabaki and Zürcher argue, 'where Reza Shah had to build a state, Atatürk, during his 15-year rule (1923–1938) could transform an existing one'.[102] Although more studies are needed to compare the capacity of the Albanian state specifically with regard to the issue of organizing and enforcing an anti-veiling campaign, interwar Albania has been generally regarded as a weak state, both economically and politically, in the literature.[103] Vickers suggests that 'during the interwar years, Albania remained Europe's least developed and poorest state by far'.[104] Although King Zog managed to unify the country in the second half of the 1920s, local tribes and landowners were still quite powerful and there was an increasing Italian penetration in the 1930s. In fact, Clayer suggests the revitalization of the unveiling debate in Albania in the mid-1930s, which resulted in the enactment of the ban on the face veil in 1937, coincided with a deep economic and political crisis in the face of rising tension with Italy. The true purpose of the law was to reinforce the idea that 'Albania should be a sovereign country among the other Western countries' at a time when Albania's sovereignty was under threat by Italy.[105]

Another important dimension to consider, which is directly related to the question of state capacity, was the institutional means through which cultural modernization was put into practice. It can be argued that the main channel used to transform the society was the national education system. Modern education was the key for the Iranian, Albanian and Turkish political elite to create patriotic, modern citizens and to integrate them into their modernist agendas. Entering the school system meant a major transformation for children, and particularly for female students, this meant the removal of the veil. This was not enough, however, for a comprehensive and rapid change in women's clothing. The question was the capacity to apply the decisions or laws issued by the central elite regarding unveiling in the provinces. In this respect, I would argue that the Kemalist regime was more capable and successful in diffusing into the local and diversifying the channels through which the targeted cultural changes could be realized, or at least, propagated and promoted. In comparisons between Turkey and Iran, this institutional capacity of the Kemalist regime has been in fact underscored by a number of scholars. Owen, for example, pointed to the importance of the establishment of a political party by Atatürk and the administrative, organizational and ideological capabilities this provided for the working of the regime.[106] Likewise, Abrahamian stressed that Atatürk ruled with the help of a political party, while Reza Shah was able to benefit from neither the support of the intelligentsia to the degree that Atatürk could nor the assistance of an organized

---

102. Atabaki and Zürcher, 'Introduction', 10.

103. Barbara Jelavich, *The History of the Balkans: Twentieth Century, Volume II* (Cambridge: Cambridge University Press, 1983), 177–84.

104. Vickers, *The Albanians*, 120.

105. Clayer, 'Behind the Veil', 234.

106. Owen, *State*, 27–9.

political party.[107] One could add to this the significance of the establishment of the People's Houses in Turkey, which provided yet another channel for the regime at the local level. Moreover, the institutional diversity in the Turkish periphery, which was highlighted in Chapter 3, was also crucial for both hosting diverse local actors and giving them opportunities to position themselves as 'local initiators' of certain reforms, such as unveiling. In other words, however limited the capacity of the local party branches, People's Houses, municipalities and local associations in interwar Turkey were when analysed on their own, comparatively speaking, they gave the Kemalist regime an advantage when it adopted the strategy of handling the issue of unveiling at the local level. Perhaps, the role that the municipalities played in the anti-veiling campaigns in the 1930s and the fact that the bans on the *peçe* and the *çarşaf* were local, and were nevertheless 'discussed' and issued by city councils – at least through a seemingly more inclusive process – should not be underestimated. This does not mean that the Kemalist regime was any less authoritarian than Iran or Albania – only that the authoritarian regime in Turkey had relatively better means available to function at the local level and to penetrate the society. The lack of this institutional capacity in Albania, for example, was perhaps one of the reasons why the anti-veiling campaign remained ineffective despite the ambitious move of the regime to enact a law on the issue.

On top of this disparity in terms of state capacity and institutional organization at the local level came the difference between the attitudes of the political leaders. In particular, Reza Shah's attitude towards the anti-veiling campaign deserves attention since it can possibly explain, at least partly, why the Iranian case has been seen as more comprehensive and repressive than it was on paper. Although there was no legislation or degree in Iran prohibiting the face veil and *chador* country-wide, the role both the regime centre and the Shah and his family played in the process was publicly very visible. The anti-veiling campaign had begun by the direct involvement of Reza Shah and his wife and daughters, as well as the family of all high-level bureaucracy in Tehran, which was probably quite influential in spreading the perception that the shah indeed ordered unveiling. For example, many sources indicate that unveiling became a state policy and was publicly launched by a speech made by Reza Shah at a ceremony at Tehran Teachers' College on 7 January 1936, which was covered by the press. Evidently, a notice was sent beforehand to all women teachers and wives of ministers, high military officials and high bureaucrats asking them to attend the ceremony having removed the *chador* and wearing European clothes and hats instead. Shah's wife and daughters had also adopted European-style attire.[108] The day of the ceremony, 7 January (the 17th of Day in the Persian calendar), would be known as 'Women's Emancipation Day' (*Rooz-e Azadi-ye Zan*).[109] In fact, even prior to this event, throughout 1935,

---

107. Ervand Abrahamian, *Iran between Two Revolutions* (Princeton: Princeton University Press, 1982), 149.

108. Amin, *The Making*, 95.

109. Sadeghi, *Women and Politics*, 86.

British and American diplomatic sources reported the possibility a ban on veiling Iran based on their observations of and communications with Reza Shah and his close circle bureaucrats.[110] Symbolic as it was, the ceremony on 7 January 1936, and further involvement of Reza Shah and his family in the process must nevertheless have played an important role in the wide-ranging form the anti-veiling campaigns took in practice in Iran, despite the more limited nature of the official directives.[111]

Revisiting un/veiling in the interwar period

The brief survey this chapter provided on the anti-veiling campaigns in Muslim contexts of the interwar period shows that they have 'broad similarities' and an 'extra-ordinary synchronicity', as Cronin suggests in her comparative account.[112] In all cases, the emphasis on the necessity of remaking the nation's women along modern lines seems to have existed side by side with an equally strong emphasis on protecting women's morality. It can be argued that the 'modern-yet-modest' formulation was valid in varying degrees in all attempts to change women's clothing in Muslim-majority contexts.[113] Since dress was also considered as a marker of the national identity, as much as it was of modernity, the removal of the face veil in particular was not presented as complete Westernization or pure adaptation to European norms. In fact, the nationalist agenda shaped the discourse on unveiling in many different ways. The increasing emphasis on the national health, for example, had its impact on the ways in which unveiling was propagated. Women's health as mothers of the nation began to be seen as indispensable for raising children with strong minds and bodies, and the idea that veiling prevents women from receiving enough sunlight, or women's seclusion prevents them from doing sports was quite widespread. In Turkey this would lead to the involvement of local health commissions in the process of banning the *peçe* and the *çarşaf*. In Iran, the directives sent by the Ministry of Education on unveiling underlined the need to increase opportunities for girls to engage in sports at schools.[114]

---

110. Amin, *The Making*, 86.

111. This was perhaps also the reason for many scholars' reading of unveiling in Iran as a compulsory policy of the regime. It is quite probable that the shah had given verbal orders, at least to the ministers who were involved in the process. Najmabadi, for example, refers to Yahya Zuka, who suggested to her in a private conversation that 'many royal orders during Riza Shah's period were verbal, dutifully communicated by obedient attendants to appropriate state officials.' Najmabadi, *Women with Mustaches*, 260, fnt. 5. Even the national news agency of Iran was reporting that there was a national 'movement' against veiling. Reporting of the Pars News Agency was translated and published in Turkish newspapers. 'İranda inkılâb hareketleri', *Cumhuriyet*, 19 January 1936.

112. Cronin, 'Introduction', 3.

113. Deniz Kandiyoti, 'Introduction', in *Women, Islam and the State*, ed. Deniz Kandiyoti (Philadelphia: Temple University Press, 1991), 1–21.

114. Rostam-Kolayi and Matin-asgari, 'Unveiling Ambiguities', 130.

Another nationalist framework used for unveiling in certain contexts was to argue that full-body covers were not dictates of Islam but a 'foreign' culture. Accordingly, the *çarşaf* in Turkey and the *chador* in Iran would be alien dresses imposed by the Arabs, whereas the *ferece* in Albania would be the symbol of Ottoman domination. There were also frequent references to initiatives for unveiling in other Muslim-majority countries, in order to be able to claim its appropriateness to Islam; other Muslims too were embracing it.

It should be pointed out that nowhere can women be seen as passive receivers. In countries like Egypt, Syria, Turkey and Iran, initial moves for unveiling came from the feminists, albeit in some cases they remained as symbolic, individual acts. However, almost everywhere, unveiling campaigns benefitted from the support of those women who had already unveiled or easily adapted themselves to the new norms and became involved in spreading unveiling. In even the most systematic attempts at unveiling, the campaigns depended heavily on the loyalty and agency of female state officials, particularly school teachers, to perform and promote the new clothing among the masses. The national education system was the most important means through which change in women's dress was realized. Even in countries where there was no systematic anti-veiling campaign, the most important momentum for unveiling came when women entered school. An increase in the number of girls' schools and their adoption of special uniforms provided the opportunity for younger generations to unveil and to dress differently than their mothers. Different cases of anti-veiling campaigns also show that the majority of the women, who were not part of the school system, tried to adopt the new dress codes and domesticate them in variety of ways; the combination of many forms of dress and veiling, especially long overcoats and headscarves became common.

Societal reactions also took many different forms. While in some cases, such as Turkey, there was no collective action or demonstration, in others, such as Albania and Afghanistan, some anti-regime uprisings used unveiling as a tool to mobilize social discontent. The fact that these authoritarian regimes were in fact more cautious about imposing unveiling than they were imagined to be is an important conclusion. One exception in this regard was the anti-veiling campaigns under the Soviet rule, where violence against unveiled women was widespread and systematic. However, even in these oppressive examples of anti-veiling campaigns, ordinary people's reactions were not as simple as passive compliance vs. active opposition. Rather, as Northrop maintains, people could utilize many different and complex strategies, 'from studied obliviousness to passive resistance to the spreading of gossip and rumors. They also included varieties of creative subterfuge around questions of law and everyday life.'[115] In fact, the role of rumour and hearsay was strikingly significant everywhere. This was probably so because the parameters of the unveiling remained a bit unclear everywhere, except, perhaps, in Albania, where it was imposed through enacting a law. Even there, however, as everywhere, the implementation process was the key, and local variations and attitudes of those

---

115. Northrop, *Veiled Empire*, 347.

who were obliged to apply the decisions on the ground were definitive. Moreover, just like they influenced inner dynamics in each country in significant ways, rumour, perceptions, exaggeration and misinformation also played an important role in assessing the experiences of other countries. As mentioned earlier, the Turkish press, both national and local, tended to exaggerate the scope of unveiling in other Muslim countries and used this as an extra motivation for promoting unveiling. Some reports in the Western press about Turkey mistakenly presented the anti-veiling campaigns as a compulsory reform based on a law or decree by the central government.[116] The impression that the veil was banned in Turkey was widespread in other Muslim contexts. For example, during the discussions in Soviet Uzbekistan on whether to ban the veil by law or decree, both opponents and proponents of the idea referred to the Turkish case, mistakenly, as an example of banning the veil by decree.[117] Similarly, the idea that the Afghan king was overthrown because he outlawed the veil was also used elsewhere as an argument supporting the necessity to be more cautious and to avoid banning the veil.[118] News claiming that Reza Shah banned the veil in Iran could be seen in the Turkish press as early as mid-1935.[119]

A comparative look at various forms of campaigns for unveiling in different Muslim contexts also reveals that dress change was as much an economic issue as it was a political and cultural one. The removal of women's conventional clothes, be it a *peştamal* in a Turkish district or a *ferece* in an Albanian town, was difficult not only because these clothes were customary, but also because they were cheap and usually local products, more easily accessible to the ordinary people, the majority of whom were poor and rural in the 1920s and 1930s. A European-style overcoat or hat was much more expensive and difficult to find. This economic side of the story shaped people's attitude towards unveiling everywhere. As Wide convincingly argues based on the economy of dress in interwar Afghanistan, what people wore was determined more by their practical concerns and conditions than they were by the ideological priorities of the state:

> A 'market place' of goods and ideas has helped connect the economic to the intellectual, the material to the cultural, and move discussions of the period beyond all-too-prevalent oppositions of 'tribalism,' 'conservatism,' 'religiosity,' 'xenophobia' on the one hand, and 'modernization,' 'Westernization,' 'secularization' and 'globalization,' on the other. It is not that these terms have

116. For example, the newspaper *New York Herald Tribune* reported on 11 September 1935 that the wearing of women's 'harem' clothes was banned by a law in Turkey, which concerned thirty-five provinces. The Turkish translation of the news was circulated among the relevant state offices. T.C. İç Bakanlığı Basın Genel Direktörlüğü Gizli Bülten, TNPA 13216-7/1, 24 September 1935.

117. Northrop, *Veiled Empire*, 286.

118. Ibid., 293.

119. For example, see 'İranda irtica', *Cumhuriyet*, 23 June 1935.

no explanatory force. But dress is a lived practice that cannot be reduced to such abstractions.[120]

The broad similarities notwithstanding, however, initiatives for unveiling in the 'Muslim world' differed from each other in crucial ways. As this chapter tried to show, from elite discussions to diverse encounters with European colonialism, many factors played a role in these differences. I argued that three countries, Albania, Iran and Turkey experienced the most systematic and comprehensive anti-veiling campaigns, which targeted the full body cover as well as the face veil. These three cases were the most analogous ones compared to the other examples during the interwar period, with strong parallels in terms of national dynamics, political regimes and modernization policies. However, they also diverged in critical ways. Albania was the only country that legislated against the face veil. Turkey and Iran, on the other hand, put more emphasis on the fight against unveiling at the local level, but still utilized different means and strategies. A comparative look at the Turkish case reveals that its greater state capacity and institutional variety at the local level set it aside from the other countries. The Kemalist regime could operate in the provinces through institutions that were greater in number and stronger. As seen in detail throughout the previous chapters, in Turkey, many actors and institutions were involved in the shaping and implementation process of the local anti-veiling campaigns, from governors to the local branches of the RPP, from city councils to People's Houses, from local newspapers to sports clubs. This did not make, I maintained, the Kemalist state any more pluralist or less authoritarian, but this institutional diversity clearly added to the dynamism of the reform process. The Pahlavi regime's strategy to impose unveiling through the ministries, while appearing to be similar to the Turkish case, could not and did not compensate for this institutional strength of the Kemalist regime and the relatively greater room this strength allowed for negotiating and domesticating the anti-veiling campaign in the periphery.

As a final remark, it should be emphasized that both national and international dynamics changed after the Second World War. Yet, the question of unveiling continued to be a source of struggle, a key axis for political debates and conflicts with strong symbolic and ideological underpinnings. The debate on banning veiling re-emerged in the Soviet Union in the 1940s.[121] In 1943, a group of Syrian women submitted a petition asking for official unveiling, which led to protests by Islamists; and Muslim women who joined the Christian women's march in Beirut in November 1943 removed their face veil.[122] In 1959, at events marking the 50th anniversary of the 1919 Revolution in Egypt and women's participation in it, 'the emancipation of Egyptian women and their freedom from the veil' were

---

120. Wide, 'Astrakhan', 193.
121. Northrop, *The Veiled Empire*, 309–11.
122. Thompson, *Colonial Citizens*, 242, 257.

also celebrated.[123] Moreover, new countries where Muslims were a minority joined the struggle against veiling: in post-war Yugoslavia, bans were issued on the use of face veil both in Serbia and Bosnia and Herzegovina; in Bulgaria, an anti-veiling campaign was launched by the new communist regime in the late 1950s.[124] And in Turkey, the debate on veiling resurfaced in almost every decade, and each time, with new dimensions and tensions added. A constant, however, was a reference to the Kemalist 'project' of women's modernization under the single-party regime, which has continued to set the parameters of the debate until today.

123. Baron, *Egypt*, 120.

124. 'Sırbistanda Müslüman kadınlarının peçe kullanması yasak', *Cumhuriyet*, 9 April 1947; 'Bosna Hersekte peçe yasak edildi', *Cumhuriyet*, 29 September 1950. For Bulgaria, see Mary Neuburger, 'Difference unveiled: Bulgarian national imperatives and the re-dressing of Muslim women, 1878–1989', in *Anti-Veiling Campaigns in the Muslim World: Gender, Modernism and the Politics of Dress*, ed. Stephanie Cronin (London: Routledge, 2014), 252–66.

CONCLUSIONS

In his pioneering work, *The Development of Secularism in Turkey*, Berkes characterizes the adoption of the Swiss Civil Code in Turkey in 1926 as 'the greatest coup of the new period' since 'the wheels of the society were thus put on a new track'.[1] In discussions on the Civil Code and family law in building up to this reform, the Kemalists favoured a unified system of codes based on secular principles, which, according to them, was a necessity if Turkey wanted to be part of the modern world. This determination can be seen in a speech of Mustafa Kemal in 1925, where he, as the leader of the new regime, made it very explicit:

> The Turkish Revolution signifies a transformation far broader than the word revolution suggests. ... It means replacing an age-old political unity based on religion with one based on another tie, that of nationality. This nation has now accepted the principle that the only means of survival for nations in the international struggle for existence lies in the acceptance of the contemporary Western civilization. The nation has also accepted the principle that all of its laws should be based on secular grounds only, on a secular mentality that accepts the rule of continuous change in accordance with the change and development of life's conditions as its law.[2]

The Minister of Justice Mahmut Esat (Bozkurt) also defended the new law based on similar lines on the day it passed in the parliament, 17 February 1926. In his speech, Mahmut Esat had in fact placed the idea and the aim behind the introduction of the new code within the larger framework of Kemalist modernization:

> We must never forget that the Turkish nation has decided to accept modern civilization and its living principles without any condition or reservation. ... If there are some points of contemporary civilization that do not seem capable of conforming to Turkish society, this is not because of the lack of capability and native capacity of the Turkish nation, but because of the medieval organization

---

1. Berkes, *The Development*, 467.
2. Ibid., 470.

and the religious codes and institutions which abnormally surround it. ... The Turkish nation, which is moving with determination to seize contemporary civilization and make it its own, is obliged not to make contemporary civilization conform to the Turkish nation, but to adjust its steps to the requirements of contemporary civilization at all costs.[3]

The determination that can be heard in Mustafa Kemal's speech and in Mahmut Esat's comments on the new Civil Code can also be traced in other Kemalist reforms and policies of the early republican era. One can refer to several other speeches of Mustafa Kemal or members of the high-level Kemalist elite, where their strong political will and the ideological motives that shaped the general frameworks of the Kemalist reforms can be examined. Such analyses have dominated the literature on Kemalist modernization; the visions of the Kemalist elite in Ankara and what they had to say about the targets and aims of the reforms they introduced have been the starting point of any analysis of the early republic. They have also been read as reflecting the ultimate character of the Kemalist modernization 'project', which has been seen as solid, well-formulated plan of a cohesive group of political elites to change the society in a top-down manner. In this line of thinking, 'social change, seen as self-propelling movement with an internal spring, has no place'; it is rather seen as promoted and shaped by the 'projects' of the elites, or as they are usually called, of the 'social engineers'.[4] As Brockett suggests, the 'assertion that what the Kemalist elite believed should happen was indeed taking place' has been very prevalent in the literature,[5] and thus far less attention has been given to the study of the implementation process of the reforms as they were translated into concrete policies and doings of the various levels of state agents in the provinces. As valuable as it is, Berkes's analysis of the new Civil Code, for example, does not offer sufficient clues to understanding why in the 1930s one could still encounter practices that were clearly against this law. In 1931, for instance, the party report on the concerns and requests raised in the local congresses of the RPP in thirty-eight provinces included notes that in the villages of some provinces, such as Artvin, Erzincan, Erzurum and Kars, marriages were carried out only by the religious hodjas, and thus these marriages were unregistered.[6] Newspapers of the 1930s, national and local alike, were full of news about such issues of unregistered marriages and births, and the many attempts by the state to have them registered

---

3. Ibid., 471.

4. Mardin, 'Projects as Methodology', 65. Mardin criticizes this dominant approach in the literature and suggests that in order to understand social change, scholars should rather look at its micro aspects and study the everyday and 'life-worlds' of social subjects. However, Mardin points at religion as the 'life-world' and sees Islam as the dominant motive in the lives of ordinary people in Turkey, which I think is an approach that narrows the concept of life-world and limits the contributions it could make to the literature.

5. Brockett, 'Collective Action', 45.

6. For the report, see BCA 030.10/79.522.2.

by granting a pardon.[7] Similarly, despite the fact that the new Civil Code clearly banned polygamy, it continued to exist in the succeeding decades.[8] Such evidence shows that the Civil Code was still contested in the periphery years after its introduction and could not be fully implemented, despite the resolute voice of the political elite in Ankara.

This book has departed from a similar discrepancy between 'fact and fiction' in the study of the Kemalist modernization. Drawing on the case of the anti-veiling campaigns of the 1930s, it reveals a more detailed and complex picture of the Kemalist reforms and policies in the periphery that takes into account the ambiguities, hesitations, contradictions, unanticipated consequences, negotiations and compromises embedded in the modernization process. Unlike many other Kemalist reforms, there was no law or central decision guiding the implementation of the anti-veiling campaigns in the provinces. Although Ankara clearly encouraged the local administrators, and tried to control and coordinate their initiatives for women's unveiling, the campaigns remained as local phenomena and were mainly fashioned by the local actors and circumstances rather than by directives coming from the centre. In fact, the directives coming from Ankara were usually weak in terms of policy guidance, and at times, vague and even inconsistent. As such, anti-veiling campaigns can be seen as an ambiguous reform agenda in terms of content and application. This ambiguity, it can be argued, created even a broader space for various actors to be involved in their shaping, and combined with their local character, turned the anti-veiling campaigns into a very rich case to observe these complex interactions between state and societal actors.

The public debate on the proper way for women to veil themselves and the characterization of the *peçe* and the *çarşaf* as uncivilized clothing originated in the late Ottoman Empire. Although the 'new woman' of the republic was promoted to symbolize a radical break with the Ottoman past, neither the search for a new womanhood nor the idea that linked social development, progress and modernity with women's emancipation and modernization of their clothing was new. The change in women's clothing and the decrease in the use of the *peçe* and the *çarşaf* were already under way among the elite women in major Ottoman urban centres. Ottoman women's increasing participation in the work force and their efforts in the war years prepared a fertile ground for their further visibility in the public sphere in the republic. The initial attempts to intervene in the clothing of women in the 1920s, which can partly be seen as a continuation of the tradition of state

---

7. For example, see 'Diyarbekirde 40 bin Mektum Nüfus Kaydedildi', *Son Posta*, 13 July 1934; 'Gizli Nüfus', *Son Posta*, 19 August 1934; 'Gizli Doğum', *Yeni Asır*, 19 November 1934; 'Gizli Nüfus Yazımı Uzatıldı', *Yeni Adana*, 20 January 1935; 'Gizli Nüfus Hakkında', *Yeni Adana*, 7 July 1936.

8. For a more detailed discussion, see Nicole A.N.M. van Os, 'Polygamy Before and After the Introduction of the Swiss Civil Code in Turkey', in *The State and the Subaltern: Modernization, Society and the State in Turkey and Iran*, ed. Touraj Atabaki (London. I.B. Tauris, 2007), 179–98.

regulation of clothing in the Ottoman era, had built on the modernist discourse and practices that emerged during the empire, but also furthered them by opening the way for direct intervention in women's veiling.

The anti-veiling campaigns in the second half of the 1920s were local, narrow in scope, limited in number and largely uninfluential in practice. While some of them seem to have been encouraged by the central elite, the campaigns were mainly the initiatives of the local elite. They emerged immediately after the enactment of the Hat Law of 1925 and were undoubtedly part of the public debate and general atmosphere the hat reform generated on modern and civilized clothing. I argued that the Hat Law functioned as a reference point and source of legitimacy for those provincial elite, men and women, who wanted to initiate a similar modernization attempt with respect to women's clothing in their localities. Particularly significant was the influence of the hat reform experience in shaping the way the question of women's veiling was handled. The Kemalist strategy of dealing with women's clothing not by issuing a law or a central degree was informed by the reactions the hat reform received. However, I also argued that part of the reason for this choice should be found in the patriarchal concerns of the Kemalist regime while trying to trigger change in women's social position and public roles. The patriarchal gender contract between the elite and non-elite male actors was to 'protect' women's morality from the ills of 'too much' Westernization. This patriarchal contract, combined with the fear of a social reaction even wider than the hat reform received, fed into the tendency of the Kemalist regime to transfer the question of unveiling to the provincial level, to trust the modernist ambitions of the local elite, and thus to be content with a more gradual change in this 'sensitive issue'.

While it can be argued that this tendency continued throughout the single-party era in broad terms, we see a bolder attempt to remove the *peçe* and the *çarşaf* in the 1930s, which I call the main wave of the anti-veiling campaigns. Local attempts to eliminate the *peçe* and the *çarşaf* would be applied in a much more comprehensive manner during this main wave, in terms of both content and the scope, and the strength of the propaganda efforts regarding it. I suggested that this main wave should be analysed in the context of 1930s Turkey, which was characterized by an increasingly authoritarian regime that consolidated its power and was more determined to penetrate the society and to intervene in ordinary people's cultural and daily practices. The new statist phase the regime entered in the 1930s was also shaped by an assertive move for cultural modernization, of which the anti-veiling campaigns were an important component alongside other bold reforms, such as the adoption of Western measures and the language reform. The year 1934 had witnessed a particularly intense reform movement in this direction, including the anti-veiling campaigns, the Surname Law, the Dress Law and women's gaining of their full political rights. The relationship between the Kemalist regime's turn to statism and the acceleration of the attempts at cultural modernization that I underlined in this book need to be analysed further based on other examples to get a more vivid picture of this 'second phase' of Kemalism in the 1930s. The anti-veiling campaigns are perhaps one of the best ways of looking at the cultural codes of the regime, which aimed at creating a more 'civilized' society, in both visual and behavioural terms. However, I think, these series of reforms that we have associated with cultural modernization should not be seen as being limited to such discursive and ideological categories of 'modern' or 'civilized' as they were frequently addressed by the Kemalists themselves. They should also be seen in a broader context of state centralization, as components of an increasing attempt by the regime in the 1930s to restore its legitimacy, to enlarge its ideological hegemony, and to increase regulation, systematization and homogenization in order to inventory various aspects of daily life of its citizens and bring them under control. It is I think in this way that we can see the integrated nature of economic, political and cultural spheres as well as the links between different policies of the single-party era more clearly.

One mechanism in the 1930s through which such parallel processes of modernization and state penetration became more deeply infused into the provinces was the municipal administration, which was significantly strengthened by the Municipal Law of 1930 and reorganized as one of the local promoters of modern life. This law and the subsequent amendments to increase further the punitive powers of the municipalities had in fact drawn the legal framework within which the anti-veiling campaigns of the 1930s were shaped and implemented. In this sense, it was no coincidence that when direct bans were issued on the use of the *peçe* and the *çarşaf* in a great majority of the anti-veiling campaigns, they were issued by the city councils acting on the basis of the Municipal Law. Yet, it would be misleading to see the anti-veiling campaigns as municipal regulations only. In fact, one of the major conclusions of this book is that there was a multiplicity of institutions and actors involved in the process leading to an anti-veiling campaign and its implementation thereafter. In other words, just as it was possible to see mayors or city council members who were unwilling to use the legal capacity of the municipalities to initiate an anti-veiling campaign, it was also common to see sport clubs, local associations, local newspapers, People's Houses, the local RPP branches or the members of the provincial councils pushing for an effective campaign. Depending on the locality, one or more of these actors and institutions could play a decisive role in the organization of an anti-veiling campaign, the ban issued by the city council being one component of the process. The implementation of the campaign was even more complex, since it was shaped by the support as well as the resistance of various actors at the local level, and simultaneously, by the interaction between Ankara and the provinces. That is why this book suggests that in order to better understand the single-party era, it is imperative to bring the local into the analysis, to keep a micro–macro balance, and to reconsider the periphery not as a locus of the 'traditional', the 'masses' or religious opposition to Kemalism but as a sphere of interaction between various actors and positions, where Kemalism and daily state practices were negotiated.

A closer look at the anti-veiling campaigns as they were experienced at the local level reveals a number of crucial insights regarding 1930s Turkey. First, the problematic aspects of focusing on high politics of the capital notwithstanding, the dominant tendency in the literature to picture a homogeneous and unified Kemalist political elite is misleading. The detailed discussion on the position of

Ankara on the anti-veiling campaigns revealed that the high-level Kemalist elite was not only in fact less monolithic than they have been imagined to be, but also could act quite hesitantly and reluctantly on certain issues. As in other policies, Ankara was involved in the anti-veiling campaigns through various channels, the main ones being the Ministry of the Interior and the RPP General Secretary. However, the nature of this involvement and the working of these channels were quite complex and they ensured neither a solid control over nor a consistent implementation of the anti-veiling campaigns. The Kemalist elite's hesitations, which clearly surfaced at the RPP congress in 1935, continued throughout the process and the basic consensus on the need for encouragement, inculcation, and propaganda regarding unveiling, which constantly appeared in the circulars sent from Ankara, had little effect in uniting the experiences in different provinces. The regime centre acted much more consistently and cohesively in cases it perceived an open resistance. It equally reacted quite steadily to those provincial administrators who pushed for an aggressive anti-veiling campaign, going beyond the authority they had been given by Ankara. It is, I think, also significant to remember in this regard that the use of force in the anti-veiling campaigns was also consistently rejected by Ankara, though it could not be avoided.

Second, the role and the attitudes of the local elite were decisive at all levels. One of the most important findings in this matter is the fact that in some of the anti-veiling campaigns, the initiative came from the local, from those who envisioned themselves as the representatives and the agents of modernization in the periphery. In other words, the anti-veiling campaigns cannot be seen as directed and imposed from Ankara only; they were supported and even initiated by some local modernists, native and appointed alike, and thus emerged as a result of more widely shared ideological premises and ambitions. Some local elites, on the other hand, varying from provincial governors to native members of city councils, were content with a more gradual change on the issue of women's veiling. There were also those who had reservations about, or even critical of, the anti-veiling campaigns. Even provincial governors, perhaps the most coherent group ideologically and educationally, could interpret the central policies and reforms in quite diverse ways. This variety forms the basis of another important argument of this book: that not only is the concept of local elite essential in analysing the Kemalist state in action, but also that the local elite should not be seen as monolithic or limited to state-appointed officials. Rather, it should be defined in an inclusive manner, as a composite group broad enough to embrace various power networks at the local level. It is crucial to remember that while salient differences like native vs. non-native or educated vs. non-educated proved important in many instances, these differences among the local elite were not as rigid and bold as they have usually been assumed in the literature.

Third, the local, or the 'periphery', had many components. Our notion of the local has to be broadened to reflect the multiplicity of the actors and voices it contains. Much like the central elite in Ankara, the local elite also did not act in a vacuum; their actions were shaped in relation to the reactions coming from the ordinary people, the real addressees of the state policies. The subordinated sectors of the society had an influence on the anti-veiling campaigns in various and creative ways, such as circulating rumours and writing anonymous letters. People's range of responses was actually quite rich. While popular resistance to the campaigns remained largely within the limits of 'secure' strategies, some anti-veiling campaigns, especially those that were enforced through the police or the gendarmerie, received violent reactions. Reactions to the campaigns also reveal that popular resistance cannot be reduced to religious or traditional reasons, as it is depicted or implicitly assumed in the literature. Popular resistance was significant, for example, particularly in making the economic aspect of the campaigns more visible to the authorities. The local producers of the *çarşaf* and the *peştamal*, as well as poor people who were unable to afford the 'modern' clothes to replace them reacted to the anti-veiling campaigns largely on the basis of economic concerns.

The multiplicity of local actors and institutions in the Turkish case and the difference this makes in terms of the relative effectiveness of the anti-veiling campaigns becomes more apparent when it is seen within the wider Muslim context. The debates on and attempts at women's unveiling in different predominantly Muslim countries during the interwar era all stemmed from a similar search for a new, modern and national woman. From the Arab countries to the Soviet Muslim republics, modernization of women, and as part of it, modernization of women's clothing, echoed modernization and development of the nation as a whole. In all experiences, though in varying degrees, unveiling was presented as a national cause rather than a pure imitation of the West, and a particular emphasis on protecting women's morality accompanied the emphasis given to their new roles as modern citizens. The reactions the anti-veiling campaigns received and the ways in which women tried to cope with them also revealed significant similarities across the cases. One important conclusion perhaps is that no matter how autocratic the political regimes in interwar 'Muslim world' were, the implementation of the authoritarian policies like the anti-veiling campaigns was never without contestation and almost never took the shape the central elite envisioned. From cultural to economic factors, many dynamics altered the original 'projects' and the end results were always shaped by an interplay between various actors and discourses. The comparison between Albania, Iran and Turkey reveals the distinctive characteristics of the Kemalist regime in 1930s more vividly in the light of its closest contemporaries. It shows that the Kemalist regime was *relatively* more capable of infusing its ideology deeper into the society, integrating *relatively* broader segments of the population to its circles of power, and providing *relatively* larger institutional variety and capacity to embrace these actors as agents at the local level. In 1930s Turkey, the Kemalist state functioned in the provinces through various institutions: the local branches of the RPP, the People's Houses, the municipalities, the city councils, the provincial councils and various associations. The anti-veiling campaigns were shaped by the initiatives and acts of these institutions, which functioned as settings accommodating different actors and positions.

It should be emphasized that this institutional diversity and capacity certainly did not make the anti-veiling campaigns in Turkey any more democratic. Nor did they make the Kemalist regime in the 1930s less authoritarian. But I think it is safe to argue that the Kemalist regime was *relatively* more capable of adjusting negotiation, domestication and variation without endangering its political power and ideological hegemony. In this sense, the findings of this book support Meeker's observation that the Kemalist regime allowed a certain degree of popular participation in governmental and non-governmental institutions in order to incorporate the local actors in the new system, much like the way the Ottoman state operated in the provinces. It is, I think, also crucial to see the capacity of Kemalism to mobilize people, from teachers to school children, from women to various local elites if we are to understand its salience as a political reference beyond the single-party era. The reading presented in this book does not diverge from the general characterization of the Kemalist single-party state as an authoritarian state, but claims to provide a better account of how this authoritarian state actually worked. There is no doubt that the Kemalist regime in the early republican period *was* an authoritarian regime, and though in varying degrees, the modernization policies initiated by this regime touched every sector of the society, as the political elite in Ankara had anticipated. However, there is also no question that the visions of the political elite in Ankara, and the policies, reforms and instruments of this authoritarian regime were influenced and shaped by its encounters with the society, with the realities and dynamics of social life it faced when operating in practice. In other words, it is the encounter and interaction of the state and the society out of which the social change, or the various 'projects' of Kemalist modernity, took their final form. Therefore, as Migdal suggests, one needs to look at those spaces where this encounter and interaction occurred; spaces where the project of modernity initiated by the elite met the society, and where they transformed one another.[9] The case of the anti-veiling campaigns in Turkey of the 1930s demonstrates that the state policies of the single-party era and the change they created could be understood fully only by looking at the interactions of the state and the society, by focusing on the concrete forms these policies took in the provinces, and by appreciating the multiplicity of actors and agencies at the local level, the central state being only one of them.

Finally, as the main target of the anti-veiling campaigns, women's roles as actors that tried to adapt, shape, modify and/or resist the change the Kemalist regime wanted to initiate, were definitive. Some women played an active role in the anti-veiling campaigns, not only as supporters but also as initiators of the bans issued by local institutions. Some women tried to resist the intervention in their clothing despite the threat of punishment, while others domesticated new clothes by adapting them to local circumstances or by embracing new forms of covering their hair. Many of them tried to deal with the multiple pressures and difficulties they were facing; the pressure for unveiling as imposed by the anti-veiling campaigns, the social and cultural pressure for keeping the veil as imposed by the local community and/or the family members, and their own preferences. For

---

9. Migdal, 'Finding the Meeting', 255.

some of them who were more educated and/or with high social status, not only the removal of the *peçe* and the *çarşaf*, but also total unveiling was happily welcomed; for some others, this was a more gradual process, a journey from wearing the *çarşaf* to covering their head with a turban or a kind of headscarf, and eventually, to opting for a modern-style hat. It is thus crucial to acknowledge this diversity of women's responses, to take into consideration the various ways through which they involved in the anti-veiling campaigns as agents, and to underline that these responses and agency shaped the process in each locality critically. A detailed look at women's reactions to and involvement in the anti-veiling campaigns shows that women's agency should be analysed and conceptualized by going beyond the poles of open resistance and passive compliance.

It is also significant to note that the anti-veiling campaigns cannot be understood within the parameters of the never-ending debate on whether they were liberating or oppressive. Women's unveiling in the early republic has been discussed by the critics of Kemalism in Turkey, particularly the conservative and Islamist critiques, as one of the most powerful symbols of Kemalist oppression, and became highly politicized, especially during the headscarf debate of the post-1980s decades. While the Kemalist narrative celebrates such policies as the emancipation of women, the critical accounts have largely represented women as victims of them. In both accounts, however, women have been characterized as passive receivers of regime's policies. As demonstrated throughout this book, this was in fact not the case. The anti-veiling campaigns turned into an opportunity space, a terrain for women to negotiate their social roles and the prevalent gender norms. And this opportunity space was not just limited to a narrow group of elite women in a few major cities. The salient feminist critique of Kemalist modernization that it failed to touch the lives of majority of women should thus be revisited. Particularly the examples where women actively participated in the anti-veiling campaigns and promoted them challenge the contention that the clothing reforms of the Kemalist regime associated political agency only with men.[10] The feminist historiography of women of the early republic should respond to some women's willingness to be part of Kemalist modernization because they thought it provided a *potentially* broader space for women's self-actualization. In other words, we can acknowledge and address the various ways women were involved in the anti-veiling campaigns, and resisted or altered them, without reducing this variety to rigid categories like full emancipation or oppression. Equally, we can scrutinize possibly empowering aspects of policies like the anti-veiling campaigns for some women, without undermining their controlling character and without ignoring the fact that some women became indeed victims of state as well as male violence because they refused to unveil, but also because, they wanted to remove the veil. It is in this complexity the actual story of women under Kemalism and their troubled relationship with it lie.

---

10. See, for example, Çınar, *Modernity*, 53–98.

APPENDIX

The table below shows the cities (provincial capitals, district capitals and sub-districts) where there was an outright ban. It does not include the cases where there was an anti-veiling campaign but the campaign did not lead to an outright ban (or cases where it is unclear whether it did or not). For example, in Diyarbakır, the campaign seems to be limited to a decision by the members of the People's House, and thus it is not included in the table below. Therefore, it should be noted that the actual number of anti-veiling campaigns was higher than the number of cases included in the table. The bans are listed chronologically, based on the time the decisions were made and declared rather than the time the bans became effective. Enforcement dates, if known, are mentioned in the Notes column. Since provincial newspapers do not specify on which day exactly the decision was made when reporting on the bans, I use only the month and the year for the date of the bans. I used the name of the issuing authority as it appears in the source. For example, if the ban was reported only as a municipal decision (*belediye kararı*), I noted the municipality as the issuing authority. If it is specifically mentioned that it was the city council (*belediye meclisi*), then I specified the city council, an organ of the municipality, as well.

It should also be noted that although the list of bans provided here is the most comprehensive list available in the literature, it is not a comprehensive one. It is based on the sources I consulted within the limits of my research. Because the campaigns and the bans were local, local sources should be consulted for every single province (and perhaps town) in order to come up with a potentially comprehensive list.

List of the Local Bans in the 1930s

Date of the Ban	City	Content	Issuing Authority	Source	Notes
August 1933	Safranbolu	*Çarşaf*	District Governor	*Cumhuriyet* 21 August 1933	
April 1934	Giresun	*Peçe*	City Council	*Cumhuriyet* 24 April 1934	
April (?) 1934	Mersin	*Çarşaf*	City Council	*Cumhuriyet* 7 April 1934	The proposal to ban the *çarşaf* was submitted to the city council in April. The ban was put into practice on 1 July. See also *Yeni Mersin*, 1 July 1934.

Date of the Ban	City	Content	Issuing Authority	Source	Notes
August 1934	Armutlu	*Çarşaf*		*Son Posta* 30 August 1934	It is not clear which institution issued the ban.
November 1934	Bergama	*Peçe, Çarşaf, Kıvrak*	City Council	*Anadolu* 7 November 1934	
November 1934	Buca	*Peçe, Çarşaf*	City Council	*Anadolu* 19 November 1934	See also *Yeni Asır*, 19 November 1934.
November (?) 1934	Kayseri	*Çarşaf*	City Council	*Yeni Asır* 27 November 1934	*Yeni Asır* reported a decision for the removal of the *çarşaf*. See also *Yeni Adana*, 4 December 1934. However, whether this initial decision included a ban is not clear. *Cumhuriyet* later reported a ban on the *çarşaf* in the district capitals and villages of Kayseri. *Cumhuriyet*, 16 September 1935.
December 1934	Bodrum	*Çarşaf, Fıta, Peçe*	City Council	*Yeni Asır* 12 December 1934	The ban was put into practice on 1 January 1935. See also *Cumhuriyet*, 12 December 1934; *Yeniyol*, 13 December 1934.
December 1934	Fethiye	*Peçe, Çarşaf*	City Council	*Yeni Asır* 12 December 1934	15 days were allowed to remove the *peçe*, and six months for the *çarşaf*.
December 1934	Kemaliye	*Peçe, Çarşaf*	City Council	*Yeni Adana* 18 December 1934	See also *Babalık*, 18 December 1934.
December 1934	Bartın	*Kafes*	Municipal Committee (*Belediye Encümeni*)	*Antalya* 20 December 1934	A period of one week was provided to remove the *kafes* in Bartın city centre.
December 1934	Bolu	*Çarşaf*	Municipality	*Yeni Asır* 21 December 1934	The decision of the municipality was put into practice in mid-June. See *Cumhuriyet*, 18 June 1935; *Yeniyol*, 19 June 1935.
February (?) 1935	Bursa	*Çarşaf, Kafes*	City Council	*Hakkın Sesi* 3 February 1935	The decision of the city council was to ban tailors from sewing the *çarşaf*. On 10 February, the *kafes* was banned. The time of the decision that banned the *çarşaf* is unclear, but it is certain that such a general ban was issued. See *Hakkın Sesi*, 10 October 1935.

Date of the Ban	City	Content	Issuing Authority	Source	Notes
February 1935	Antalya	*Peçe, Çarşaf, Kafes*	City Council	*Antalya* 16 February 1935	All *kafes*es were to be removed by the end of February, while for the removal of the *peçe* and the *çarşaf*, women had time until the end of April. See also *Yeniyol*, 14 February 1935; *Yeni Asır*, 14 February 1935.
February 1935	Adana	*Peçe, Çarşaf*	City Council	*Cumhuriyet* 13 February 1935	The ban was put into practice on 16 March. See *Yeni Asır*, 13 March 1935.
February 1935	Akşehir	*Peçe, Çarşaf*	Municipality	*Babalık* 13 February 1935	
February (?) 1935	Erzincan	*Peçe, Çarşaf, Kafes*	Provincial Council	*İkbal* 22 February 1935	
February 1935	Rize	*Peçe, Çarşaf*	City Council	*Yeni Asır* 1 March 1935	Women were given a period of one year to replace their *çarşaf* with an overcoat. The decision of the city council also asked women not to use umbrella to hide themselves.
March 1935	Artvin	*Peçe, Çarşaf*	City Council	*Yeni Asır* 7 March 1935	See also *Halk*, 7 March 1935.
April 1935	Muğla	*Peçe, Çarşaf*	City Council	*Cumhuriyet* 25 April 1935	The ban was put into practice in June. See also BCA 490.01/17.88.1, 15 October 1935.
April 1935	İnegöl	*Peçe, Çarşaf, Kafes*	City Council	*Cumhuriyet* 25 April 1935	Non-compliance would be fined, ranging from 5 to 50 liras. See also *Hakkın Sesi*, 23 April 1935.
April 1935	Ereğli	*Peçe, Çarşaf*	City Council	*Babalık* 10 August 1935	The ban was put into practice on 1 August 1935.
May 1935	Nevşehir	*Peçe, Çarşaf, Yaşmak*	Municipality	*Cumhuriyet* 18 May 1935	*Peçe* and *Yaşmak* were to be removed immediately.
July 1935	Sungurlu	*Peçe, Çarşaf, Kafes*	Municipality	*Cumhuriyet* 10 July 1935	Both the local party administration and the District Health Council (*Sağlık Kurulu*) were part of the decision making.
August (?) 1935	Zile	*Peçe, Çarşaf*	City Council	*Cumhuriyet* 2 August 1935	See also *Yeniyol*, 3 August 1935.
August 1935	Kastamonu	*Peçe, Çarşaf*	City Council	*Yeniyol* 3 August 1935	See also *Halk*, 3 August 1935.

Date of the Ban	City	Content	Issuing Authority	Source	Notes
August 1935	Konya	*Peçe, Çarşaf, Şelme*	City Council	*Babalık* 7 August 1935	The ban was put into practice on 15 September 1935. See also *Cumhuriyet*, 9 August 1935.
August 1935	Ilgın	*Peçe, Çarşaf*	City Council	*Babalık* 10 August 1935	
August 1935	Kadınhan	*Peçe, Çarşaf*	City Council	*Babalık* 13 August 1935	
August 1935	Karaman	*Peçe, Çarşaf*	City Council	*Babalık* 15 August 1935	See also *Cumhuriyet*, 21 August 1935.
August 1935	Aydın	*Peçe, Çarşaf, Peştamal*	City Council	EGM 13216-7/1 17 August 1935	
August 1935	Tosya	*Peçe, Çarşaf*	City Council	EGM 13216-7/1 21 August 1935	
August 1935	Göynük	*Peçe, Çarşaf*	City Council	*Cumhuriyet* 23 August 1935	
August 1935	Afyon	*Peçe, Çarşaf*	City Council	*Cumhuriyet* 24 August 1935	See also *Son Posta*, 24 August 1935.
August 1935	Sivas	*Peçe, Çarşaf*	City Council	*Cumhuriyet* 26 August 1935	
August 1935	Isparta	*Peçe, Çarşaf*		*Cumhuriyet* 26 August 1935	It is not clear which institution issued the ban.
August 1935	Çorum	*Çarşaf*	Municipality	EGM 13216-7/1 20 August 1935	
August (?) 1935	Seyitgazi	*Peçe, Çarşaf*	Municipality	EGM 13216-7/1 7 February 1936	
September 1935	Erdek	*Peçe, Çarşaf*	City Council	*Cumhuriyet* 1 September 1935	

Date of the Ban	City	Content	Issuing Authority	Source	Notes
September 1935	Soma	*Peçe, Çarşaf*	City Council	*Cumhuriyet* 10 September 1935	
September 1935	Karacasu	*Peçe, Çarşaf, Peştamal*	City Council	*Cumhuriyet* 13 September 1935	
September 1935	Elaziz	*Peçe, Çarşaf*	City Council	*Cumhuriyet* 13 September 1935	
September 1935	Çermik	*Peçe, Çarşaf*		*Cumhuriyet* 16 September 1935	It is not clear which institution issued the ban.
September 1935	Denizli	*Peçe, Çarşaf, Peştamal*	Governor	*Babadağ* 24 September 1935	See Uyar, 'Tek-Parti'.
September 1935	Kilis	*Peçe, Çarşaf*	City Council	*Son Posta* 23 September 1935	Women were given time to remove their *çarşaf* until December 1935. See also *Cumhuriyet*, 27 January 1936.
September 1935	Yozgat	*Peçe, Çarşaf*	Governor (?)	BCA 490.01/17.88.1 13 November 1935	
September 1935	Sinop	*Çarşaf*	City Council	*Cumhuriyet* 3 October 1935	
September (?) 1935	Çankırı	*Peçe, Çarşaf*	City Council	EGM 13216-7/1 4 November 1935	
October 1935	Bitlis	*Peçe, Çarşaf*	City Council	*Son Posta* 2 October 1935	
October (?) 1935	Uşak	*Peçe, Çarşaf*	City Council	*Cumhuriyet* 3 October 1935	The *peçe* was to be removed immediately, whereas the *çarşaf* was allowed only until 29 October, Republic Day.
October (?) 1935	Mardin	*Peçe*	Municipality	*Cumhuriyet* 3 October 1935	*Cumhuriyet* reported that there was a decision by the municipality. However, whether the decision included a ban on the *peçe* is not clear.
October 1935	Siirt	*Peçe, Çarşaf*	Municipality	*Son Posta* 13 October 1935	The campaign was initiated by the People's House earlier in March. See *Halk*, 25 March 1935.

Date of the Ban	City	Content	Issuing Authority	Source	Notes
November 1935	Adıyaman	*Peçe, Çarşaf*	City Council	*Cumhuriyet* 7 November 1935	
November 1935	Maraş	*Peçe, Çarşaf, Karadon*	City Council	BCA 490.01/17.88.1 5 November 1935	*Karadon* was a type of baggy trouser common among local men in Maraş. See also *Cumhuriyet*, 11 November 1935.
November 1935	Gümüşhane	*Peçe, Çarşaf*	City Council	*Cumhuriyet* 13 November 1935	
November 1935	Bayburt	*Peçe, Çarşaf*	City Council	*Cumhuriyet* 29 November 1935	
November 1935	Akçaabat	*Peçe, Çarşaf*	Municipality	*Halk* 25 November 1935	
December 1935	Maçka	*Peçe, Çarşaf, Peştamal*	Municipality	*Halk* 12 December 1935	
February 1936	Trabzon	*Peçe, Çarşaf*	City Council	*Halk* 10 February 1936	
February 1936	Of	*Peçe, Çarşaf*	City Council	*Halk* 24 February 1936	
March 1937	Ordu	*Peçe, Çarşaf, Peştamal*	Governor	EGM 13216-7/1 5 March 1937	The *peçe*, the *çarşaf* and the *peştamal* were banned as of 23 April 1937.
November 1938	Hakkari	*Peçe*	Municipality	EGM 13216-7/2 20 November 1938	It was the municipality of Çölemerik, the provincial centre of the province of Hakkari that decided to ban the *peçe*. Cited in Yılmaz, *Becoming Turkish*.

BIBLIOGRAPHY

Archival Sources

Ministry of the Interior of the Republic of Turkey, Directorate General of Security
Archives (*Emniyet Genel Müdürlüğü Arşivi* - EGM)
Presidency of State Archives of the Republic of Turkey, Republican Period (*Devlet Arşivleri
Başkanlığı Cumhuriyet Arşivi* - BCA)
The National Archives of the United Kingdom Foreign Office Records (FO)
United States National Archives and Records Administration (NARA)
Turkish Grand National Assembly Minute Book (*TBMM Zabıt Ceridesi*)

Newspapers and Periodicals

Ak Günler (Adana)
Anadolu (Izmir)
Antalya (Antalya)
Babalık (Konya)
Cumhuriyet
Halk (Trabzon)
Hakimiyeti Milliye
Hakkın Sesi (Bursa)
İkbal (Trabzon)
Kars (Kars)
Resimli Ay
Son Posta
Yeni Adana (Adana)
Yeni Asır (Izmir)
Yeni Mersin (İçel)
Yeniyol (Trabzon)

Books and Articles

Abadan-Unat, Nermin. ed. *Women in Turkish Society*. Leiden: Brill, 1981.
Abrahamian, Ervand. *Iran between Two Revolutions*. Princeton: Princeton University
Press, 1982.
Abu-Lughod, Lila. ed. *Remaking Women: Feminism and Modernism in the Middle East*.
New Jersey: Princeton University Press, 1998.
Adak, Sevgi. 'Kemalist Laikliğin Oluşum Sürecinde Ramazanlar (1923–1938)'. *Tarih ve
Toplum Yeni Yaklaşımlar* 11 (Fall 2010): 47–88.

Adak, Sevgi. 'Anti-veiling Campaigns and the Local Elites in Turkey of the 1930s: A View from the Periphery'. In *Anti-Veiling Campaigns in the Muslim World: Gender, Modernism and the Politics of Dress*, edited by Stephanie Cronin, 59–85. London: Routledge, 2014.

Adak, Sevgi. 'Women in the Post-Ottoman Public Sphere: Anti-Veiling Campaigns and the Reshaping of the Urban Space in Early Republican Turkey'. In *Women and the City, Women in the City: A Gendered Perspective on Ottoman Urban History*, edited by Nazan Maksudyan, 36–67. New York: Berghahn, 2014.

Adak, Sevgi. 'Women, the *Kafes* and the City. Gendering Urban Transformation in Early Turkish Republic'. In *Nation, Body and Visuality in the Post-Ottoman Urban Space: Turkish and Yugoslav Cities in the Interwar Period*, edited by Nataša Mišković and Karl Kaser. Oxford: Berghahn, forthcoming.

Ahmed, Leila. *Women and Gender in Islam: Historical Roots of a Modern Debate*. New Haven: Yale University Press, 1992.

Ahmed-Ghosh, Huma. 'A History of Women in Afghanistan: Lessons Learnt for the Future or Yesterdays and Tomorrow: Women in Afghanistan'. *Journal of International Women's Studies* 4, no. 3 (May 2003): 1–14.

Akarlı, Engin Deniz. 'The State as a Socio-Cultural Phenomenon and Political Participation in Turkey'. In *Political Participation in Turkey*, edited by Engin D. Akarlı and Gabriel Ben-Dor, 135–55. Istanbul: Boğaziçi University Publications, 1975.

Akın, Yiğit. 'Reconsidering State, Party and Society in Early Republican Turkey: Politics of Petitioning'. *International Journal of Middle East Studies* 39 (2007): 435–57.

Akkent, Meral and Gaby Frager. *Başörtü*. Frankfurt: Dağyeli, 1987.

Akşit, Elif Ekin. *Kızların Sessizliği: Kız Enstitülerinin Uzun Tarihi*. Istanbul: İletişim, 2005.

Aktaş, Cihan. *Tanzimat'tan 12 Mart'a Kılık-Kıyafet ve İktidar*. 2nd ed. Istanbul: Kapı, 2006.

Alp, Tekin. *Kemalizm*. Istanbul: Cumhuriyet Gazete ve Matbaası, 1936.

Alus, Servet Muhtar. 'II. Abdülhamid Devrinde Kadın Kıyafetleri'. *Resimli Tarih Mecmuası* 2, no. 13 (January 1951): 544–7.

Amin, Camron. *The Making of the Modern Iranian Woman: Gender, State Policy, and Popular Culture, 1865–1946*. Florida: University Press of Florida, 2002.

Aslan, Senem. '"Citizen Speak Turkish!" A Nation in the Making'. *Nationalism and Ethnic Politics* 13, no. 2 (2007): 245–72.

Aslan, Senem. *Nation Building in Turkey and Morocco: Governing Turkish and Berber Dissent*. Cambridge: Cambridge University Press, 2014.

Apak, Melek Sevüktekin, Filiz Onat Gündüz and Fatma Öztürk Eray. *Osmanlı Dönemi Kadın Giyimleri*. Ankara: Türkiye İş Bankası Kültür Yayınları, 1997.

Arat, Zehra F. 'Turkish Women and the Republican Reconstruction of Tradition'. In *Reconstructing Gender in the Middle East: Tradition, Identity and Power*, edited by Fatma Müge Göçek and Shiva Balaghi, 57–78. New York: Columbia University Press, 1995.

Arat, Yeşim. 'Women's Movement of the 1980s in Turkey: Radical Outcome of Liberal Kemalism?'. In *Reconstructing Gender in the Middle East: Power, Identity and Tradition*, edited by Fatma Müge Göçek ve Shiva Balaghi, 100–12. New York: Columbia University Press, 1994.

Arat, Yeşim. 'The Project of Modernity and Women in Turkey'. In *Rethinking Modernity and National Identity in Turkey*, edited by Sibel Bozdoğan and Reşat Kasaba, 95–112. Seattle: University of Washington Press, 1997.

Arat, Zehra F. 'Kemalizm ve Türk Kadını'. In *75 Yılda Kadınlar ve Erkekler*, edited by Ayşe Berktay Hacımirzaoğlu, 51–70. Istanbul: Tarih Vakfı Yayınları, 1998.

Asım, Selahaddin. *Türk Kadınlığının Tereddisi yahud Karılaşmak*. Istanbul: Resimli Kitab Matbaası, n.d.

Atabaki, Touraj and Erik J. Zürcher. 'Introduction'. In *Men of Order: Authoritarian Modernization under Atatürk and Reza Shah*, edited by Touraj Atabaki and Erik J. Zürcher, 1–12. London: I.B. Tauris, 2004.

Atatürk'ün Söylev ve Demeçleri I-III. Ankara: Atatürk Kültür, Dil ve Tarih Yüksek Kurumu Atatürk Araştırma Merkezi, 1989.

Atauz, Sevil. 'Cumhuriyet'in İlk Yıllarında Gaziantep'te Gündelik Yaşamın Dönüşümü: Bir Sözlü Tarih Çalışması'. In *Bilanço 1923-1998, Türkiye Cumhuriyeti'nin 75 Yılına Toplu Bakış Uluslararası Kongresi Vol. I: Siyaset, Kültür, Uluslararası İlişkiler*, edited by Zeynep Rona, 217–29. Istanbul: Tarih Vakfı Yurt Yayınları, 1999.

Atay, Falif Rıfkı. *Niçin Kurtulmamak*. Istanbul: Varlık, 1953.

Atay, Falih Rıfkı. *Çankaya*. Istanbul: Bateş Atatürk Dizisi, 1998.

Aybars, Ergün. *İstiklal Mahkemeleri I-II (1920-1927)*. Izmir: Dokuz Eylül Üniversitesi Yayınları, 1988.

Aydın, Cemil. *The Idea of the Muslim World: A Global Intellectual History*. Cambridge, MA: Harvard University Press, 2017.

Azak, Umut. 'A Reaction to Authoritarian Modernization in Turkey: The Menemen Incident and the Creation and Contestation of a Myth, 1930–31'. In *State and the Subaltern: Modernization, Society and the State in Turkey and Iran*, edited by Touraj Atabaki, 143–58. London: I.B. Tauris, 2007.

Azak, Umut. *Islam and Secularism in Turkey: Kemalism, Religion, and the Nation State*. London: I.B. Tauris, 2010.

Badran, Margot. *Feminists, Islam, and Nation: Gender and the Making of Modern Egypt*. Princeton: Princeton University Press, 1995.

Baiza, Yaiha. *Education in Afghanistan: Developments, Influences and Legacies since 1901*. London: Routledge, 2013.

Balsoy, Gülhan. *The Politics of Reproduction in Ottoman Society, 1838-1900*. London: Pickering & Chatto, 2013.

Baker, Patricia L. 'The Fez in Turkey: A Symbol of Modernization?' *Costume* 20 (1986): 72–85.

Baker, Patricia L. 'Politics of Dress: The Dress Reform Laws of 1920–1930s Iran'. In *Languages of Dress in the Middle East*, edited by Nancy Lindisfarne-Tapper and Bruce Ingham, 178–92. London: Curzon Press, 1997.

Baron, Beth. 'Unveiling in Early Twentieth Century Egypt: Practical and Symbolic Considerations'. *Middle Eastern Studies* 25, no. 3 (July 1989): 370–86.

Baron, Beth. 'Nationalist Iconography: Egypt as a Woman'. In *Rethinking Nationalism in the Arab Middle East*, edited by James Jankowski and Israel Gershoni, 105–24. New York: Columbia University Press, 1997.

Baron, Beth. *Egypt as a Woman: Nationalism, Gender and Politics*. Berkeley: University of California Press, 2005.

Bayart, Jean-François. 'Republican Trajectories in Iran and Turkey: A Tocquevillian Reading'. In *Democracy without Democrats? The Renewal of Politics in the Muslim World*, edited by Ghassan Salamé, 282–300. London: I.B. Tauris, 1994.

Baydar, Oya and Feride Çiçekoğlu. eds. *Cumhuriyet'in Aile Albümleri*. Istanbul: Tarih Vakfı Yurt Yayınları, 1998.

Ben-Dor, Gabriel and Engin D. Akarlı. 'Comparative Perspectives'. In *Political Participation in Turkey*, edited by Engin D. Akarlı and Gabriel Ben-Dor, 157–62. Istanbul: Boğaziçi University Publications, 1975.

Berkes, Niyazi. *The Development of Secularism in Turkey*. Montreal: McGill University Press, 1964.

Berkes, Niyazi. *Türkiye'de Çağdaşlaşma*. Ankara: Bilgi Yayınevi, 1973.

Berktay, Fatmagül. 'Cumhuriyet'in 75 Yıllık Serüvenine Kadınlar Açısından Bakmak'. In *75 Yılda Kadınlar ve Erkekler*, edited by Ayşe Berktay Hacımirzaoğlu, 1–11. Istanbul: Tarih Vakfı Yayınları, 1998.

Berktay, Fatmagül. 'Osmanlı'dan Cumhuriyet'e Feminizm'. In *Modern Türkiye'de Siyasi Düşünce I: Tanzimat ve Meşrutiyet'in Birikimi*, edited by Mehmet Ö. Alkan, 348–61. Istanbul: İletişim, 2001.

Blumi, Isa. *Rethinking the Late Ottoman Empire: A Comparative Social and Political History of Albania and Yemen 1878-1918*. Istanbul: The Isis Press, 2003.

Bozarslan, Hamit. 'Kemalism, Westernization and Anti-liberalism'. In *Turkey beyond Nationalism: Towards Post-Nationalist Identities*, edited by Hans-Lukas Kieser, 28–34. London: I.B. Tauris, 2006.

Bozdoğan, Sibel. *Modernism and Nation Building: Turkish Architectural Culture in the Early Republic*. Seattle: University of Washington Press, 2001.

Brockett, Gavin D. 'Collective Action and the Turkish Revolution: Towards a Framework for the Social History of the Atatürk Era, 1923-38'. *Middle Eastern Studies* 34, no. 4 (October 1998): 44–66.

Brockett, Gavin D. 'A View from the Periphery: The Provincial Press as a Source for Republican Turkish Social History'. In *Towards a Social History of Modern Turkey: Essays in Theory and Practice*, edited by Gavin D. Brockett, 123–53. Istanbul: Libra, 2011.

Brummet, Palmira. *Image and Imperialism in the Ottoman Revolutionary Press, 1908-1911*. Albany: State University of New York Press, 2000.

Bruinessen, Martin van. *Agha, Shaikh and State: The Social and Political Structures of Kurdistan*. London: Zed Books, 1992.

C.H.P. Dördüncü Büyük Kurultayı Görüşmeleri Tutulgası, 9-16 Mayıs 1935. Ankara: Ulus Basımevi, 1935.

Caporal, Bernard. *Kemalizmde ve Kemalizm Sonrasında Türk Kadını (1919-1970)*. Ankara: Türkiye İş Bankası Kültür Yayınları, 1982.

Certeau, Micheal de. *The Practice of Everyday Life*. Berkeley: University of California Press, 1984.

Chaturvedi, Vinayak. 'Introduction'. In *Mapping Subaltern Studies and the Postcolonial*, edited by Vinayak Chaturvedi, vii–xix. London: Verso, 2000.

Chehabi, Houcheng. 'Staging the Emperor's New Clothes: Dress Codes and Nation-Building under Reza Shah'. *Iranian Studies* 26, no. 3-4 (Summer/Fall 1993): 209–29.

Chehabi, Houcheng. 'Banning of the Veil and Its Consequences'. In *The Making of Modern Iran: State and Society under Riza Shah, 1921-1941*, edited by Stephanie Cronin, 193–210. London: Routledge, 2003.

Chehabi, Houcheng. 'Dress Codes for Men in Turkey and Iran'. In *Men of Order: Authoritarian Modernization under Atatürk and Reza Shah*, edited by Touraj Atabaki and Erik J. Zürcher, 209–37. London: I.B. Tauris, 2004.

Childress, Faith J. 'Taking Side Roads: Researching Mid-level Elites as Turkish Social History'. In *Towards a Social History of Modern Turkey: Essays in Theory and Practice*, edited by Gavin D. Brockett, 97–122. Istanbul: Libra, 2011.

Clayer, Nathalie. 'Adapting Islam to Europe: The Albanian Example'. In *Islam und Muslime in (Südost)Europa im Kontext von Transformation und EU-Erweiterung*, edited by Christian Voss et Jordanka Telbizova-Sack, 53–69. München: Verlag Otto Sagner, 2010.

Clayer, Nathalie. 'Behind the Veil: The Reform of Islam in Interwar Albania or the Search for a "Modern" and "European" Islam'. In *Anti-Veiling Campaigns in the Muslim World: Gender, Modernism and the Politics of Dress*, edited by Stephanie Cronin, 231–51. London: Routledge, 2014.

Clayer, Nathalie, Fabio Giomi and Emmanuel Szurek. eds. *Kemalism: Transnational Politics in the Post Ottoman World*. London: I.B. Tauris, 2018.

Cleveland, William L. 'Atatürk Viewed by His Arab Contemporaries: The Opinions of Sati'al-Husri and Shakib Arslan'. *International Journal of Turkish Studies* 2, no. 2 (1982): 15–23.

Cronin, Stephanie. 'Introduction'. In *Subalterns and Social Protest: History from Below in the Middle East and North Africa*, edited by Stephanie Cronin, 1–22. London: Routledge, 2008.

Cronin, Stephanie. 'Introduction: Coercion or empowerment? Anti-veiling Campaigns in Comparative Perspective'. In *Anti-Veiling Campaigns in the Muslim World: Gender, Modernism and the Politics of Dress*, edited by Stephanie Cronin, 1–36. London: Routledge, 2014.

Cumhuriyet Half Fırkası Genel Kâtipliğinin Fırka Teşkilâtına Umumî Tebligatından Halkevlerini ilgilendiren kısım, cilt 5, Temmuz 1934 den Birincikânun 1934 sonuna kadar. Ankara: Ulus Matbabası, 1935.

Cündioğlu, Dücane. *Türkçe Kur'an ve Cumhuriyet İdeolojisi*. Istanbul: Kitabevi, 1998.

Cündioğlu, Dücane. *Bir Siyasi Proje Olarak Türkçe İbadet 1*. stanbul: Kitabevi, 1999.

Çakır, Serpil. *Osmanlı Kadın Hareketi*. 2nd ed. Istanbul: Metis, 2011.

Çalışlar, İpek. *Latife Hanım*. Istanbul: Doğan Kitap, 2007.

Çağaptay, Soner. 'Reconfiguring the Turkish Nation in the 1930s'. *Nationalism and Ethnic Politics* 8, no. 2 (Summer 2002): 67–82.

Çağaptay, Soner. 'Kemalist Dönem'de Göç ve İskan Politikaları: Türk Kimliği Üzerine Bir Çalışma'. *Toplum ve Bilim* 93 (Summer 2002): 218–41.

Çapa, Mesut. 'Giyim Kuşamda Medeni Kıyafetlerin Benimsenmesi ve Trabzon Örneği'. *Toplumsal Tarih* 30 (June 1996): 22–8.

Çınar, Alev. *Modernity, Islam, and Secularism in Turkey: Bodies, Places and Time*. Minneapolis: University of Minnesota Press, 2005.

Davis, Fanny. *The Ottoman Lady: A Social History from 1718 to 1918*. New York: Greenwood Press, 1986.

Demirci, Tuba and Selçuk Akşin Somel. 'Women's Bodies, Demography, and Public Health: Abortion Policy and Perspectives in the Ottoman Empire of the Nineteenth Century'. *Journal of the History of Sexuality* 17, no. 3 (2008): 377–420.

Demirdirek, Aynur. *Osmanlı Kadınlarının Hayat Hakkı Arayışının Bir Hikayesi*. Ankara: İmge, 1993.

Demirel, Ahmet. *Tek Partinin İktidarı: Türkiye'de Seçimler ve Siyaset (1923–1946)*. Istanbul: İletişim, 2013.

Duman, Doğan. *Ulusal Ekonominin Yapılanmasında Yerli Malı Haftaları*. Izmir: Dokuz Eylül Yayınları, 2001.

Durakbaşa, Ayşe. 'Taşra Burjuvazisinin Tarihsel Kökenleri'. *Toplum ve Bilim* 118 (2010): 6–38.

Duverger, Maurice. *Political Parties*. London: Methuen, 1951.

Efrati, Noga. *Women in Iraq: Past Meets Present*. New York: Columbia University Press, 2012.

Ekmekçioğlu, Lerna. *Recovering Armenia: The Limits of Belonging in Post-Genocide Turkey*. Stanford: Stanford University Press, 2016.

Eldeniz, Perihan Naci. 'Atatürk ve Türk Kadını'. *Belleten* XX, no. 80 (1956): 739–45.

Ellison, Grace. *Ankara'da Bir İngiliz Kadın*. Translated by Osman Olcay. Ankara: Bilgi Yayınevi, 1999.

Emirbayer, Mustafa. 'Manifesto for a Relational Sociology'. *The American Journal of Sociology* 103, no. 2 (1997): 281–317.

Emrence, Cem. 'Politics of Discontent in the Midst of the Great Depression: The Free Republican Party of Turkey (1930)'. *New Perspectives on Turkey* 23 (Fall 2000): 31–52.

Emrence, Cem. *99 Günlük Muhalefet Serbest Cumhuriyet Fırkası*. Istanbul: İletişim, 2006.

Emrence, Cem. *Remapping the Ottoman Middle East: Modernity, Imperial Bureaucracy and the Islamic State*. London: I.B. Tauris, 2011.

Erdoğan, Necmi. 'Devleti "İdare Etmek": Maduniyet ve Düzenbazlık'. *Toplum ve Bilim* 83 (Winter 1999/2000): 8–31.

Ettehaideh, Mansoureh. 'The Origins and Development of the Women's Movement in Iran, 1906–41'. In *Women in Iran from 1800 to the Islamic Republic*, edited by Lois Beck and Guity Nashat, 85–106. Chicago: University of Illinois Press, 2004.

Fischer, Bernd J. 'Introduction'. In *Balkan Strongmen: Dictators and Authoritarian Rulers of Southeast Europe*, edited by Bernd J. Fischer, 1–18. London: C. Hurst & Co. Publishers, 2006.

Fischer, Bernd J. ed. *Balkan Strongmen: Dictators and Authoritarian Rulers of Southeast Europe*. London: C. Hurst & Co. Publishers, 2006.

Frey, Frederick W. *The Turkish Political Elite*. Cambridge, MA: The M.I.T. Press, 1965.

Frey, Frederick W. 'Political Development, Power and Communications in Turkey'. In *Communications and Political Development*, edited by Lucian W. Pye, 298–316. Princeton: Princeton University Press, 1967.

Gençosman, Kemal Zeki. *Altın Yıllar*. Istanbul: Hür Yayınları, 1981.

Georgeon, François. 'Kemalizm ve İslam Dünyası (1919–1938): Bazı İşaret Taşları'. In *Kemalizm ve İslam Dünyası*, edited by İskender Gökalp and François Georgeon, 11–53. Istanbul: Arba, 1990.

Gingeras, Ryan. *Sorrowful Shores: Violence, Ethnicity, and the End of the Ottoman Empire, 1912–1923*. Oxford: Oxford University Press, 2009.

Gologlu, Mahmut. *Üçüncü Meşrutiyet 1920*. Ankara: Başnur Matbaası, 1970.

Gologlu, Mahmut. *Türkiye Cumhuriyeti Tarihi I: Devrimler ve Tepkileri (1924–1930)*. Istanbul: Türkiye İş Bankası Kültür Yayınları, 2007.

Gökaçtı, M. Ali. *Dünyada ve Türkiye'de Belediyecilikç*. Istanbul: Ozan Yayıncılık, 1996.

Graham-Brown, Sarah. *Images of Women, The Portrayal of Women in Photography of the Middle East, 1860–1950*. New York: Columbia University Press, 1988.

Guha, Ranajit. 'Preface'. In *Subaltern Studies I. Writings in South Asian History and Society*, edited by Ranajit Guha, vii–viii. Delhi: Oxford University Press, 1982.

Halide Edip. *Turkey Faces West: A Turkish View of Recent Changes and Their Origin*. New Haven: Yale University Press, 1930.

Heper, Metin. *The State Tradition in Turkey*. Beverley: Eothen Press, 1985.

Heyat, Farideh. *Azeri Women in Transition: Women in Soviet and Post-Soviet Azerbaijan*. London: Routledge, 2002.

Hirschon, Renée. ed. *Crossing the Aegean: An Appraisal of the 1923 Compulsory Population Exchange between Greece and Turkey*. Oxford: Berghahn Books, 2003.

Hobsbawm, Eric. 'Peasant and Politics'. *Journal of Peasant Studies* 1, no. 1 (1973): 3–22.

Hobsbawm, Eric. *On History*. London: Weidenfeld & Nicolson, 1997.

Huntington, Samuel P. and Clement H. Moore. eds. *Authoritarian Politics in Modern Society: The Dynamics of Established One-Party Systems*. New York: Basic Books, 1970.

Işın, Ekrem. 'Tanzimat, Kadın ve Gündelik Hayat'. *Tarih ve Toplum* 51 (March 1988): 22–7.
Jelavich, Barbara. *The History of the Balkans: Twentieth Century, Volume II*. Cambridge: Cambridge University Press, 1983.
Kal, Nazmi. *Atatürk'le Yaşadıklarını Anlattılar*. Ankara: Bilgi Yayınevi, 2001.
Kamp, Marianne. *The New Woman in Uzbekistan: Islam, Modernity, and Unveiling under Communism*. Seattle: University of Washington Press, 2006.
Kamp, Marianne. 'Feminicide as Terrorism: The Case of Uzbekistan's Unveiling Murders'. In *Sexual Violence in Conflict Zones: From the Ancient World to the Era of Human Rights*, edited by Elizabeth Heineman, 56–70. Philadelphia: University of Philadelphia Press, 2011.
Kamp, Marianne. 'Women-Initiated Unveiling: State-Led Campaigns in Uzbekistan and Azerbaijan'. In *Anti-Veiling Campaigns in the Muslim World: Gender, Modernism and the Politics of Dress*, edited by Stephanie Cronin, 205–28. London: Routledge, 2014.
Kandiyoti, Deniz. 'Emancipated but Unliberated? Reflections on the Turkish Case'. *Feminist Studies* 13, no. 2 (Summer 1987): 317–39.
Kandiyoti, Deniz. 'Bargaining with Patriarchy'. *Gender and Society* 2, no. 3 (September 1988): 274–90.
Kandiyoti, Deniz. 'Introduction'. In *Women, Islam and the State*, edited by Deniz Kandiyoti, 1–21. Philadelphia: Temple University Press, 1991.
Kandiyoti, Deniz. 'End of Empire: Islam, Nationalism and Women in Turkey'. In *Women, Islam and the State*, edited by Deniz Kandiyoti, 22–47. Philadelphia: Temple University Press, 1991.
Kandiyoti, Deniz 'Gendering the Modern: On Missing Dimensions in the Study of Turkish Modernisty'. In *Rethinking Modernity and National Identity in Turkey*, edited by Sibel Bozdoğan and Reşat Kasaba, 113–32. Seattle, WA: University of Washington Press, 1997.
Kandiyoti, Deniz. 'Locating the Politics of Gender: Patriarchy, Neoliberal Governance and Violence in Turkey'. *Research and Policy on Turkey* 1, no. 2 (2016): 103–18.
Karadağ, Meltem. 'Taşra Kentlerinde Yaşam Tarzları Alanı: Kültür ve Ayrım'. *Toplum ve Bilim* 118 (2010): 39–58.
Karakışla, Yavuz Selim. *Women, War and Work in the Ottoman Empire: Society for the Employment of Ottoman Muslim Women (1916–1923)*. Istanbul: Ottoman Bank Archives and Research Centre, 2005.
Kashani-Sabet, Firoozeh. *Conceiving Citizens: Women and the Politics of Motherhood in Iran*. Oxford: Oxford University Press, 2011.
Kashani-Sabet, Firoozeh. 'Dressing Up (or down): Veils, Hats and Consumer Fashions in Interwar Iran'. In *Anti-Veiling Campaigns in the Muslim World: Gender, Modernism and the Politics of Dress*, edited by Stephanie Cronin, 149–62. London: Routledge, 2014.
Keddie, Nikki. *Modern Iran: Roots and Results of Revolution*. New Haven: Yale University Press, 2006.
Kılıçzade Hakkı. 'Pek Uyanık Bir Uyku'. *İctihad* 55 (February 1328[1912]).
Kılıçzade Hakkı. 'Kılıçzade Hakkı'nın Tesettüre İlan-ı Harbi'. *Toplumsal Tarih* 66 (June 1999): 34–6.
Knöbl, Wolfgang. 'Theories That Won't Pass Away: The Never-Ending Story of Modernization Theory'. In *Handbook of Historical Sociology*, edited by Gerard Delanty and Engin F. Işın, 96–107. London: Sage Publications, 2003.
Kocabıçak, Ece. 'What Excludes Women from Landownership in Turkey? Implications for Feminist Strategies'. *Women's Studies International Forum* 69 (July–August 2018): 115–25.

Koçak, Cemil. 'Siyasal Tarih (1923-1950)'. In *Türkiye Tarihi 4: Çağdaş Türkiye 1908-1980*, edited by Sina Akşin, 84–173. Istanbul: Cem Yayınevi, 1997.

Koçak, Cemil. *Umûmî Müfettişlikler (1927-1952)*. Istanbul: İletişim, 2003.

Koçak, Cemil. *Belgelerle İktidar ve Serbest Cumhuriyet Fırkası*. Istanbul: İletişim, 2006.

Koçak, Cemil. *Tek-Parti Döneminde Muhalif Sesler*. Istanbul: İletişim, 2011.

Koçu, Reşat Ekrem. *Türk Giyim Kuşam ve Süslenme Sözlüğü*. Istanbul: Sümerbank Kültür Yayınları, 1969.

Koloğlu, Orhan. *İslamda Başlık*. Ankara: Türk Tarih Kurumu Basımevi, 1978.

Köksal, Duygu and Anastasia Falierou. 'Introduction: Historiography of Late Ottoman Women'. In *A Social History of Late Ottoman Women: New Perspectives*, edited by Duygu Köksal and Anastasia Falierou, 1–27. Leiden: Brill, 2013.

Lamprou, Alexandros. '"CHP Genel Sekreterliği Makamına": 30'lu ve 40'lı Yıllarda Halkevleri'yle İlgili CHP'ye Gönderilen Şikayet ve Dilek Mektupları Hakkında Kısa Bir Söz'. *Kebikeç* 23 (2007): 381–92.

Lamprou, Alexandros. 'Negotiating Gender Identities during Mixed-Gender Activities: Amateur Theatre in the 1930s and 1940s in Turkey'. *British Journal of Middle East Studies* 42, no. 4 (2015): 618–37.

Lamprou, Alexandros. *Nation Building in Modern Turkey: The 'People's Houses', the State and the Citizen*. London: I.B. Tauris, 2015.

Lewis, Bernard. *The Emergence of Modern Turkey*. Oxford: Oxford University Press, 1961.

Lewis, Geoffrey. *The Turkish Language Reform: A Catastrophic Success*. Oxford: Oxford University Press, 2000.

Libal, Kathryn, 'Staging Turkish Women's Emancipation: Istanbul, 1935'. *Journal of Middle East Women's Studies* 4, no. 1 (Winter 2008): 31–52.

Libal, Kathryn. 'Specifying Turkish Modernity: Gender, Family and Nation-State Making in the Early Republic'. In *Towards a Social History of Modern Turkey: Essays in Theory and Practice*, edited by Gavin D. Brockett, 81–96. Istanbul: Libra, 2011.

Libal, Kathryn. 'From face veil to cloche hat: The backward ottoman versus New Turkish Woman in Urban Public Discourse'. In *Anti-Veiling Campaigns in the Muslim World: Gender, Modernism and the Politics of Dress*, edited by Stephanie Cronin, 39–58. London: Routledge, 2014.

Linke, Lilo. *Allah Dethroned: A Journey through Modern Turkey*. London: Constable & Co LTD, 1937.

MacLeod, Arlene E. 'Hegemonic Relations and Gender Resistance: The New Veiling as Accommodating Protest'. *Signs* 17, no. 3 (1992): 533–57

Mahmood, Saba. 'Feminist Theory, Embodiment and the Docile Agent: Some Reflections on the Egyptian Islamic Revival'. *Cultural Anthropology* 16, no. 2 (2001): 202–36.

Marcosson, Issac F. *Turbulent Years*. New York: Dodd, Mead & Company, 1938.

Mardin, Şerif. 'Center-Periphery Relations: A Key to Turkish Politics?' *Daedalus* 102, no. 1 (Winter 1973): 169–90.

Mardin, Şerif. 'Religion and Secularism in Turkey'. In *Atatürk: Founder of a Modern State*, edited by Ali Kazancıgil and Ergun Özbudun, 191–219. London: C. Hurst & Co., 1981.

Mardin, Şerif. 'Projects as Methodology: Some Thoughts on Modern Turkish Social Science'. In *Rethinking Modernity and National Identity in Turkey*, edited by Sibel Bozdoğan and Reşat Kasaba, 64–80. Seattle: University of Washington Press, 1997.

Mazıcı, Nurşen. 'Menemen Olayı'nın Sosyo-kültürel ve Sosyo-ekonomik Analizi'. *Toplum ve Bilim* 90 (Fall 2001): 131–46.

Meeker, Michael. 'The Black Sea Turks: Some Aspects of Their Ethnic and Cultural Background'. *International Journal of Middle East Studies* 2, no. 4 (October 1971): 318–45.

Meeker, Michael. *A Nation of Empire: The Ottoman Legacy of Turkish Modernity*. Berkeley: University of California Press, 2002.

Metinsoy, Murat. 'Kemalizmin Taşrası: Erken Cumhuriyet Taşrasında Parti, Devlet ve Toplum'. *Toplum ve Bilim* 118 (2010): 124–64.

Metinsoy, Murat. 'Everyday Resistance to Unveiling and Flexible Secularism in Early Republican Turkey'. In *Anti-Veiling Campaigns in the Muslim World: Gender, Modernism and the Politics of Dress*, edited by Stephanie Cronin, 86–117. London: Routledge, 2014.

Migdal, Joel. 'Finding the Meeting Ground of Fact and Fiction: Some Reflections on Turkish Modernization'. In *Rethinking Modernity and National Identity in Turkey*, edited by Sibel Bozdoğan and Reşat Kasaba, 252–60. Seattle: Washington University Press, 1997.

Migdal, Joel. *State in Society: Studying How States and Societies Transform and Constitute One Another*. Cambridge: Cambridge University Press, 2001.

Migdal, Joel S., Atul Kohli and Vivienne Shue. 'Introduction: Developing a State-in-society Perspective'. In *State Power and Social Forces: Domination and Transformation in the Third World*, edited by Joel S. Migdal, Atul Kohli and Vivienne Shue, 1–6. Cambridge: Cambridge University Press, 1994.

Milani, Farzaneh. *Veils and Words: The Emerging Voices of Iranian Women Writers*. London: I.B. Tauris, 1992.

Minault, Gain. *The Khilafat Movement: Religious Symbolism and Political Mobilization in India*. New York: Columbia University Press, 1982.

Moghadam, Valentine M. 'Nationalist Agendas and Women's Rights: Conflicts in Afghanistan in the Twentieth Century'. In *Feminist Nationalism*, edited by Lois A. West, 75–100. New York: Routledge, 1997.

Najmabadi, Afsaneh. 'Hazards of Modernity and Morality: Women, State and Ideology in Contemporary Iran'. In *Women, Islam and the State*, edited by Deniz Kandiyoti, 48–76. Philadelphia: Temple University Press, 1991.

Najmabadi, Afsaneh. 'Crafting an Educated Housewife in Iran'. In *Remaking Women: Feminism and Modernism in the Middle East*, edited by Lila Abu-Lughod, 91–125. New Jersey: Princeton University Press, 1998.

Najmabadi, Afsaneh 'From Supplementarity to Parasitism'. *Journal of Women's History* 16, no. 2 (Summer 2004): 30–5.

Najmabadi, Afsaneh. *Women with Mustaches and Men without Beards: Gender and Sexual Anxieties of Iranian Modernity*. Berkeley: University of California Press, 2005.

Najmabadi, Afsaneh. 'Authority and Agency: Revisiting Women's Activism during Reza Shah's Period'. In *State and the Subaltern: Modernization, Society, and the State in Turkey and Iran*, edited by Touraj Atabaki, 159–77. London, I. B. Tauris, 2007.

Nereid, Camilla Trud. 'Domesticating Modernity: The Turkish Magazine *Yedigün*, 1933–9'. *Journal of Contemporary History* 47, no. 3 (2012): 48–504.

Neuburger, Mary. 'Difference Unveiled: Bulgarian National Imperatives and the Re-dressing of Muslim Women, 1878–1989'. In *Anti-Veiling Campaigns in the Muslim World: Gender, Modernism and the Politics of Dress*, edited by Stephanie Cronin, 252–66. London: Routledge, 2014.

Northrop, Douglas. *Veiled Empire: Gender and Power in Stalinist Central Asia*. Ithaca: Cornell University Press, 2004.

Norton, John. 'Faith and Fashion in Turkey'. In *Languages of Dress in the Middle East*, edited by Nancy Lindisfarne-Tapper and Bruce Ingham, 149–77. London: Curzon Press, 1997.

Oğuz, Çiğdem. ed. 'Women's Agency in the Late Ottoman Empire'. Special issue, *Journal of Ottoman and Turkish Studies Association* 6, no. 2 (2019): 9–130.

Ortaylı, İlber. *Tanzimattan Cumhuriyete Yerel Yönetim Geleneği*. Istanbul: Hil Yayın, 1985.

Os, Nicole A.V.M. van. 'Millî Kıyafet: Ottoman Women and the Nationality of Their Dress'. In *The Turks, vol. 4*, edited by Hasan Celal Güzel, C. Cem Oğuz and Osman Karatay, 580–92. Ankara: Yeni Türkiye Yayınları, 2002.

Os, Nicole A.V.M. van. 'Polygamy Before and After the Introduction of the Swiss Civil Code in Turkey'. In *The State and the Subaltern: Modernization, Society and the State in Turkey and Iran*, edited by Touraj Atabaki, 179–98. London. I.B. Tauris, 2007.

Os, Nicole A.V.M. van. 'Feminism, Philanthropy and Patriotism: Female Associational Life in the Ottoman Empire'. PhD diss., Leiden University, 2013.

Owen, Roger. *State, Power and Politics in the Making of the Modern Middle East*. New York: Routledge, 1992.

Öksüz, Hikmet and Veysel Usta. *Mustafa Reşit Tarakçıoğlu, Hayatı, Hatıratı ve Trabzon'un Yakın Tarihi*. Trabzon: Serander, 2008.

Önder, Mehmet. *Atatürk'ün Yurt Gezileri*. Istanbul: İş Bankası Kültür Yayınları, 1998.

Önen, Nizam and Cenk Reyhan. *Mülkten Ülkeye: Türkiye'de Taşra İdaresinin Dönüşümü (1839-1929)*. Istanbul: İletişim, 2011.

Özbudun, Ergun. *Türkiye'de Sosyal Değişme ve Siyasal Katılma*. Ankara: Ankara Üniversitesi Hukuk Fakültesi Yayınları, 1975.

Özbudun, Ergun. 'The Continuing Ottoman Legacy and the State Tradition in the Middle East'. In *Imperial Legacy: The Ottoman Imprint on the Balkans and the Middle East*, edited by L. Carl Brown, 133–57. New York: Columbia University Press, 1996.

Özbudun, Ergun. 'The Nature of the Kemalist Political Regime'. In *Atatürk: Founder of a Modern State*, edited by Ali Kazancıgil and Ergun Özbudun, 79–102. London: Hurst&Company, 1997.

Paidar, Parvin. *Women and the Political Process in Twentieth-Century Iran*. Cambridge: Cambridge University Press, 1995.

Parla, Taha. *Türkiye'de Siyasal Kültürün Resmî Kaynakları, Vol. 3: Kemalist Tek-Parti İdeolojisi ve CHP'nin Altı Ok'u*. Istanbul: İletişim, 1992.

Parla, Taha and Andrew Davison. *Corporatist Ideology in Kemalist Turkey: Progress or Order?* Syracuse: Syracuse University Press, 2004.

Pearson, Owen. *Albania in the Twentieth Century: A History, Vol. I, Albania and King Zog: Independence, Republic and Monarch, 1908-1939*. London: I.B. Tauris, 2004.

Poullada, L.B. 'Political Modernization in Afghanistan'. In *Afghanistan: Some New Approaches*, edited by George Grassmuck, Ludwing W. Adamec and Frances H. Irwin, 99–148. Ann Arbor: University of Michigan Press, 1969.

Price, G. Ward. *Extra-Special Correspondent*. London: Harrap, 1957.

Quataert, Donald. 'Clothing Laws, State, and Society in the Ottoman Empire, 1720–1829'. *International Journal of Middle East Studies* 29, no. 3 (1997): 403–25.

Rinaldo, Rachel. 'Pious and Critical: Muslim Women Activists and the Question of Agency'. *Gender and Society* 28, no. 6 (December 2014): 824–46.

Rostam-Kolayi, Jasamin and Afshin Matin-asgari. 'Unveiling Ambiguities: Revisiting 1930s Iran's *Kashf-e Hijab* Campaign'. In *Anti-Veiling Campaigns in the Muslim World: Gender, Modernism and the Politics of Dress*, edited by Stephanie Cronin, 121–39. London: Routledge, 2014.

Sadeghi, Hamideh. *Women and Politics in Iran: Veiling, Unveiling, and Reveiling*. Cambridge: Cambridge University Press, 2007.

Saikal, Amin. 'Kemalism: Its Influence on Iran and Afghanistan'. *International Journal of Turkish Studies* 2, no. 2 (1982): 25–32.

Saikal, Amin. *Modern Afghanistan: A History of Struggle and Survival*. London: I.B. Tauris, 2012.

Saktanber, Ayşe. 'Kemalist Kadın Hakları Söylemi'. In *Modern Türkiye'de Siyasî Düşünce, Vol. II, Kemalizm*, edited by Ahmet İnsel, 323–33. Istanbul: İletişim, 2001.

Sanasarian, Eliz, *The Women's Rights Movement in Iran: Mutiny, Appeasement, and Repression from 1900 to Khomeini*. New York: Praeger, 1982.

Sayarı, Sabri. 'Some Notes on the Beginning of Mass Political Participation in Turkey'. In *Political Participation in Turkey*, edited by Engin D. Akarlı and Gabriel Ben-Dor, 121–33. Istanbul: Boğaziçi University Publications, 1975.

Scott, James C. *Weapons of the Weak: Everyday Forms of Resistance*. New Haven: Yale University Press, 1985.

Scott, James C. *Seeing Like a State: How Certain Schemes to Improve the Human Condition Have Failed*. New Haven: Yale University Press, 1998.

Scott, Joan W. 'Women in History: The Modern Period'. *Past & Present* 101 (November 1983): 141–57.

Scott, Joan W. 'Gender: A Useful Category of Historical Analysis'. *The American Historical Review* 91, no. 5 (December 1986): 1053–75.

Scott, Joan W. 'Feminism's History'. *Journal of Women's History* 16, no. 2 (Summer 2004): 10–29.

Serçe, Erkan. *Tanzimat'tan Cumhuriyet'e İzmir'de Belediye (1868-1945)*. Izmir: Dokuz Eylül Yayınları, 1998.

Shakry, Omnia. 'Schooled Mothers and Structured Play: Child Rearing in Turn-of-the-Century Egypt'. In *Remaking Women: Feminism and Modernity in the Middle East*, edited by Lila Abu-Lughod, 126–70. Princeton: Princeton University Press, 1998.

Sharma, Aradhana and Akhil Gupta. 'Introduction: Rethinking Theories of the State in an Age of Globalization'. In *The Anthropology of the State: A Reader*, edited by Aradhana Sharma and Akhil Gupta, 1–41. Oxford: Blackwell Publishing, 2006.

Shissler, A. Holly. 'Beauty Is Nothing to Be Ashamed of: Beauty Contests as Tools of Women's Liberation in Early Republican Turkey'. *Comparative Studies of South Asia, Africa and the Middle East* 24, no. 1 (2004): 107–22.

Szurek, Emmanuel. '"Yan, Of, Ef, Viç, İç, İs, Dis, Pulos … ": the Surname Reform, the "Non-Muslims," and the Politics of Uncertainty in Post-genocidal Turkey'. In *Arabic and Its Alternatives: Religious Minorities and Their Languages in the Emerging Nation States of the Middle East (1920-1950)*, edited by Heleen Murre-van den Berg, Karène Sanchez Summerer and Tijmen Baarda, 77–110. Leiden: Brill, 2020.

Şeni, Nora. 'Fashion and Women's Clothing in the Satirical Press of Istanbul at the End of the 19th Century'. In *Women in Modern Turkish Society*, edited by Şirin Tekeli, 25–45. London: Zed Books, 1995.

Taşçıoğlu, Muhaddere. *Türk Osmanlı Cemiyetinde Kadının Sosyal Durumu ve Kadın Kıyafetleri*. Ankara: Akın Matbaası, 1958.

Taşkıran, Tezer. *Cumhuriyetin 50. Yılında Türk Kadın Hakları*. Ankara: Başbakanlık Basımevi, 1973.

Tepeyran, Ebubekir Hazım. *Belgelerle Kurtuluş Savaşı Anıları*. Istanbul: Çağdaş Yayınları, 1982.

Tekeli, İlhan. *Cumhuriyetin Belediyecilik Öyküsü (1923-1990)*. Istanbul: Tarih Vakfı Yurt Yayınları, 2009.

Tekelioğlu, Orhan. 'Modernizing Reforms and Turkish Music in the 1930s'. *Turkish Studies* 2, no. 1 (2001): 93–108.

Thompson, Elizabeth. *Colonial Citizens: Republican Rights, Paternal Privilege, and Gender in French Syria and Lebanon*. New York: Columbia University Press, 2000.

Tomes, Jason Hunter. *King Zog of Albania: Europe's Self-Made Muslim Monarch*. New York: New York University Press, 2004.

Torab, Azam. 'Piety as Gendered Agency: A Study of Jalaseh Ritual Discourse in an Urban Neighborhood in Iran'. *The Journal of the Royal Anthropological Institute* 2, no. 2 (June 1996): 235–52.

Toynbee, Arnold J. *Survey of International Affairs 1925, Vol. I: The Islamic World since the Peace Settlement*. London: Oxford University Press, 1927.

Tunaya, Tarık Zafer. *Türkiye'de Siyasi Partiler I: İkinci Meşrutiyet Dönemi 1908–1918*. Istanbul: Hürriyet Vakfı Yayınları, 1984.

Tunçay, Mete. *T.C.'nde Tek-Parti Yönetimi'nin Kurulması (1923–1931)*. 2nd ed. Istanbul: Cem Yayınevi, 1992.

Turan, Murat. *CHP'nin Doğu'da Teşkilatlanması*. Istanbul: Libra, 2011.

Uyar, Hakkı. 'Çarşaf, Peçe ve Kafes Üzerine Bazı Notlar'. *Toplumsal Tarih* 33 (September 1996): 6–11.

Uyar, Hakkı. 'Tek Parti Döneminde Denizli'de Siyasal Hayat'. In *Uluslararası Denizli ve Çevresi Tarih ve Kültür Sempozyumu: Bildiriler 1*, edited by Ayfer Özçelik et al., 561–79. Denizli: Pamukkale Üniversitesi Fen Edebiyat Fakültesi Tarih Bölümü Yayınları, 2006.

Ülker, Erol. 'Assimilation, Security and Geographical Nationalization in Interwar Turkey: The Settlement Law of 1934'. *European Journal of Turkish Studies* 7 (2008). https://doi.org/10.4000/ejts.822.

Üngör, Uğur Ümit. *The Making of Modern Turkey: Nation and State in Eastern Anatolia, 1913-1950*. Oxford: Oxford University Press, 2011.

Üstel, Füsun. *İmparatorluktan Ulus-Devlete Türk Milliyetçiliği: Türk Ocakları (1912–1931)*. Istanbul: İletişim, 1997.

Varlık, M. Bülent. ed. *Umumî Müfettişler Toplantı Tutanakları – 1936*. Istanbul: Dipnot, 2010.

Vickers, Miranda. *The Albanians: A Modern History*. London: I.B. Tauris, 2001.

Weiker, Walter F. *Political Tutelage and Democracy in Turkey: The Free Party and Its Aftermath*. Leiden: Brill, 1973.

Wide, Thomas. 'Astrakhan, Borqa', Chadari, Dreshi: The Economy of Dress in Early-Twentieth-Century Afghanistan'. In *Anti-Veiling Campaigns in the Muslim World: Gender, Modernism and the Politics of Dress*, edited by Stephanie Cronin, 163–201. London: Routledge, 2014.

Yakut, Kemal. 'Tek Parti Döneminde Peçe ve Çarşaf'. *Tarih ve Toplum* 220 (April 2002): 23–32.

Yeğenoğlu, Meyda. *Colonial Fantasies: Towards a Feminist Reading of Orientalism*. Cambridge: Cambridge University Press, 1998.

Yılmaz, Hale. *Becoming Turkish: Nationalist Reforms and Cultural Negotiations in Early Republican Turkey, 1923-1945*. Syracuse: Syracuse University Press, 2013.

Zihnioğlu, Yaprak. *Kadınsız İnkılap: Nezihe Muhittin, Kadınlar Halk Fırkası, Kadın Birliği*. Istanbul: Metis, 2003.

Zürcher, Erik J. *Political Opposition in the Early Turkish Republic: The Progressive Republican Party*. Leiden: Brill, 1991.

Zürcher, Erik J. *Turkey: A Modern History*. 3rd ed. London: I.B. Tauris, 2004.

Zürcher, Erik J. 'The Ottoman Legacy of the Kemalist Republic'. In *The State and the Subaltern: Modernization, Society and the State in Turkey and Iran*, edited by Touraj Atabaki, 95–110. London: I.B. Tauris, 2007.

Zürcher, Erik J. 'Turkey in the First World Crisis: From Authoritarianism to Totalitarianism'. In *Routes into the Abyss: Coping with Crises in the 1930s*, edited by Helmut Konrad and Wolfgang Waderthaner, 127–38. Oxford: Berghahn Books, 2013.

INDEX